D1741607

The Lexicogrammar of Adjectives

Functional Descriptions of Language Series

Series Editor: Robin Fawcett, University of Wales, College of Cardiff

There is a large and growing interest in functional descriptions of the languages of the world. This series – conceived as a sister to the Open Linguistics Series – provides a forum for descriptions of selected aspects of languages (and occasionally for descriptive overviews of whole languages) that approach the problem of explaining language from an explicitly functional perspective.

The series offers a natural home for the publications of those working in, or in sympathy with, one or more of the following theoretical frameworks: systemic functional linguistics, functional grammar, Firthian description (for example, work in the tradition of Quirk, Leech and colleagues), functional sentence perspective, role and reference grammar, cognitive grammar, tagmemics, stratificational grammar, and the various 'West Coast functionalists' and others with similar views.

The Lexicogrammar of Adjectives

A Systemic Functional Approach to Lexis

GORDON H. TUCKER

CASSELL

London and New York

Cassell

Wellington House, 125 Strand, London WC2R 0BB
370 Lexington Avenue, New York, NY 10017 – 6550

First published 1998

© Gordon H. Tucker 1998

All rights reserved. No part of this publication may be reproduced or transmitted
in any form or by any means, electronic or mechanical, including photocopying,
recording or any information storage or retrieval system, without permission in
writing from the publishers.

British Library Cataloguing in Publication Data

A catalogue record for this book is available from the British Library.

ISBN 0–304–33903–2

Library of Congress Cataloging-in-Publication Data

Tucker, Gordon H. (Gordon Howard), 1945–
    The lexicogrammar of adjectives: a systemic functional approach to
lexis/Gordon H. Tucker.
        p.   cm. – (Functional descriptions of language)
    Includes bibliographical references and index.
    ISBN 0–304–33903–2 (hardcover)
    1. Grammar, Comparative and general – Adjectives.   2. Lexicology.
3. Systemic grammar.   I. Title.   II. Series.
P273.T83   1998   97–52313
415—dc21   CIP

Contents

Acknowledgements

The author and publisher are grateful to the authors and publishers of the following publications who have given their kind permission for the use of copyright material reproduced in this book:

Berry, M. (1997) *Introduction to systemic linguistics, Vol. 2: Levels and links*. London: Batsford, on page 14.

Cross, M. (1993) Collocation in computer modelling of lexis as most delicate grammar. In M. Ghadessy (ed.) *Register Analysis: Theory and Practice*. London: Pinter Publishers, on page 23.

Fawcett, R.P. (1980) *Cognitive Linguistics and Social Interaction: Towards an Integrated Model of a Systemic Functional Grammar and the Other Components of an Interacting Mind*. Heidelberg: Julius Groos and Exeter University, on page 17.

Hasan, R. (1987) The grammarian's dream: lexis as most delicate grammar. In Halliday, M.A.K., and Fawcett, R.P. (eds) (1987) *New Developments in Systemic Linguistics, Vol. 1: Theory and Description*. London: Pinter, on page 17.

Martin, J.R. (1992) *English Text: System and Structure*. Amsterdam: John Benjamins, on pages 28, 29, 30 and 31.

Matthiessen, C.M.I.M. (1990) Lexico(grammatical) choice in text generation. In C.L. Paris, W.R. Swartout and W.C. Mann (eds), *Natural Language Generation in Artificial Intelligence and Computational Linguistics*. Dordrecht: Kluwer Academic Publishers, on pages 25 and 30.

Preface

There has been and will continue to be an abundance of books on both grammar and lexis. The subject matter of this book, however, is, exclusively, neither one nor the other. Its central concern is lexicogrammar, albeit the lexicogrammar associated with a specific lexical category, the adjective. It was Michael Halliday who, as far as I am aware, first introduced the term 'lexicogrammar' into the study of language, a term which is not to be interpreted as a replacement for 'grammar', or as shorthand for the simple banding together of grammatical and lexical forms in linguistic organization. This is made clear in another idea of Halliday's, namely that lexis is 'most delicate grammar'. Others – and especially John Sinclair – would argue the converse, that grammar is 'most generalized lexis'. Yet I believe these two positions to be complementary, differing only in the direction from which they come at language. Both positions suggest an integrated approach, one in which there is no rigid compartmentalization of grammar and lexis.

The theoretical framework in which one works – in this case of this book, Systemic Functional Grammar – both determines and is determined by the kind of questions that one asks and attempts to answer. If the scope of this book could be reduced to a single question, it would be, 'What is involved linguistically in the selection of one or other adjective as part of the overall meaning potential of English?' And that is clearly not just a question of choice between one lexical item and another. A speaker's knowledge of a language involves knowing the contexts in which adjectives are possible and appropriate expressions of meaning and the consequences, both structural and lexical, of selecting one or another adjective. Among the consequences of any such choice is the potential for the elaboration and extension of meaning through modification and complementation of the adjective itself. Furthermore, if one is concerned with language as meaning potential – and this is a central concern of systemic functional linguistics – the thorny problem of the semantic organization of the lexical resource cannot be avoided. These are all issues which are addressed in this book.

If it is no longer fashionable in linguistic theory to write large explicit grammars of a particular language, there are still at least three valid reasons for doing so. Firstly, there is the research activity of computational natural language generation, with which this book is integrally associated, through being a part of the computationally implemented Cardiff Grammar. If computational grammars are to be of use, they must provide extensive coverage of both structure and lexis. Secondly, if linguistics has a responsibility for the development of large descriptive grammars, then again, one cannot stop at theoretical principles and limited exemplifications. Finally, it is partly through the process of pushing ideas to the limit that we can assess their validity. It is now almost forty years since Michael Halliday first wrote of the idea of treating lexis as 'most delicate grammar'. If nothing else, this book is an extensive exploration of this challenging notion.

There are numerous colleagues to whom I am indebted and who have, directly or indirectly, influenced the ideas set out in this book. First and foremost, Robin Fawcett gave me the unique opportunity of making a contribution to the development of his model of systemic functional grammar, particularly in respect of lexis, and to the computational implementation of what has come to be known as the Cardiff Grammar. Robin's ideas and mine – like structure and lexis – have become fully integrated in my own work. Yet without his model, developed over three decades of earnest and dedicated scholarship, there would have been little to build upon. Secondly, no systemic functional linguist could fail to acknowledge the immense debt owed to Michael Halliday. In many respects, all developments in systemic functional linguistics are a response to one or other seminal idea of Michael's, and my own work is no exception. Thirdly, there are those who have, like myself, taken up the challenge of 'lexis as most delicate grammar', in particular Margaret Berry, Marilyn Cross, Ruqaiya Hasan, Jim Martin and Christian Matthiessen. Their respective contributions have proved invaluable in interpreting and developing Michael Halliday's original concept. Fourthly, in their first existence as a doctoral dissertation, the ideas presented here were scrutinized by Chris Butler and Geoffrey Turner, and it was their critical comments and encouragement that persuaded me to present them to a wider readership. Despite the contribution of those mentioned above, I alone am responsible for any inadequacies and shortcomings that the book may be considered to have.

Books also depend on the contribution and support of others, who, refreshingly, are not involved personally in the subject matter. In this sense, I would especially like to express my gratitude to Marion Blake of Cassell Academic who looked after my manuscript and guided me patiently and considerately through the processes of producing a book. I should add that I was more apprehensive of Marion's reading of my manuscript that I was of most others'. Finally, there are those who simply believe in you and give you the important support that any such enterprise requires, regardless of the cost to themselves. To Christine, for this, as always, thank you. This book is dedicated to my dear mother and my dear late father.

Gordon Tucker
Cardiff
May 1998

1 Introduction

The grammarian's dream is (and must be, such is the nature of grammar) of constant territorial expansion. He would like to turn the whole of linguistic form into grammar, hoping to show that lexis can be defined as 'most delicate grammar'. (Michael Halliday: 'Categories of the theory of grammar', 1961)

The lexicon – if I may go back to a definition I used many years ago – is simply the most delicate grammar. In other words, there is only one network of lexicogrammatical options. (Michael Halliday: *Language as Social Semiotic*, 1978)

1.1 STRUCTURE AND LEXIS

The study of linguistic form has by and large favoured a separation between syntactic and lexical description. Indeed, this separation is prevalent in the popular conception of how a language works: there is 'grammar' and there is 'vocabulary', and one consults the reference grammar for an account of how language is structured and the dictionary for information about words, their meanings and usage. Any compartmentalization of language into levels or components is, however, a convenience of linguists.

The only transparent 'components' of linguistic form are words. They are certainly the only formal linguistic entities that we might expect people other than linguists to readily recognize. The rest, as far as form is concerned, is simply the way words are put together, interact and pattern. Syntax is an abstraction of the patterning of words. Like most 'scientific' investigators, linguists are happy when they find regular patterns, since this allows them to generalize and make claims about the underlying organization of language. The reasons for investigating the formal properties of language differ, of course, between theoretical schools. For the Chomskyan school the aim is to uncover the universal linguistic properties, thereby throwing light on the language faculty in a psychological (and neuro-biological) sense. For the Hallidayan school the aim is to explore how language is organized to make social meanings, where the structural potential of a language is in a non-arbitrary relationship to its (social) meaning potential.

These different perspectives on formal linguistic organization need not be considered irretrievably incompatible and irreconcilable. Language is, after all, both a psychological and a social phenomenon. It is unfortunate that intellectual (and no doubt other forms of) politics has led to situations of proprietorial imperialism and at times heavy-handed appropriation of the domain and goals of linguistic theory. In the long run, it is the particular insights that theories offer humanity that will ultimately decide their usefulness.

One consequence of the choice between the Chomskyan psychological perspective and the Hallidayan social perspective is the treatment of lexis. In a theory whose goal it is to establish Universal Grammar – that biological endowment, genetically transmitted and present in our pre-natal brains – lexis can have little role to play. Lexis is language and culture specific, and the social and semiotic function of a word can only be acquired through human interaction. If there are universal aspects of individual words, they are cultural and social universals. Even if one were to argue that the presence of an expression for 'water' is found in every language because of our individual physical dependence on water to survive (hence individual rather than social), the expression only has value in social interaction and comes into being through it. All life depends on water, yet only humans talk about it.

The investigation of Universal Grammar must sideline individual tokens of lexis, even though their general properties can only be uncovered by taking them as a point of departure. On the other hand, a theory which sets out to explain the relationship between language and meaning potential in the social context cannot but consider lexis. If the difference, for example, between active and passive voice is explained in terms of the social semiotic, so must the difference between *chair* and *stool*, between *give* and *donate*. Of course, it is possible to describe the linguistic system in terms of its structural potential and go no further (a purely form-oriented endeavour) but then the relationship with its social function would remain unexplained. Once function and meaning are introduced into the equation, however, lexis cannot be avoided.

Alternatively, one could claim that structure and lexis are both central to meaning potential but constitute different levels of description. A theory could be developed to provide an account of the role and organization of structure in this process and a separate account of the role and organization of lexis. Indeed, if one cannot find a way of unifying the two, this is perhaps inevitable. Halliday himself initially appeared to accept this conclusion (see Chapter 2). The problem arises, however, when one comes to explain how the two levels interact to give one unified language system that provides the full meaning potential.

The difficult of accounting for the relationship between structure and lexis has also beset other paradigms. If a theory sets up (1) a syntactic component which contains the rules and principles of syntactic structures, and (2) a separate lexicon which contains individual lexical entries, how does it relate the two, if only for the purposes of generating all and only all the sentences of a language? What relevant information is to be assigned to which component so that – to use an idiom from the language of contemporary computer science – the two components can 'talk to each other'? The answer, in simple terms, is that a syntactic component must know how words behave and a lexicon must know how individual words behave syntactically. And as this involves rules and principles which are common to both parts, where do they belong?

Compartmentalization of this kind is a way of generalizing. The rules of syntax can only be expressed as generalizations if individual lexis is not taken into account. Our example of the active/passive voice is a generalization, both in purely structural terms and in terms of meaning potential. One might extend the generalization to cover all clauses which contain verbs with at least two arguments (e.g. *hit, kiss, give, known,* etc.). Unfortunately, there are two-argument verbs, such as *be, become, belong,* which do not interact with the active/passive alternation. Furthermore, there are verbs which are found in passive constructions, but not in all of their potential environments. The verb *want,* for example, is found passively in *you're wanted on the telephone,* but not in **you're wanted to start work tomorrow.* Finally, some verbs amongst those that have the active/passive potential are found to be more frequent in passive constructions than others.

This last point is crucial. Generalizations on the structure of language tell us little about how people actually use the language, and consequently how a language really is. The patterns of structural and lexical behaviour are not revealed by the linguist's introspection or from a few examples chosen to fit the pattern. This is the conclusion that increasingly is being drawn from a growing body of linguistic research on large computer corpora or databases. It is only when we come to investigate a language from samples of millions of words of running text that we can really begin to understand how words and structures behave and interact.

The incontrovertibility of many of the findings of language description based on large computer corpora draws us back both to the question of accounting for structure and lexis and also to the goals of linguistic enquiry and the choice of theory. Generative linguists in the Chomskyan Universal Grammar paradigm will continue to factor out the idiosyncrasies of actual linguistic behaviour and especially of lexis. As we have observed, the aim of this type of linguistic enquiry is ultimately to throw light on the biological basis of linguistic organization as a modular faculty of the mind and brain. It is open to speculation what advances might develop from the isolation of the language gene. Yet even such ambitious goals have engendered numerous important contributions to language description, much of which cannot be ignored by anyone interested in language. Whilst Universal Grammarians have concentrated on the principles and parameters underpinning formal language systems, others who espouse the same general theoretical paradigm have been active in important work on lexis, and in particular lexical semantics. Two notable contributors to this area are Levin in her work arising from the MIT lexicon project (Levin 1985, 1993) and Pustejovsky in his development of a theory of qualia and the generative lexicon (1991).

For many researchers, the goal of linguistic enquiry remains that of describing language and languages and the principles of linguistic organization in terms of language use. If we are concerned with language as a social semiotic system, we are interested in both how language is organized to serve this function in society and how speakers use it, maintain it and change it for social ends.

1.2   A UNIFIED APPROACH TO LEXIS AND STRUCTURE

Arguably, any theory of linguistic organization must ultimately take into account at least how its formal properties accommodate the particular social functions that it serves. A theory of language or a model of a particular language which does not fully incorporate lexis cannot do this. Moreover, it has to account for use as attested by corpus linguistic research. If such a theory purports to give rise to language description, it must have the potential to incorporate the vagaries and idiosyncrasies of lexicogrammatical behaviour and the cryptotypical phenomena which are uncovered by the observation of language use on a significantly large scale.

The approach to lexis explored in this book constitutes an attempt to develop a theoretical model of language in which this is potentially achievable, and in particular in the case of lexis. The theory which underpins it is systemic functional grammar (SFG), associated primarily with Michael Halliday. The particular model, whilst remaining substantially within general Hallidayan principles, is that developed by Robin Fawcett and myself at the University of Wales, Cardiff, and henceforth referred to as the Cardiff Grammar.

The tendency that has emerged in SFG is of a **unified approach** to grammar and lexis, witnessed by the use of the term **lexicogrammar**, reflected in Halliday's claim at the head of this chapter (Halliday 1978: 43). There is consequently no separate lexicon organized as a list of lexical entries. Instead, a single network of options represents the meaning potential of the language and specifies simultaneously the structural and lexical (and indeed intonational) organization corresponding to the set of choices in meaning that a speaker can make.

1.3 LEXIS AT LARGE

It is outside the scope of this book to consider in detail the considerable number of disciplinary areas which contribute to our understanding of lexis. Moreover, approaches to lexis in these areas are determined by their own objectives and purposes. Wherever they have been a source of insight into the particular approach adopted in this book, they are introduced at relevant points in the discussion. All that is provided here is a brief general overview of some of the important areas of interest.

A broad categorization of approaches to lexis needs to include at least the following:

(a) lexis in linguistic theory (e.g. Chomsky 1981, Hudson 1984)
(b) lexical semantics as a subcomponent of general semantics (e.g. Lyons 1977, Cruse 1986, Ferris 1993)
(c) lexicographical studies (e.g. Sinclair 1987b, Ilson 1985)
(d) corpus linguistics (e.g. Hoey 1993, Sinclair 1991, Stubbs 1996)
(e) computational lexicography, lexicons for natural language processing and lexical databases, machine translation, machine-readable dictionaries (e.g. Boguraev and Briscoe 1989)
(f) conceptual and knowledge representation, belief systems, ontologies (e.g. Findler 1979, Dahlgren 1988)

Lexis is a central concern in a number of other areas which include **first and second language lexical acquisition** (e.g. Meara 1980, Clark 1994), **literary stylistics** (e.g. Carter and Burton 1982), **cognitive models and the organization of the**

mental lexicon (e.g. Johnson-Laird 1983, Aitchison 1987, Lakoff 1987, Levelt 1993).

There is, understandably, considerable overlap between these disciplinary areas. Much research in contemporary lexical semantics is to a greater or lesser degree associated with major linguistic theories (e.g. Jackendoff 1985; Levin 1985, 1993; Levin and Pinker 1992; Pustejovsky 1991, all with Chomskyan generative theory, e.g. Chomsky 1981). Computational linguistic research on lexicons and the exploitation of machine-readable dictionaries is associated both with individual linguistic theories and with contemporary lexicography (e.g. Boguraev and Briscoe 1989 with the theory of Generalized Phrased Structure Grammar (Gazdar *et al.* 1985) and with the *Longman Dictionary of Contemporary English* (LDOCE)). The use of corpus linguistics in contemporary lexicography is exemplified by the work of the COBUILD Project (Sinclair 1987a).

In much contemporary linguistic theory, the dominant focus of attention is on syntax rather than lexis. As we have observed, the general tendency is to recognize separate components, namely a **syntactic component** and a **lexicon**. Major theories which follow this tendency are the various developments within the Chomskyan paradigm, Lexical-Functional Grammar (Kaplan and Bresnan 1982), and Generalized Phrase Structure Grammar and Head-driven Phrase Structural Grammar (Gazdar *et al.* 1985, Pollard and Sag 1987). Within general accounts of such theories, the treatment of lexis is usually restricted to a discussion of the features which entries in the lexicon must contain in order to account for appropriate lexical insertion into syntactic structures.

There is, however, a substantial body of research on the lexicon within the framework of such theories. This tends to be represented as lexical semantics. Levin's work, in particular, originating in the MIT Lexicon Project (Levin 1985) has produced valuable insights into the behaviour of classes of lexical items, especially verbs and their argument structures. Another valuable contribution has come from Pustejovsky's work on the 'Generative Lexicon' (Pustejovsky 1991) in which he proposes a 'theory of qualia' to account for the generation and interpretation of sentences such as *I've finished the book* where, clearly, aspects of the semantic structure of *book* allow us to understand how to interpret its co-occurrence with the verb *finish*.

A significant departure from the dual component model is found in the work of Hudson (1984) and Starosta (1988). This represents an alternative approach to the mainstream theories within the paradigm of generative grammar, in advocating what Hudson terms 'pan-lexicalism' (Hudson 1979). For Starosta, 'Grammar is lexicon' and all grammatical rules are to be viewed as generalizations about the lexicon (1988: 38–9). Yet if these approaches are 'word grammars' and give priority to lexis in the explanation of structure, they still constitute syntactic or grammatical theories and have little place for the discussion of lexical behaviour beyond the generalizations which are derived from lexis as a starting point. Furthermore, they are representatives of 'minority' theories and consequently are not associated with any major research into lexis proper.

Much of the most interesting research on lexis has developed within **computational linguistics** (CL) in its widest sense. The area of **computational**

lexicography may be seen to fall both within and outside the strict domain of computational linguistics. It constitutes a major branch of computational linguistics through research on extracting lexical information from machine-readable dictionaries (MRDs) (e.g. work on the LDOCE MRD by Boguraev and Briscoe 1987, 1989, Vossen *et al.* 1989, and by Wilks *et al.* 1987). Computational lexicography, or lexical computing, in the preparation of dictionaries (e.g. the COBUILD Project, Sinclair 1987c, 1991) tends to be associated with Corpus Linguistics. Computer corpora, as again in the case of the COBUILD corpus and more recently the British National Corpus, serve both the purpose of informing standard lexicography – and are now widely adopted by major dictionary publishers (e.g. Oxford University Press and Longman) – and for more general work on language description (cf. Stubbs 1996).

The primary concern of computational lexical research is the development of large-scale lexical resources known as lexicons or lexical databases. Natural language systems capable of parsing and understanding a wide range of natural language texts depend crucially on the size and organization of their lexicon.

Both computational and theoretical linguistics draw substantially on work in **lexical semantics**. In the former of these areas there is clearly a need to relate natural language representation to underlying knowledge representation. Researchers in this field are either linguistic semanticists, e.g. Pustejovsky (1991), who are attempting to throw light on lexical phenomena with computational linguistics in mind, or conceptual semanticists and researchers in knowledge representation, e.g. Dahlgren (1988), who see lexical information as a valuable source of insight for conceptual and knowledge structure. As I made clear in the preceding section, there is no generally agreed distinction or strict compartmentalization between these different areas of research.

Attempts to explicate the senses of words have traditionally fallen into one of two general approaches: the 'semantic primitives' approach and the 'lexical semantic relations' approach. Various sets of primitives have been suggested, notably by Shank (1972), by Wilks himself (1975a, 1977) and by Wierzbicka (1980a).

The debate on the validity of decomposing lexical items into primitives is one which may ultimately never be resolved. There are numerous arguments which weaken the case for the decomposition approach. These range from the apparent impossibility of establishing a definitive set of primitives (*pace* Wierzbicka), to the difficulty of decomposing certain lexical items such as colours, e.g. *red* decomposes into [+coloured] (and what else?). The view of primitives as necessary and sufficient conditions for the representation of the meaning of lexical items is challenged both by Wittgenstein's (1953) notion of 'family resemblances' and by Rosch's work on 'prototype theory' (Rosch 1978). Despite the counter-arguments, decompositional approaches continue to be incorporated into semantic theories (e.g. Jackendoff 1985, 1990).

The principal alternative to primitives in lexical semantics involves sense relations such as synonymy, hyponymy, meronymy and oppositeness (e.g. Lyons 1977: 270ff, Leech 1974: 95–125, Cruse 1986).

Finally, most approaches to lexis and the lexicon are based on the correspondence of lexical meaning and single word forms. Dictionaries themselves, as

Cumming (1987) points out, are primarily organized around small linguistic units. Such approaches cannot easily account for meanings which are realized through lexical and grammatical units larger than the word. These include fixed and semi-fixed phrases, in terms of both idioms, e.g. *that takes the biscuit, to pull someone's leg*, and the extensive use of what one might refer to as 'grammatical metaphor' (Halliday 1994: 342), e.g. *I haven't the faintest idea, he took his time coming*, etc. All such types of realization involve lexical and grammatical co-occurrence, and are in many respects related to collocational phenomena. Once again, research on large computer corpora is constantly reminding us of the massive presence of complex co-occurrence phenomena. One approach to this problem is the **phrasal lexicon**, first proposed by Becker (1975), in which lexical entries are given as entire phrases.

1.4   THE FOCUS OF THIS BOOK: ADJECTIVES

The central aim of this book is to explore and demonstrate the feasibility of an integrated approach to lexis. Yet it is not a discussion of lexis *tout court*. Had it been, it might well have contributed once again to the perception of structure and lexis as separate linguistic 'entities'. No account of lexical phenomena in a model of language, however, can be comprehensive, unless it remains at the level of theoretical generalization. Furthermore, the validity of general theoretical and descriptive principles is put to the test in the development of explicit models of language.

In considering lexis from a traditional word class perspective, the major classes of **verb, noun, adjective** and **adverb** are all candidates for individual treatment. They constitute the **open set** word classes which have been the central concern of lexicologists and lexical semanticists. Other classes such as **prepositions, determiners, conjunctions**, etc. have been perceived as having a primarily grammatical function.

I have chosen to limit the greater part of this discussion of the treatment of lexis in an SFG to the lexicogrammar of **adjectives**. This choice is the outcome of a number of considerations. First and foremost, adjectives have generally received less attention than the other open set classes. There is undoubtedly a 'pecking order' in lexical matters, seen from the grammarian's point of view, and this reflects, above all, the extent to which lexis encroaches upon grammar. First in this pecking order are **verbs**. These are central to clause structure and intimately related to the discussion of transitivity, case, semantic role (argument) structure, tense and aspectual type. In second place come **nouns**, not only for their role in realizing the arguments associated with verbs, but also because speakers refer predominantly to 'things' in an external reality which is composed of 'things'. Finally, adjectives relate to 'qualities' or 'attributes' of the 'things' which participate in the events and processes which language serves to represent. The study of adjectives, their structures and meanings, has therefore tended to constitute a third order of lexical enquiry.

Nevertheless, adjectives raise a considerable number of interesting problems, from the point of view both of their grammar and of their lexical semantic organization. Investigation into their behaviour as 'heads of phrases' reveals the structural and functional complexity that has been typically associated with verbs and nouns. The semantic organization of adjectives, in terms of classes and subclasses, and the relations between senses and their grammatical implications, are phenomena equally deserving of the kind of attention that has often been given to verbs and nouns. Finally, an attractive reason for examining adjectival organization is that such a study covers some at least of the fourth of the open set word classes, **adverbs**. As will be seen in later chapters, these two classes share many structural and semantic properties which affect the general organization of the lexicogrammar.

What is proposed here, therefore, is a **lexicogrammar of adjectives** – or in somewhat more overtly semantic terms, a lexicogrammar of **Quality**. It represents at the same time an investigation of the general problems of incorporating lexis in a systemic functional model of language and the specific problems associated with one area of lexis.

Finally, in terms of the scope of this work, it should be emphasized that what is being proposed is not a theory of lexical semantics *per se*, although lexical semantics is central to the organization of the model. Such a disclaimer may be felt to be inconsistent with the self-declared semantic orientation of a systemic functional grammar. Yet I would claim that there is a difference between a model of language which attempts to make explicit 'how differences in meaning are formally realized' and a model of the structure of meaning and how meanings are interpreted. A systemic functional grammar of a language, and in particular here the Cardiff model, provides an account of the semantic potential from the point of view of how it is linguistically expressed. To claim that in so doing a systemic functional grammar explicates all aspects of meaning would be a serious exaggeration of its overall explanatory power.

1.5   THE ORGANIZATION OF THIS BOOK

Chapter 2 provides a survey of approaches to lexis within the systemic functional tradition. It therefore serves as a background to the particular model described in the book. The model itself, the Cardiff Grammar, is described in Chapter 3. Given the integrated approach to structure and lexis, it is not possible to discuss lexis independently from the overall model. Chapter 4 provides the checklist of adjectival phenomena which a grammar needs to address. Chapter 5 introduces the functional structure required to express the various phenomena. In Chapter 6, I discuss the question of system networks in which the systems are predominantly concerned with lexical difference. Chapter 7 then provides a detailed account of the system network for Quality, that is, where the meaning potential expressed by adjectives and their structures is specified. The realization rules for this system network are described and discussed separately in Chapter 8. The following two chapters look respectively at the relationship between adjectives and structure in terms of intensification and complementation (Chapter 9) and the function of adjectival structures in the clause and in the nominal group (Chapter 10).

2 Approaches to lexis in systemic linguistics

2.1 OVERVIEW

In this chapter we shall examine the predominant approaches to lexis within recent systemic functional linguistics and the earlier 'scale and category' framework, excluding, however, the current Cardiff Grammar approach itself, which forms the basis of the proposals set out in this book.

In the treatment of lexis, several tendencies have emerged: the 'lexis as most delicate grammar' tendency (Halliday 1961, Berry 1977, Fawcett 1980, 1987, Hasan 1987, Cross 1991, Tucker 1996), the collocation tendency associated primarily with Sinclair (e.g. 1987b, 1991), the metafunctional approach to lexis (Matthiessen 1990) and textual aspects of lexis, in particular lexical cohesion (Halliday and Hasan 1976, Martin 1992). As with accounts of structural and functional relations, there has been a notable progression in the treatment of lexis over the last thirty years of systemic theory.

2.2 THE ORIGINS OF THE 'LEXIS AS MOST DELICATE GRAMMAR' APPROACH

The development of systemic approaches to lexis in linguistic theory finds its origins in the ideas expressed by Halliday (1961) in his influential paper 'Categories of the theory of grammar'. One idea in particular – largely unexplored at the time – has come to represent the predominant systemic view of lexical organization. It is the idea that lexis is, in Halliday's words, 'most delicate grammar' (Halliday 1961: 267).

The expression 'most delicate grammar' is far from self-evident, as will be seen from the discussion below. Yet, in whatever way it has come to be interpreted within systemic linguistics, it represents a departure from the more generally accepted traditional approach which sees 'grammar' (or 'syntax') and 'lexis' (or the 'lexicon') as two separate, albeit related, components of a model of language. Essentially, it removes the strict demarcation between the two, incorporating them into one unified resource for the expression of meaning, the lexicogrammar.

Two points of clarification are necessary, however, before embarking upon the development of the 'most delicate grammar' view. Firstly, Halliday's original formulation was largely speculative, and indicative of what he, as a grammarian, would wish to do:

> The grammarian's dream is (and must be, such is the nature of grammar) of constant territorial expansion. *He would like to turn the whole of linguistic form into grammar* [my

> emphasis], hoping to show that lexis can be defined as 'most delicate grammar'. (Halliday 1961: 267)

Halliday's approach *qua* grammarian is reiterated thirty years later in another statement that itself is highly significant in the debate on lexis:

> Sinclair is by nature a lexicographer, whose aim is to construct the grammar out of the dictionary. I am by nature a grammarian, and my aim (the grammarian's dream, as I put it in 1961) is to build the dictionary out of the grammar. (Halliday 1991)

Secondly, the original formulation was set in the context of the 'scale and category' approach to linguistic theory. At this early stage, the category of 'system' had not gained the prime theoretical importance that it has now, as reflected in the name of the theory itself. It is essentially the evolution of this category and the gradual semanticization of systemic functional grammars that has led to a better understanding of how to model lexis as 'most delicate grammar'.

Halliday, in 1961, was unable to see a way forward in expressing lexical organization in terms of more delicate systems of grammatical description. The finer distinctions that language permits, those reflected by the difference between lexical items, could not be captured in terms of grammatical delicacy. Thus, the point where grammatical description reaches maximum delicacy marks the beginning of lexical organization, in terms of open sets of distinctions:

> There comes a point, however, when one is forced out to the exponents; and this happens in one of two ways. In the first case the description yields a system in which the formal exponents themselves operate as terms. Here we have gone all the way in grammar; the formal items are grammatically contrastive (and do not belong to the dictionary). In the second case the description yields a class where no further breakdown by grammatical categories is possible, a class whose exponents make up an open set. Here we must leave grammar; *the relations between the exponents must be accounted for as lexical relations* [my emphasis]. (Halliday 1961: 266)

It should be made clear that this is not an admission of the untenability of the 'most delicate grammar' position. For Halliday, at that time, it was a question of the unavailability of data and evidence that might allow such systems to be described:

> No description has yet been made so delicate that we can test whether there really comes a place where increased delicacy yields no further systems: relations at this degree of delicacy can only be tested statistically, and serious statistical work in grammar has hardly begun. (Halliday 1961: 247)

The consequence of the inability to propose a description of this kind led to what might be seen as a 'holding position':

> *For the moment* [my emphasis] it seems better to treat lexical relations ... as on a different level, and to require a different theory to account for them. (Halliday 1961: 267)

Despite this apparent postponement of 'the grammarian's dream' project, Halliday had sown the seed of what is now considered the 'orthodox' position on the treatment of lexis in contemporary systemic functional theory. While Halliday does not himself pursue the project in his own descriptive work, it is taken up by other systemicists, whose work is surveyed in later sections of this chapter.

2.3   A DIFFERENT EMPHASIS: COLLOCATION

The alternative approach to lexis which Halliday suggests in 'Categories' is Firth's theory of collocation. Firth introduced the term as part of his linguistic theory as set out in Firth (1957: 194ff) and Palmer (1968: 179–81). However, as Palmer observes, Firth seems to have restricted his interest to specialized collocations – to examples such as *silly* with *ass*, to *cow* with *milk* (Palmer 1968: 6).

Collocation is essentially the study of the syntagmatic relations that hold between words. For Firth, an essential aspect of the meaning of a word is 'the company it keeps' (Palmer 1968: 179). It is matched in Firth's theory by a grammatical equivalent, i.e. colligation, the syntagmatic relation between grammatical classes (Palmer 1968: 181). Halliday develops his major statement on collocation appropriately in an article among a collection written in memory of J.R. Firth (Halliday 1966a). The same volume also includes an article by Sinclair, who, more than any other scholar from the 'scale and category' tradition, develops the study of collocation (Sinclair 1966) (see also Section 2.4). Here Sinclair takes up the point made earlier by Halliday, that there are fundamental differences in the behaviour of grammatical and lexical contrasts:

> One lexical item is not chosen rather than another one, lexical items do not contrast with each other in the same sense as grammatical classes contrast. (Sinclair 1966: 411)

What Sinclair appears to mean by this is that lexical systems, in terms of what items may be selected in a given context, are open-ended, unlike many systems of grammatical alternatives, which are expressed through binary choices or at least a small number of choices. The collocationally determined occurrence of a lexical item is a function of the statistical likelihood of its being found in the syntagmatic context of other lexical items. Clearly, this is different from the syntagmatic relations which hold between elements of structure in a grammatical unit. Consider, for example, the fact that items that are not strong collocates one of the other may co-occur in the same stretch of language without any resultant infringement of the 'rules' of the language. This is not true of grammatical structures, all of which must colligate with each other.

The central notions associated with collocational phenomena are 'collocate', 'span', 'scatter', 'cluster' and 'set'. Collocates are lexical items that have a high probability of co-occurrence with a given item under examination, the node. The environment of co-occurrence for collocates is the span, established usually by counting a given number of words either side of the node. The term lexical item here does not refer to a simple lexical form such as *ripe*, but to its scatter which includes *riper*, *ripest*, *ripen* and *ripeness*. It is therefore the lexical content of an item, and not its grammatical form, which enters into collocational relations, as can be seen from the examples (1) to (3) below:

(1)   the fruit was ripe
(2)   the sun helps ripen the fruit
(3)   the fruit was succulent in its ripeness

Each node examined will yield a cluster of collocates. By extracting from the clusters of a number of nodes those collocates which have a greater generality of co-occurrence than any individual cluster, we obtain a lexical set. In this sense the set is seen as a close lexical parallel to the grammatical category of system (Halliday 1966a: 152–3). Berry (1977), in her discussion of lexis, attempts to draw closer parallels between grammatical categories and lexical categories in terms of collocation, although with limited success. This attempt is described and evaluated in 2.4.2.

2.4   LATER DEVELOPMENTS IN SYSTEMIC LEXIS

2.4.1   The emergence of the lexicogrammatical model

If it appears that Halliday postponed a deeper exploration of his 1961 account of lexis as most delicate grammar, he did not in any sense abandon the notion. This is clear from an interview with Herman Parret in which he states:

> The lexical system is not something that is fitted in afterwards to a set of slots defined by the grammar. The lexicon – if I may go back to a definition I used many years ago – is simply the most delicate grammar. In other words, there is only one network of lexico-grammatical options. And as these become more and more specific, they tend more and more to be realized by the choice of lexical item rather than by the choice of a grammatical structure. But it is still part of a single system. (Halliday 1978: 43)

This statement is highly significant and is representative of a somewhat evolved position on lexis, one that leads more naturally to the attempts of other systemicists to explore 'most delicate grammar' solutions to lexis. Its significance lies in the expression 'only one network of lexicogrammatical options'. Halliday is now talking of 'lexicogrammar' and of 'options'. This is the unified language system of resource, of meaning potential, in which grammar and lexis are distinguished in terms of more or less specific choices. Reference to the term 'network' also signals, indirectly, the more privileged status of 'system' and, by extension, of 'system network'. It clearly indicates a contrasting view with the traditional distinction made in linguistics between the 'syntax' and the 'lexis' or in the generative linguistic tradition between the 'syntactic component' and the 'lexicon' (Chomsky 1965). Halliday sees these two aspects of form to be one and the same thing; the meanings which a language makes available to its speakers are realized either in grammatical structures or in lexical items, and these two types of realization are not essentially different, at least in their representation within the system network.

Exploration of the 'grammarian's dream' approach is taken up in the late 1970s and the 1980s in the work of Berry, Fawcett and Hasan. Whilst there are considerable similarities in the overall proposals of these scholars, a number of differences are observable. Given their attention to lexis, each proposal is outlined individually in the sections below. Berry's and Fawcett's treatments of lexis are also reviewed by Butler (1985: 133–5). What is perhaps surprising is that Halliday himself, as author of the concept of 'lexis as most delicate grammar', has never published even a prototype lexical system network. Even in Kress (1976), where many of Halliday's early 'English system networks' are brought together, descriptions stop short of lexis. His well-developed system network for the nominal group, for example, does not extend into lexis beyond the inclusion of the feature [noun] in the system for 'CLASS AT HEAD' (Kress 1976: 131). As quoted in Section 2.2, Halliday is 'by nature a grammarian', even though as such, (one of) his professed aims is 'to build the dictionary out of the grammar'. To exaggerate the significance of this lacuna in Halliday's description would be ungenerous. We cannot reasonably expect the architect both to produce the blueprint and then proceed to construct the whole of the edifice, brick by brick.

2.4.2 M. Berry's approach to lexis

Berry (1977), whilst incorporating collocation in her account of systemic theory, attempts to draw parallels between lexical and structural organization. In her approach, collocations of lexical items 'occurring one after another in sequence' are likened to elements of grammatical structure. She then attempts to postulate rank for lexical organization, i.e. lexical units of different sizes on a rank scale, but as she concludes:

> Since there is only one unit which can be delimited with any degree of confidence, it is difficult to apply the concept of rank to lexis, though theoretically there must be a rank scale, with the lexical item as the lowest unit and with a higher unit which consists of lexical items. (Berry 1977: 60–1)

It is difficult to understand Berry's insistence on the theoretical necessity of a rank scale for lexis. As she admits, there is little evidence for the application of this concept to 'lexical units'. Clearly, lexical senses are not all co-extensive with the unit of word on the postulated rank scale for grammatical description. But this is precisely the point. Lexis does not need its own rank scale when it can exploit grammatical units above the word. Thus, for example, the lexical sense in the expression *pull someone's leg* – synonymous in broad terms with the single word *tease* – exploits the structure of the clause for its realization. It is perfectly reasonable, in examining the patterning of lexis, to attempt to abstract away from the forms, and that appears to me to be what research on collocation attempts to do. Collocations, however, are relationships between senses and not evidence of rank scale phenomena in respect of 'lexical units'.

A significant question raised by Berry is what the stretches of language that carry collocation are. This is again the problem of attempting to set up 'lexical units' that are parallel to grammatical units. Whereas the units of grammatical description have been satisfactorily identified and defined, collocation has remained associated with the rather loose notion of span, that is, an arbitrary number of words over which collocational tendencies are measured. It is indeed difficult to claim, without invoking grammatical criteria, that a certain number of words either side of the lexical item under attention constitutes any kind of unit. Again, Berry concludes that these are questions which have so far proved difficult to answer. The solution to the problem is perhaps that these are the wrong questions and that in lexis there is not a parallel with grammar in terms of unit and rank.

Berry (1977), however, constitutes the first published attempt to implement Halliday's 'most delicate grammar' approach to lexis by setting out a system network which represents the meaning distinctions which are carried by individual lexical items. She provides partial, tentative system networks for 'Things' (nouns) and 'Qualities' (adjectives/adverbs). The most fully developed of these are in a network for types of animal (Berry 1977:62), (Figure 2.1).

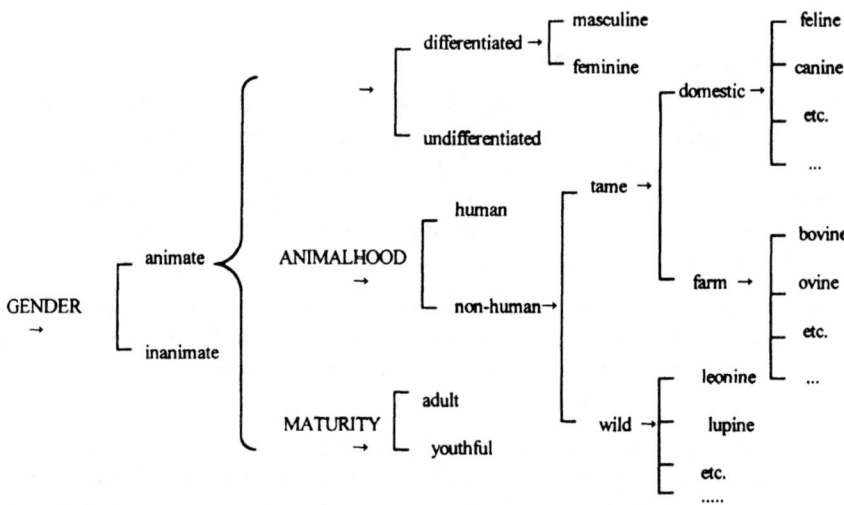

Figure 2.1. Berry's system network of 'gender systems' (Berry 1977: 62)

An immediate observation is that the feature labels in Berry's networks are overtly semantic in nature, with perhaps the exception of the term GENDER itself, which has clear grammatical consequences. This ties in with the growing emphasis at the time on meaning potential, and is in tune with the approach to be presented here. Secondly, the network progresses directly to parallel systems such as DIFFERENTIATION ([differentiated] versus [undifferentiated]), ANIMALHOOD ([human versus non-human]) and MATURITY ([adult] versus [youthful]). The outcome from a traversal of the system network is a set of features, e.g. [animate], [differentiated], [feminine], [non-human], [tame], [domestic], and [canine], which would specify the lexical item bitch. As Butler rightly observes (1985: 134), a network set out in this way is a systemic formalization of the componential analysis approach to lexical meaning (for a discussion see Chapter 6). But there is here a serious issue for systemic theory, because the parallel arrangement of componential distinctive features is a source of problems; such an arrangement requires the introduction of a considerable number of constraints to ensure that any set of possible features that may constitute a selection expression ultimately lead to a lexical item. It is clear from examining Berry's network that there are combinations of features that do not in fact have any realization. And she does not provide any kind of formalism in which the necessary constraints might be stated. I shall take this issue up in relation to this and other networks in Chapter 6.

Although Berry does not provide realization statements to accompany her system network, she does, however, discuss the kind of statement which she claims is needed. These, she states, are like the 'particularization statements' that she posits for structure – but they differ in two ways. First, grammatical particularization statements 'narrow choice of formal item to a particular class or sub-class', whereas in lexis they 'narrow choice of formal item to a particular individual unique item' (Berry 1977: 69). Second, lexical particularization statements, unlike those for structure, are attached not to a single feature but to a combination of features. Thus, we might have a rule of the kind: if [feminine] and [adult] and [bovine] then select [*cow*].

It would be unfair to conclude, however, that Berry – in what is essentially an introductory textbook on systemic linguistics – unconditionally espouses the 'most delicate grammar' approach. Although she makes reference to Halliday's notion, stating that 'This school of thought envisages the possibility of lexis eventually being subsumed under grammar' (Berry 1977: 71), she reflects, as did Halliday sixteen years earlier, that, given the inexperience of linguists in this area, the school of thought concedes the necessity to treat lexis and grammar as separate levels. Between this view of lexis and the belief that 'lexis will never be subsumed under grammar' (Berry 1977: 71), she suggests an intermediate position – that grammar and lexis differ only by degree, related on a cline, with no sharp division between them. This intermediate view itself begins to resemble the 'most delicate grammar' position.

Ultimately, her own position recognizes grammar and lexis as distinct yet related levels, and she posits the possibility of fusing their system networks and realization processes. In this conceptual framework she offers two possible solutions. The first would be to map functions specified in the lexical systems onto those specified by the grammatical systems, by means of 'discontinuity' and 'conflation' statements. The second is to allow features in the lexical system networks to operate directly, independently of the realization processes, and to map the formal realizations from both processes at the surface end by means of a new set of discontinuity and conflation statements. But it has to be said that there is no published account, either in Berry (1977) or in any publication since, of how this programmatic proposal would work out in practice.

In concluding her discussion, Berry rightly points out that the relationship between lexis and grammar has often been largely irrelevant to the various purposes for which systemic linguistics has been used. This points to the predominant use of systemic linguistics as a descriptive and analytical tool. Berry goes on to say:

> The problem only arises in general linguistic studies primarily concerned with showing exactly how the surface forms of language are derived from their meanings. (Berry 1977: 75)

As I stated at the outset, it is this application of systemic functional grammar that is the topic of this book: my assumption is that a good generative grammar can be the source of a good text-descriptive grammar. Berry, like Halliday earlier, does at least leave the debate open. As Butler points out:

> Berry's discussion does not provide us with any cut-and-dried answers to the theoretical problem of integrating lexis into a semantically based model. It does, however, constitute the only serious attempt in the literature to examine the possibilities available. In particular, it gives due consideration to both the similarities and the differences between grammatical and lexical patterning. (Butler 1985: 135)

2.4.3 R.P. Fawcett (1980) and cultural classification

Fawcett's (1980) approach to lexis can be seen as the precursor to the work presented here. The comments made are therefore limited to his account at that time. His current position is represented by the treatment of lexis in the Cardiff Grammar, as implemented computationally in the GENESYS generator and described, in relation to noun senses, in Fawcett (1994). The lexical aspects of the Cardiff Grammar are the result of contributions made by Robin Fawcett and myself over the last seven years; there are many aspects of our current work where it is impossible to credit either researcher with the innovations.

In a short discussion of 'lexicalism' and systemic grammar, Fawcett claims that what is needed in order to capture lexical specificity without losing sight of grammatical generalization is:

> a model that makes an appropriate connection between the syntactico-semantic generalizations associated with units such as the clause and the facts associated with given lexical items. (Fawcett 1980: 271)

He goes on to claim that his model, amongst possible others, provides the framework for this connection and does so through two features in particular: (1) the notion of delicacy in system networks and (2) the concept of re-entry to the system network.

In general, Fawcett (1980) considers lexis as the representation of the cultural classification of 'Processes', 'Things' and 'Qualities'. Cultural classification is modelled as the more delicate part of relevant sub-networks, and he gives examples of networks for both verbs and nouns.

The lexis of verbs, for example, appears in various parts of the TRANSITIVITY network after the subclassification of Processes into action, mental and relational types and further sub-classification according to their association with Participant Roles. The networks that he uses to illustrate this are (1) a system

16

network for action Processes within TRANSITIVITY, and (2) a 'very tentative and partial' system network for the cultural classification of 'affected-centred Processes' in English (1980: 137, 153). The realization rules associated with features of the TRANSITIVITY network occur right through the network, down to the most delicate choices in cultural classification. These specify the clause elements to be inserted, the conflation of Participant Roles with these elements, and the item which is to expound the Main Verb. As in Hasan's realization statements (2.4.4), features in the network for 'Thing' are preselected by realization rules through the process of re-entry. In his 1980 account, the specific details of preselection in this respect are not spelled out – though they are later, for example in Fawcett *et al.* (1993).

For the lexis of nouns, Fawcett sketches out a partial account of the cultural classification of things. As with the cultural classification of Processes in the system of transitivity, cultural classification of 'things' is represented as a sub-network within the overall system network for the expression of 'Thing', which specifies all semantic options realized through the structure of the nominal group. The option of expressing 'Thing' as a noun, together with the potential for particularization (through determiners) and *ad hoc* classification (through modifiers and qualifiers), is one option alongside others such as naming (e.g. *Ike, Ivy*, etc.), token classification (pronouns) and seeking classification (*who, what*, etc.). The cultural classification sub-network (Figure 2.2) develops out of

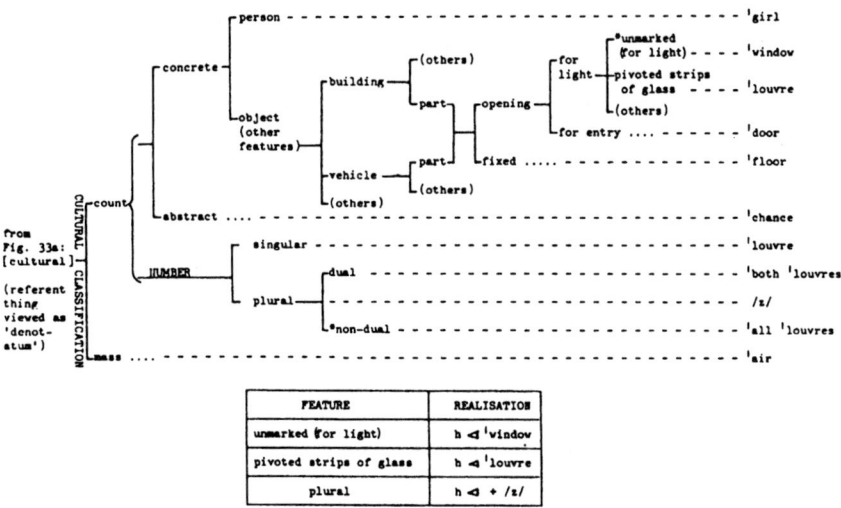

FEATURE	REALISATION
unmarked (for light)	h ◁ 'window
pivoted strips of glass	h ◁ 'louvre
plural	h ◁ + /z/

Figure 2.2. Fawcett's system network for the cultural classification of things in English (Fawcett 1980: 218)

features such as [count] and [mass], [concrete] and [abstract], and increases in delicacy on a taxonomical basis, in which the relations of hyponymy and meronymy play a central role. Fawcett does not develop his cultural classification network further or justify its shape, as Butler (1985: 134) points out. Fawcett admits these limitations, and also points out that the network 'probably reflects overmuch the somewhat narrow view of semantic features that dominated semantics in the 1960s and early 1970s' (Fawcett 1980: 219).

Fawcett's lexical networks tend to be free from the extensive parallelism that is found in the work of Hasan and Cross (2.4.4 and 2.4.5). Moreover, unlike Hasan, for whom the array of features in a selection expression specifies the lexical item, Fawcett places the realization rule for specification of the lexical verb on terminal features in the network (cf. Hasan 1987).

As I suggested at the beginning of this section, Fawcett's 1980 systemic functional grammar formed the basis for the large computationally implemented Cardiff Grammar, which has been under development in the COMMUNAL Project (Fawcett *et al.* 1993), an overview of which is given in Chapter 3. The work presented here, within the current Cardiff Grammar framework, is therefore the natural successor to Fawcett's earlier work. One notable intervening development of the model, also in terms of 'lexis as most delicate grammar', is his account of relational Processes in the semantics of clause and verb in English (Fawcett 1987). This paper offers a new interpretation of the lexicogrammar of relational processes to 'set alongside the approach taken by Halliday 1985' (Fawcett 1987: 131). It offers an extensive treatment of the lexicogrammar of Processes in which are included locational Processes such as *go, come* and *leave*, possessive Processes such as *have, buy* and *sell* (cf. Hasan 1985) and attributive Processes such as *be, become* and *make.* As in his 1980 model, the realization statements, which here are for relational Processes, are on terminal features in the network. This can be exemplified by one of the terminal features in the possessive Process subnetwork, [unmarked-pos-ca], which has the realization rule:

M < have (expound the Main Verb by the item have)
/Ca BY S (conflate the Participant Role of Carrier with Subject)
FOR S: RE [thing] (for Subject re-enter at [thing])
/Pos BY C (conflate the Participant Role of Possessed with Complement)
FOR C: RE [thing] (for Complement re-enter at [thing]) (Fawcett 1987: 167)

Fawcett's recent work on lexis (1994), in the context of the current Cardiff Grammar situated in a computational system for natural language generation, makes special reference to the relationship between the organization of the lexis of nouns within system networks and ontological modelling in the belief system. This work reflects the need to posit other 'components' in such a system in order to account for the organization of, and relationships between, entities at a conceptual level which cannot be adequately modelled at the lexicogrammatical level. It therefore echoes the view (expressed in Chapter 6) that a system network approach to lexis cannot, and should not, be expected to handle all aspects of lexical semantic and conceptual semantic organization, and that consequently some theory of such organization is required.

Although Fawcett's 1980 system network approach to lexis paves the way for the current work in the Cardiff Grammar, it is clearly only suggestive of the way in which lexis can be modelled. Little more could be expected in a work which attempts to give a general overview of the lexicogrammar. It is only by implementing system networks that their 'generative' validity can be assessed. The luxury of 'partial and tentative' networks is not afforded to the lexicogrammarian working on an explicit computational grammar of English. Even the best of 'pencil and paper' networks and realization rules turn out to be generatively inadequate. It is therefore unsurprising that many aspects of Fawcett's original proposal have undergone at times considerable modification in the light of their implementation in the Cardiff Grammar.

2.4.4 R. Hasan and the 'grammarian's dream'

Hasan's 1987 paper was the first publication which focused solely on exploring the reality of Halliday's 'grammarian's dream' of turning the whole of linguistic form into grammar. Her exploration is in terms of two fundamental questions: (1) is this project feasible and (2) what are the consequences? By way of exemplification, she gives detailed accounts of three areas of transitivity: the lexicogrammar of what she terms 'acquisition' (with the processes *gather*, *collect* and *accumulate*; of 'deprivation 1' (*scatter*, *divide* and *distribute*); and of 'deprivation 2' (*strew*, *spill* and *share*).

Hasan sets out to explore the features which are associated with each of the verbal processes in the sets above, and to demonstrate their uniqueness as lexical items, a concept recognized, as she points out, by authors such as Berry (1977), Fawcett (1980), Fillmore (1977), Leech (1974) and Lyons (1977). The uniqueness that is referred to is not simply their individual identities *qua* lexical items with some individual semantic correlate, but their intra-linguistic uniqueness. Lexical items are different because each one entails a unique set of lexicogrammatical correlates. On this basis, the features which determine lexical items have formal consequences, which are expressed by a set of realization statements (Hasan 1987: 185). This view is consonant with Fawcett's statement that features in a system network are motivated by some reflex in form (Fawcett 1973: 157 and 1980: 101, reiterated in Martin 1987: 16). Furthermore, recognition of the lexicogrammatical uniqueness of each lexical item accords with the view of corpus linguists such as John Sinclair and Gill Francis that grammar is the grammar of individual words and is only revealed through extensive lexis-oriented corpus investigation. Tucker (1996) attempts a reconciliation of the grammarian's and corpus linguist's positions, arguing that they are complementary, rather than diametrically opposed.

Hasan's system network for [disposal] within TRANSITIVITY is given here in Figure 2.3. Like Berry's network for GENDER, it contains parallel systems. Thus for example, the feature [action] entails selection in both the ACT system and the BENEFACTION system, and [disposal] entails selection from both ACCESS and CHARACTER. Each feature in the network is associated with one or more types of realization statement, which Hasan gives as: (1) insertion of a structural function *x*, (2) conflation of two or more functions into one element, (3) ordering of elements *a* and *b* (and ... *n*) *vis-à-vis* each other, (4) subcategorization of

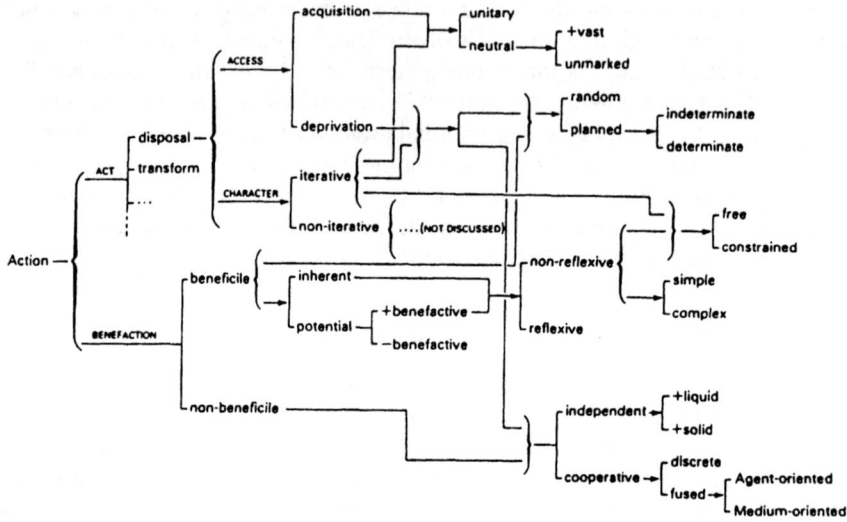

Figure 2.3. Hasan's system network for processes of [disposal] (Hasan 1987: 189)

some function or feature, (5) pre-selection of some feature as a concomitant of some insertion/subcategorization, and (6) outclassification of some function/feature as incompatible with some insertion/subcategorization (Hasan 1987: 185). The realization statements for [disposal], for example, are:

1. sub-categorize Event as /(material action) of disposal involving change in location of Medium/
2. sub-categorize Medium Thing as /alienable object/
3. sub-categorize Agent Thing as /human, person(s) or institutions/

The subcategorization statements resemble the selectional restrictions of Chomsky's Standard Theory (1965). Hasan warns, however, against equating the two by specifying that, unlike selectional restrictions, subcategorization statements do not operate on items, possess directionality or lead to 'linguistic malaise' if not observed (Hasan 1987: 188). Selectional restrictions, however, were removed from lexical entries in later versions of generative grammar for the reasons summarized by Horrocks as follows:

> The features in terms of which the selectional restrictions are stated seem to have more to do with semantics than syntax, and indeed could only be regarded as having syntactic import in a theory which required the syntax and lexicon together to generate all the grammatical sentences of a language, and no non-sentences, without assistance from other components. (Horrocks 1987: 36)

It is precisely this kind of observation which distinguishes grammars within the generative tradition from systemic functional grammars. In Hasan's approach described here, and in the Cardiff Grammar, the semantics reflected in selectional behaviour of this kind **is** part of the lexicogrammar (i.e syntax and lexicon) and not the responsibility of some other 'component'. Hasan admits to stating subcategorization informally, for 'lack of formal information'. As I understand this statement, she is indicating that she has not developed a formal representation of the features from other networks which are required to state subcategorization. The features she uses for the subcategorization of Participant Roles, such as 'Agent', are overtly semantic, e.g. 'human', 'person(s) or institutions'. Ideally, it seems, Hasan would wish to subcategorize according to features that have the same lexicogrammatical status as those she uses in the TRANSITIVITY network. To take one example, statement 3 above subcategorizes the Agent Thing as '/human, person(s) or institutions/'. These features must refer to features in the system network for Thing. However informally they may be expressed here, in the more formal statement required for Hasan's network a set of lexicogrammatically significant features would presumably need to be identified. And this is perhaps the crux of the problem in the development of 'lexis as most delicate grammar'. The question still remains as to how nouns, adjectives and adverbs can be expressed in the same lexicogrammatical terms as are used for verbs. (This is taken up in Chapter 6.)

Hasan's network highlights a series of systemic oppositions which are necessary, she claims, to account for the individual behaviour of each member of a set of Process types. She is able to show how a particular selection expression – the list of features specified by traversing the network from left to right – (a) requires that an EVENT be expressed by a given lexical verb and (b) specifies the grammatical context in which that verb is found. The minimal difference between two lexical verbs will be expressed by their sharing the same selection expression with the exception of one feature. An example of this is the opposition of [+solid] and [+liquid] which distinguishes the two verbs *strew* and *spill*.

In her conclusion, Hasan provides an important clarification of the value of the features found in her network. She stresses that:

> The options of the networks are not 'universals', 'primitives' or god-given truths: they are schematic pointers to man-made meanings which can be expressed verbally. The options are presented in certain relations to each other because this is how I understand English ways of meaning; they are not there because the making of any other kind of relation is impossible ... The networks REPRESENT a language; they do not INVENT it. (Hasan 1987: 207)

It is the claim of systemic linguistics that these feature options lie at the heart of what systemic grammars set out to do. They express, through the system networks, those meanings and the relations between them which the resource of a particular language makes available.

Hasan's 1987 paper is an important contribution to the 'grammarian's dream' project. It is, however, a highly specific and circumscribed account. Its relevance is, yet again, to the area of the lexicogrammar of verbs, and therefore clauses. While such contributions, like Fawcett's 1987 account of relational Processes, throw light on the complexity of this area of the lexicogrammar, they offer us little insight into how the grammarian's dream can be realized in 'second- and third-order lexis' as I referred to it in Chapter 1, namely, the lexi-cogrammar of nouns and adjectives.

2.4.5 M. Cross

Cross's work on lexis, as part of a larger project HORACE, falls within the frame-work of computational linguistics, and in particular of computational text generation (Cross 1991, 1993). Its aims are therefore similar to those of the PENMAN Project, including the NIGEL grammar (Mann and Matthiessen 1983, 1985, Matthiessen and Bateman 1991) and the COMMUNAL Project, including the Cardiff Grammar (Fawcett *et al.* 1993), to which the work reported here relates. Cross in fact takes the NIGEL grammar as a basis for her work and develops and extends it appropriately for the purposes of her own text generation. The register domain for the text generation that Cross undertakes is that of environmental texts involving the 'water cycle'. She is therefore pri-marily concerned with lexical senses from the ideational metafunction, although some lexical choices based on tenor are allowed for by 'extra-network' means, along the lines described in Matthiessen (1990) and discussed in 2.4.6.

In discussing her approach to lexical generation, Cross explores taxonomic perspectives and metalinguistic representation in terms both of semantic prim-itives and of underlying conceptual bases. The approach which she ultimately adopts is that of 'register-based most delicate grammar', with feature-based net-works of the metalinguistic type rather than the lexical taxonomic type. This means, in essence, that she claims to be using cross-classifying componential fea-ture terms, such as [metamorphosis] versus [no metamorphosis] and [initial solid] versus [initial liquid], rather than using features based on lexical seman-tic relations such as hyponymy, meronymy, opposition, etc. It is not clear, how-ever, that Cross succeeds in maintaining this distinction in the case of nominal lexis. She provides detailed accounts of the networks for 'process', 'thing', and for what she refers to as the 'adjectival group' and the 'adverbial group'. The network for process is also responsible for both verbal and nominal forms; thus, for example, the feature [evaporate] serves as the entry condition to two 'lex-ification gates' (cf. Matthiessen 1988) which re-introduce the difference between Process and Thing, and lead to its 'lexification' as either *evaporate* or *evaporation*.

Much of Cross's classification concerns extensions to the small NIGEL pro-cess network in the areas of transformation (*heat, cool, melt, crack,* etc.), behaviour (*drink, eat, farm,* etc.), motion (*come, go, rise,* etc.), occurrence (*suffer, undergo, occur,* etc.), and relocation (*get, obtain, supply,* etc.), with the first of these given most attention, due to the nature of the lexis in the 'water cycle' texts. The networks themselves are inspired principally by Hasan's approach (1987), as dis-cussed in 2.4.4. The central issue raised by an analysis of Cross's work concerns the role of systemic choices in the specification of certain lexical verbs. Let us take her network for 'transformation material processes', which is given in Figure 2.4.

As is the case in a number of Cross's networks, the initial entry condition leads to parallel (or simultaneous) systems. The feature [transformation]

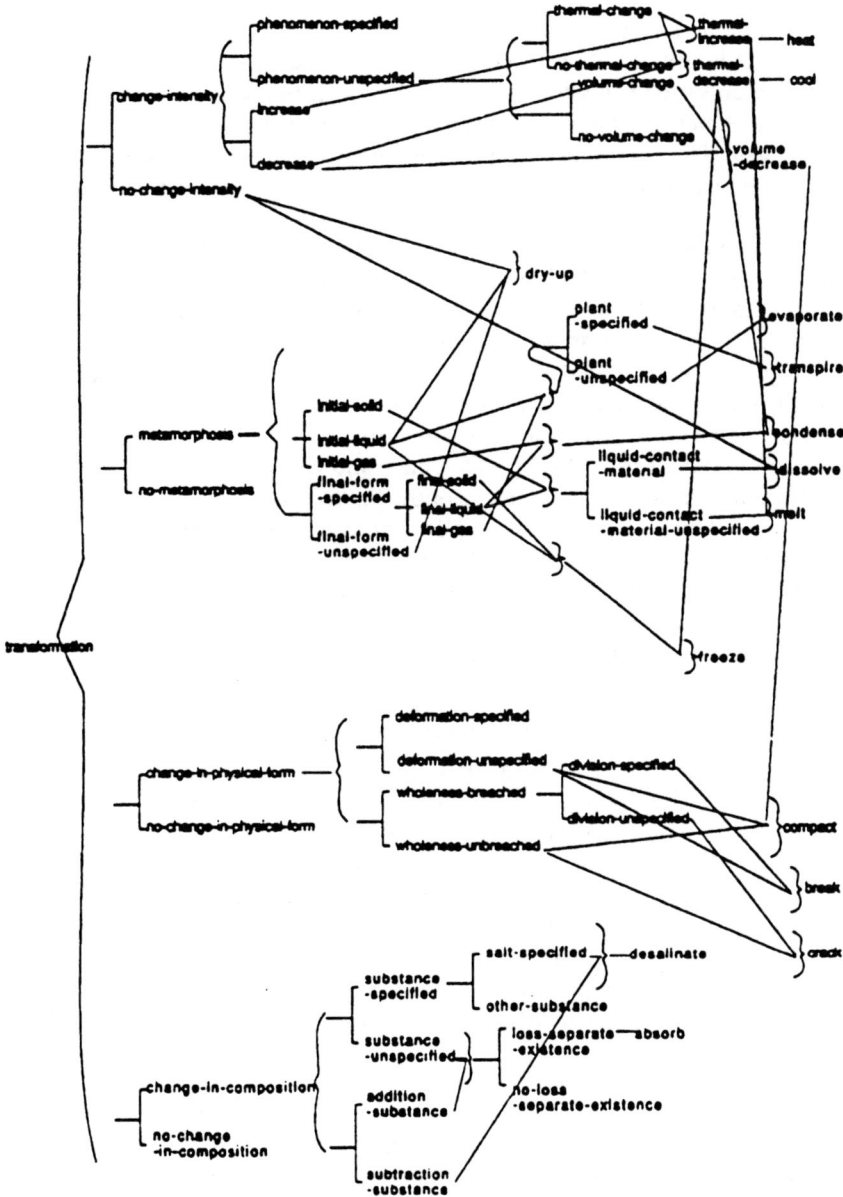

Figure 2.4. Cross's network for 'transformation material processes' (Cross 1993: 211)

specifies that four systems must be entered in parallel: [change-intensity] / [no-change-intensity], [metamorphosis] / [no-metamorphosis], [change-in-physical-form] / [no-change-in-physical-form] and [change-in-composition] / [no-change-in-composition]. These feature oppositions are clearly found necessary in the specification of the grammar and lexis of Processes such as *heat, cool, evaporate, dissolve*, etc. However, it will be observed that in the case of the Processes *desalinate* and *absorb* only the final system involving 'change in composition' is utilized. The network specifies that choices must be made in all four systems. Now EITHER the other systems have no influence on the grammar of the two Processes above OR their various combinations specify other Processes which have been omitted from the network. If, as it would appear, the former state of affairs holds, then, although no lexicogrammatical infelicity will result, the network requires selection of features from oppositions which are in no way reflected in the form. In terms of Cross's network the opposition [metamorphosis] / [no-metamorphosis] is irrelevant to the lexicogrammar of *absorb*. It appears, therefore, that the 'change of composition' system should EXCLUDE entry into the other systems which are entered in parallel. The large issue of systemic constraint, which this example illustrates, is discussed more fully in Chapter 9.

Cross's networks for 'Things', 'Qualities' and 'Adverbials' are rather more sketchy. This is, again, a consequence of the limited domain-specific lexis in the 'water cycle' texts. As one might expect, the partial Thing networks that she proposes rely heavily in places on thesaurus-type metalinguistic features and a predominance of hyponymy relations. Although Cross discusses lexification with respect to her partial Thing network, little else is provided in the way of realization statements referring to the grammar of nominal lexis.

2.4.6 C.M.I.M. Matthiessen and lexical choice

Like Fawcett's recent work, much of Matthiessen's work on lexis is centred on computational text generation and in particular on the problem of lexical choice in text generation (Matthiessen 1990). In this context, Matthiessen has been primarily concerned with the development of the NIGEL grammar in the PENMAN Project (Mann and Matthiessen 1985, Matthiessen 1985, 1988, Matthiessen and Bateman 1991) and, more recently, with multi-lingual text generation. Constraints imposed upon the NIGEL grammar, through collaboration with other projects during its early development, led to the adoption of the more 'conventional' RUS lexicon. Reasons for this choice are given in Cumming (1986).

However, in Matthiessen (1990) a systemic approach to lexis is explored. The model that Matthiessen discusses is again founded on the 'grammarian's dream' notion of Halliday 1961, exemplified by Hasan's 1987 network (2.4.4). He therefore adopts the thesaurus model rather than the dictionary model (lexicon), whilst specifying the basic differences between thesaurus organization (following Roget) and the system network approach. Essentially, according to Matthiessen, there are three differences: (1) system networks are not simple discrimination networks, since they have parallel systems (and therefore involve cross-classification); (2) systemic lexis is ordered in terms of the categories of the grammar, rather than 'fields of experience', as in the case of Roget's thesaurus; (3) systemic lexis also takes into account the interpersonal and textual metafunctional organization of lexis, rather than simply reflecting its ideational organization (Matthiessen 1990: 259).

It is this third area of difference that Matthiessen emphasizes. This reflects the view (one which is endorsed in my own approach) that the lexicogrammar realizes meanings from all three metafunctions. According to Matthiessen, interpersonal and textual lexis may either make independent contributions, or combine with ideational lexis. The independent contribution of interpersonal lexis is in terms of modal lexis (modality, polarity, attitude, etc.), whilst that of textual lexis is in terms of phoric lexis (reference, substitution and conjunction). Interpersonal lexis combines with ideational through connotation (affect and formality) whilst textual lexis and ideational lexis combine in terms of lexical cohesion (repetition, etc.) (see Halliday and Hasan 1976 and Martin 1992). Examples of each are given from Matthiessen (1990: 267) (Figure 2.5).

The other two areas of difference between thesaurus and system network which Matthiessen draws attention to are more problematic. Although cross-classification is a natural feature of system networks, there is no real proposal in the systemic literature on lexical networks that does not contain large areas of lexis discriminated purely by taxonomic relations, i.e. without overt

	interpersonal	textual
(i) Independent	modal lexis (modality, polarity, attitude, etc.)	phoric lexis (reference, substitution, conjunction)
	But surely, my dear Mrs. Warren, you know the reason.	But surely, my dear Mrs. Warren, you know the reason. Anyway I suggested Ian tried to stay with him and he did.
(ii) In combination with ideational lexis	'connotation': affect formality	lexical cohesion: repetition, etc.
	Anyway I suggested Ian tried to stay with him and he did and I meanwhile I'd told Ian all about how daft this bloke was so Ian goes and stays with him and then he goes and tells him all about it.	Anyway I suggested Ian tried to stay with him and he did and I meanwhile I'd told Ian all about how daft this bloke was so Ian goes and stays with him and then he goes and tells him all about it.

Figure 2.5. Interpersonal and textual lexis (Matthiessen 1990: 267)

cross-classification. Matthiessen's own example of lexical organization in a system network (1990: 260) clearly suggests that 'species of animal' are distinguished simply by taxonomy, e.g. [feline], [canine], [equine], etc. and [canine] is distinguished by the hyponyms [alsatian], [terrier], [spaniel], etc., Moreover, it could be argued that cross-classification is at least implicit, if not explicitly expressed, in a thesaurus. The use of lexical semantic classification, as is the case in Matthiessen's network – and indeed in the 'noun' system networks proposed by other systemicists – suggests that such networks are not organized entirely on the basis of categories of the grammar, rather than according to 'fields of experience'. The important issue of how 'lexical' system networks are organized is discussed fully in Chapter 6.

Matthiessen also points out the influence of contextual factors on the lexical resource. He suggests, following Halliday (1978: 141–5), that the choice of functions realized lexically is influenced by aspects of the situation. Thus field (the type of social action) influences choice within the ideational metafunction, tenor (the role relationships) within the interpersonal metafunction, and mode (the symbolic organization) within the textual metafunction. Matthiessen clarifies these relationships by giving brief examples for each. Field, for example, in terms of 'technicality of field' influences the organization of ideational taxonomies. Tenor, through 'affect, formality, expertise, etc.' influences the choice of 'formal and attitudinal items'. Finally, mode, in terms of the distinction between 'spoken' and 'written', influences the 'degree of lexical specificity and the 'density' of lexical items per unit of running text' (Matthiessen 1990: 273).

In most respects, Matthiessen's general account of lexis in a systemic model differs little from the account I present in this book. There are, of course, differences of emphasis. Much has been made of the distinction between the three metafunctions, especially in terms of how they are reflected by three (fairly) independent areas of system network organization. This degree of independence in respect of lexis is less clear in Matthiessen's account. Furthermore, the overriding functional organization of Matthiessen's lexical system networks is ideational. Yet this itself is not an unreasonable position. Textually influenced choices (such as the choice of *animal* rather than *dog*) at some point in the construction of a text are made possible because there is a lexical semantic relation of hyponymy between the two. Similarly, although perhaps to a lesser extent, the interpersonally motivated choice of the metaphor *pig* in *what a pig you are!* relies upon the ideational classification of pigs and the encyclopaedic knowledge associated (unfairly!) with these creatures. One might argue, therefore, that the 'ideational denotation' makes the 'interpersonal connotations' and the 'textual inferences' possible. However, this might be seen as a dangerous line of enquiry, since by pursuing it, one could easily reach Leech's conclusion that only ideational meaning is the subject of semantics, whereas interpersonal and textual meaning fall into the domain of pragmatics (Leech 1983).

What is important in the insistence on the 'metafunctional hypothesis' is that it reminds us that there is more than one kind of meaning, and that provision has to be made for this in modelling 'meaning potential'. A purely ideational account of lexical relations is inadequate for this purpose. A lexical system network must make explicit the choice between *friend* and *mate*, for example, which is clearly an interpersonal one. The approach presented here differs from Matthiessen's in that, in generative terms, the metafunctions take a back seat; they are not explicitly represented in the lexicogrammar. In various parts of the lexical system network of the Cardiff Grammar choices will be represented which involve interpersonal and textual meaning. Yet they are not separated out as such, and no reference is made to them in these terms. Moreover, the Cardiff Grammar emphasizes the **interdependency** of the metafunctions rather than their **independence**. An account of these considerations is given in Chapter 8.

2.4.7 J.R. Martin and lexical cohesion

Martin's prime interest in lexis is in its role in contributing to the 'textuality' of text. He sets out to analyse the contribution of the resource of lexical relations to textual cohesion. For this purpose, he examines lexis under the heading of 'ideation'. He proposes that lexical relations can be approached from four different perspectives: collocation, lexis as most delicate grammar, lexical cohesion and field taxonomies. He relates these relations to the planes and strata of linguistic organization, assigning field-specific taxonomies of 'lexical meanings' to context, cohesion to discourse semantics and field-neutral taxonomies (delicate grammar) and collocation to lexicogrammar.

Taking Halliday's notion of field of discourse, Martin proposes that fields may be defined as 'sets of activity sequences oriented to some global institutional purpose' (Martin 1992: 292). He then suggests breaking down these sequences into:

i. taxonomies of actions, people, places, things and qualities.
ii. configurations of actions with people, places, things and qualities and of people, places and things with qualities.
iii. activity sequences of these configurations.

On the basis of these field characterizations, Martin sets up a unit at the level of 'discourse semantics' which he calls the 'message part'. The message part realizes aspects of the level of field, as illustrated above, and is itself realized in the lexicogrammar by lexical items organized in terms of experiential meanings. Although Martin wishes to distinguish between meanings at the level of discourse semantics and those at the level of lexicogrammatical organization, he makes no proposal as to how the latter may be formally distinguished. There is thus no further specification of the message part beyond the labelling 'message part'. Martin suggests, however, that ultimately 'it will prove necessary to differentiate technically among the different meanings at this level' (1992: 325). The relationship between three levels of field, discourse semantics and (experiential) lexicogrammar is illustrated in a table (Martin 1992: 325), which is reproduced here as Table 2.1.

Thus, by way of illustration, the lexical item *rink*, as selected from the lexical resource for 'Thing' in the grammar, is a realization of a 'message part', which itself realizes the category 'Thing' at the level of field.

Table 2.1. Ideational labelling across levels (Martin 1992: 325)

FIELD	DISCOURSE SEMANTICS	EXPERIENTIAL GRAMMAR
activity sequence	(unnamed)	clause complex (temporal)
activity	message	Process (& TRANSITIVITY roles)
activity	message part	Event
people & things	message part	Thing
place	message part	Circumstance
quality	message part	Epithet; Manner adverb

In his treatment of lexical organization within the lexicogrammar, Martin distinguishes between 'taxonomic relations' and 'nuclear relations' (configurations). The former subsume the familiar relations of hyponymy, synonymy, meronymy and opposition (as set out, for example, in Lyons 1977 and Cruse 1986). Nuclear relations, less well understood, reflect 'The ways in which actions, people, places, things and qualities are configured as activities in activity sequences' (Martin 1992: 309).

Nuclear lexical relations represent, therefore, the syntagmatic organization of lexical meaning, whereas taxonomic relations represent their paradigmatic organization. As Martin points out, in earlier approaches to lexical cohesion, nuclear relations were handled under the heading of collocation. What Martin attempts to do is to examine and identify more precisely the semantic relations which hold between elements of lexical organization on this axis. This would seem to be his justification for a new technical term, rather than collocation, which has not generally been explored specifically in terms of its relationship to discourse-semantic and field organization. In order to explain nuclear relations Martin exploits Halliday's treatment of clause complexes in terms of 'expansion', and its three relations of 'elaboration', 'extension' and 'enhancement' (Halliday 1994: 215ff). Martin presents a revised and expanded account of these relations, extending their coverage to 'action' and 'signifying' processes and to the experiential structure of the clause and the nominal and verbal groups. This approach uses these relations to re-describe phenomena such as: 'Process–Range' and 'Process–Medium' (play + tennis, play + the ball), 'phrasal processes' (look at/after/over) and 'Epithet–Thing' in the nominal group (*red car, hungry puppy*). The range of these relations is shown as a taxonomy (Figure 2.6).

Through this analysis of clauses and groups, Martin seeks to refine and extend Matthiessen's 1992 account of nuclearity and peripherality (Figure 2.7) in terms of the relationship between Process, Participant Role and Circumstantial Role. Finally, in Martin's revision of Matthiessen's account, four bands of nuclearity and peripherality are posited: centre, nucleus, margin and periphery (Martin 1992: 319) (Table 2.2).

At first sight, Martin's analysis may seem to be relevant solely in terms of the lexical relations which hold in terms of the semantic configurations expressed

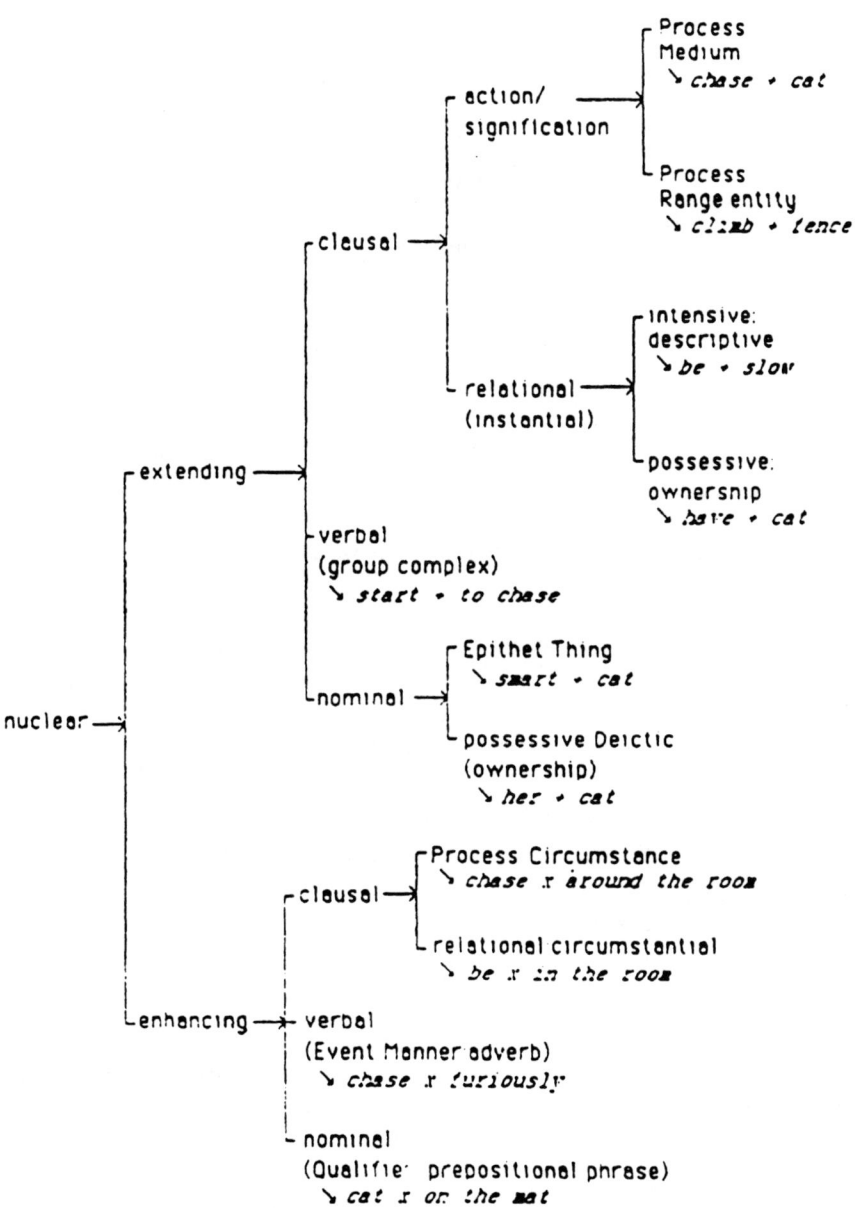

Figure 2.6. Martin's taxonomy of nuclear relations (Martin 1992: 320)

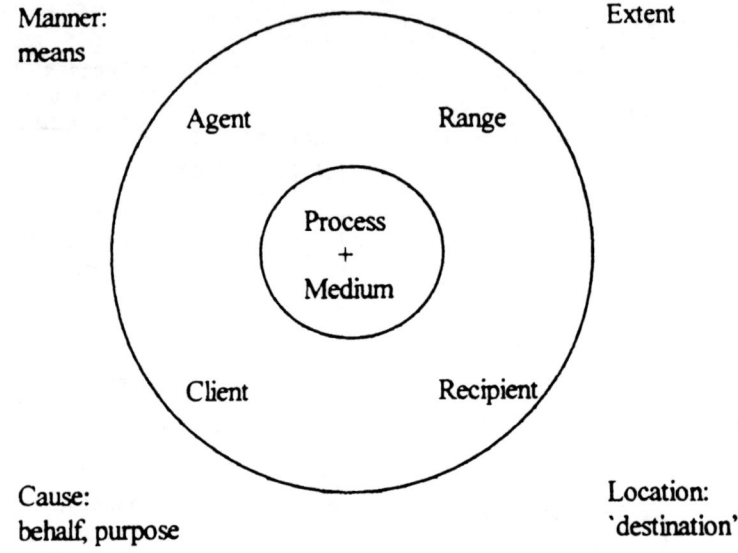

Manner: means

Extent

Agent   Range

Process
+
Medium

Client   Recipient

Cause: behalf, purpose

Location: 'destination'

Figure 2.7. Nuclearity and peripherability in Matthiessen (1992)

Table 2.2. Martin's alternative model of nuclearity (Martin 1992: 319)

CENTRE	NUCLEUS	MARGIN	PERIPHERY
Process =	+ Medium	+ x Agent	x Circumstance
Range:process	+ Range:entity	+ x Beneficiary	
Classifier = Thing	+ Epithet	(+ x Numerative?)	x Qualifier
Event = Particle	+ Event (event complex)	(+ x causative?)	x Manner adverb

within the lexicogrammar of clauses and groups. But, as Martin points out, these relations are not limited to the grammatical structure itself. As an example of this, Martin gives the relation between *serve* and *ace* in the 'Process–Medium' configuration (elaboration/extension). Although they are lexicogrammatically related in the clause *Ben served another ace*, the two message parts may be found in separate clauses in *Ben serves . . . That's his fifth ace of the match*, or metaphorically realized in *Ben's serve produced very few aces today* (Martin 1992: 309).

Thus Martin establishes, through the taxonomic and the nuclear relations which hold between message parts, an important instrument for analysing lexical cohesion in texts from an ideational point of view. His analysis is therefore able to proceed in terms of both the syntagmatic (nuclear) and the

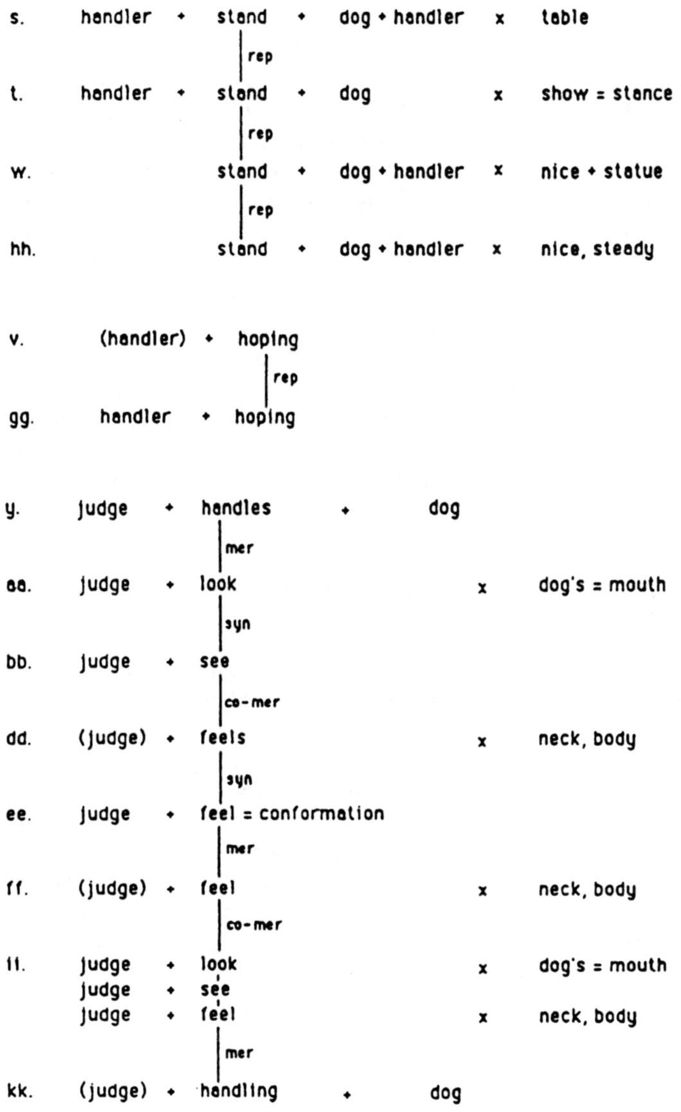

```
s.     handler   →   stand    →   dog → handler   x   table
                      |
                      | rep
t.     handler   →   stand    →   dog             x   show = stance
                      |
                      | rep
w.                   stand    →   dog → handler   x   nice → statue
                      |
                      | rep
hh.                  stand    →   dog → handler   x   nice, steady


v.     (handler)  →  hoping
                      |
                      | rep
gg.    handler    →  hoping


y.     judge     →   handles          →   dog
                      |
                      | mer
aa.    judge     →   look                 x   dog's = mouth
                      |
                      | syn
bb.    judge     →   see
                      |
                      | co-mer
dd.    (judge)   →   feels                x   neck, body
                      |
                      | syn
ee.    judge     →   feel = conformation
                      |
                      | mer
ff.    (judge)   →   feel                 x   neck, body
                      |
                      | co-mer
ii.    judge     →   look                 x   dog's = mouth
       judge     →   see
       judge     →   feel                 x   neck, body
                      |
                      | mer
kk.    (judge)   →   handling         →   dog
```

Figure 2.8. An example of Martin's analysis of lexical cohesion (Martin 1992: 336–7)

31

paradigmatic (taxonomic) axes. An example of Martin's analysis is given in Figure 2.8.

Martin's work, as we have seen, is firmly situated in the context of textual analysis and interpretation. He is not primarily concerned with the lexicogrammar as a 'generative' device which allows the producer of text to make meanings. Therefore, whereas his account provides a useful checklist of aspects of lexical organization which are textually significant (in both paradigmatic and syntagmatic terms), there is no proposal as to how the lexicogrammar, or a fuller model of an interacting mind, is to provide for these. The numerous examples of system network fragments indicate the kind of organization that is needed, yet are never explicit enough to state the lexicogrammatical consequences of the systems and features represented. Justification for the shape of networks for 'Thing', for example, is no more explicit than the earlier attempts of Fawcett (1980), criticized for this reason by Butler (1985: 134). It is also significant that Martin refers to the study of material Processes in Hasan 1987 (see 2.4.4) as 'the most important study in this area'. Hasan herself produces no system network for 'Thing' and only hints informally at what kind of systemic features it might contain. What can be gained from Martin's account, therefore, is support for a 'thesaurus-oriented' model of lexical organization which incorporates lexical semantic and collocational relations.

2.4.8 The contemporary work of J. Sinclair on collocation: the COBUILD approach

Sinclair was one of Halliday's close collaborators in the period of 'scale and category grammar', the precursor to SFG. For a number of years now, however, as founder of the COBUILD Project, he has been primarily concerned with corpus-based research in the area of computational lexicography. He has explored the implications of collocation within linguistic theory and has consistently emphasized the importance of appealing to computationally and statistically based work in the development of natural language grammars and dictionaries. The statistical nature of lexical collocation has always called out for extensive text analysis, and this has now become feasible in the era of large machine-readable corpora of natural language. Thus the work on collocation that Sinclair embarked upon in the 1960s (Sinclair 1966) has been developed and found to be increasingly significant through research in lexical computing.

The lexicographical work of Sinclair and his COBUILD colleagues constitutes an important challenge to grammarians in a number of ways. Firstly, it militates against the application of what Sinclair terms 'the open choice principle':

> This is the way of seeing language text as the result of a very large number of complex choices. At each point where a unit is completed (a word or a phrase or a clause), a large range of choice opens up, and the only restraint is grammaticalness. (Sinclair 1987b: 319–20)

Sinclair suggests that virtually all grammars are based on the open choice principle. It remains to be seen whether Sinclair includes in this approach the 'lexis as most delicate grammar' notion or the modification developed at Cardiff presented here. Halliday (1978: 43) claims that 'the lexical system is not something that is fitted in afterwards to a set of slots defined by the grammar'. Sinclair, on the other hand, does not reject outright the open choice principle, but relegates it to the status of 'secondary model':

> It thus appears that a model of language which divides grammar and lexis, and which used the grammar to provide a string of lexical choice points, is a secondary model. (1987b: 32–4)

The 'primary' model that Sinclair seems to suggest is based on the idiom principle:

> It is clear that words do not occur at random in a text, and that the open choice principle does not provide substantial enough restraints. (1987b: 320)

Sinclair's 'principle of idiom' concerns the availability to speakers of a large number of semi-preconstructed phrases that constitute single lexical choices. Collocation is illustrative of the idiom principle, in the sense that it involves the simultaneous selection of pairs or groups of lexical items that are not necessarily syntactically adjacent. There is – and it is this that cannot be accommodated by an open choice account – an underlying rigidity of phraseology, based on the co-selection of certain items of lexis in given contexts.

Sinclair also forwards the hypothesis, supported by his own extended investigation of corpora, that there is a close correlation between the different senses of a word and the structures in which they occur. The notion of structure is also extended to 'lexical structure', in terms of collocation and similar patterns (Sinclair 1988: 74). An illustrative example given by Sinclair is the relation between the three most common senses of the lemma YIELD and their respective realizations as intransitive verb, noun and transitive verb. He concludes from this example that there is seemingly a 'strong tendency for sense and syntax to be associated' (Sinclair 1988: 86). And if this is a central feature of language, then as he suggests,

> it can be turned to provide valuable evidence for lexicography – suggesting sense divisions, and phraseology – identifying phrase units with distinctive patterning. The traditional domain of syntax would be invaded by lexical hordes. (1988: 87)

Renouf and Sinclair (1991) reinforce this challenge to the grammarian's approach to structure in their examination of certain collocational patternings which involve common grammatical words, such as the context (a) A + ? + OF and (b) TOO + ? OF. These grammatical contexts, they suggest, offer a firm basis for studying collocation. They conclude that the 'choice of word class and collocate is specific, and governed by both elements in the framework' (Renouf and Sinclair 1991: 143). The exploration of such item-based frameworks constitutes an eminently sensible way of presenting language patterning, beyond the traditional approach of linguists which sees language as divisible into coherent units. The next stage is to complement such studies by matching them with the proposals of functionally oriented grammarians. Again, Sinclair is not concerned with producing formal generative models. Much of the work of the researchers on the COBUILD Project is closely linked with the production of dictionaries and descriptive grammars in which strict formalization is unnecessary and of little use to consumers. The task of modelling the lexico-grammatical patternings uncovered by such research is consequently left to formal grammarians, with a fair degree of scepticism on the part of Sinclair and close co-researchers as to the feasibility of the enterprise.

As I have pointed out elsewhere (Tucker 1996), Sinclair's strongly lexis-oriented approach – 'constructing the grammar out of the dictionary', as Halliday puts it – may well be reconcilable with the kind of systemic functional approach represented by the practical implementation of the grammarian's dream, as proposed in this book. If this is in fact so, it is clear that systemic grammars must show that they are capable of representing collocational relations – or what lexical semantic organization underlies them – and the phenomenon of semi-preconstructed phrases that Sinclair and his co-researchers are eager to point out. Tucker (1996) demonstrates how this can be done for idioms such as *I haven't the faintest idea*. It is a major concern of this book – and of the Cardiff Grammar as a whole – to show how lexis and grammar can be most appropriately interwoven.

2.5 SUMMARY: FROM TEXT DESCRIPTION TO TEXT PRODUCTION

This chapter has surveyed the main systemic approaches to lexis other than current work at Cardiff, and has highlighted some of the trends. What emerges is the need for a model which:

(a) incorporates the lexicogrammatical nature of lexis (i.e. the lexical and grammatical 'meaning potential' in a unified network of lexicogrammatical options);

(b) incorporates the taxonomical lexical semantic relations (hyponymy, synonymy, meronymy and opposition);

(c) takes account of the syntagmatic relations discussed earlier under the headings 'collocation' and 'nuclear relations'.

The traditional strength of systemic linguistics, in comparison with other theories as practised by hundreds of linguists throughout the world, is its explanatory power in **analysing** text, in 'unpacking' (to use a current popular metaphor) the polysystemic range of meanings which are encoded in text. The point which I shall emphasize at various places in the present work is that an account of the lexicogrammar of a language must also make explicit how it is organized as a resource for **producing** text, and how such a resource is exploited in the production of such meanings. Here I shall be emphasizing this second perspective, so that the account of lexis given here is integrated into a 'generative' model. The primary aim of such a model is to explicate the resource as such and the process by which it generates – or produces – meanings.

Most syntactically oriented theories of language give short shrift to lexis. In terms of the relationship between syntax and the lexicon, it is often considered that it is enough to state what the role of each is, and what each must contain in terms of linguistic organization.

In a similar vein, within systemic linguistics, it seems to have been initially considered appropriate to concentrate on grammar, and then as a supplement to show how lexis might be modelled in the ways discussed above. Thus Halliday could state the principle of 'lexis as most delicate grammar', and then, by modelling fragments of lexicogrammar, illustrate how it can be put into practice, as was done most fully for given areas of lexis by Hasan (1987), Fawcett (1987) and Cross (1991, 1993). The problem with this approach to modelling lexis is this: 'At what point do we stop in any substantial and extensive model of the lexicogrammar?' In the syntax–lexicon approach typical of generative grammarians, it is a more feasible enterprise to exhaust the grammatical description without much attention to the lexis, since they are considered separate components, even if interacting ones. And, if we are to entertain the view of corpus linguists such as Sinclair that the grammar is revealed by the behaviour of lexical items, any grammatical description will be seriously incomplete unless there is substantial modelling of lexis itself.

3 The Cardiff Grammar

3.1 OVERVIEW

A discussion of lexis within an integrated approach to structure and lexis must necessarily include an account of the overall model. This chapter outlines the general characteristics of the Cardiff Grammar – the particular model of systemic functional grammar (SFG) that provides the framework for the present treatment of lexis. Many readers will have some familiarity with systemic functional grammar, notably through the work of M.A.K. Halliday. Although the model described here falls clearly within the systemic functional paradigm, it differs in a number of ways from the Hallidayan approach. This brief overview of the Cardiff Grammar model is therefore a necessary preliminary to the treatment of lexis explored in this book.

As I have already made clear, the Cardiff Grammar has no identifiably separate 'lexicon' component. Realization both in (lexical) items and in structure is a consequence of the selection of semantic features from a **single unified system network**. It is therefore impossible to present lexical aspects of the model without reference to its overall design. Furthermore, much of the later descriptive sections of the book are formulated using the specific terms and notations of the Cardiff Grammar. An account of the particular theoretical and technical aspects of the grammar will enable readers to clearly understand and evaluate the descriptions and discussion, as well as to compare the proposals with other systemic descriptions.

3.2 HISTORICAL BACKGROUND

All contemporary approaches to systemic grammar have a common ancestry in Halliday's seminal work 'Categories of the theory of grammar' (Halliday 1961). In this paper, Halliday formulates a set of theoretical principles, many of which are still fully accepted by systemic linguists more than thirty years later. A fundamental development in the theory, and the emergence of **Systemic Grammar**, comes with Halliday (1966b). It is here that Halliday first explores the idea of **system** – one of the original 'categories' in his 1961 paper – as an expression of 'deep grammar', of paradigmatic choices in a given environment (see also 3.3.2). By applying the notion of delicacy to systemic relations, rather than to structural relations – as again was the case in Halliday's original formulation – the organization of systems into **system networks** became possible, as Butler (1985: 40) points out. The system network was therefore the expression of the relationship between systems in terms of either **dependence** or **simultaneity**. Although Halliday saw the system as 'semantic choice', the feature terms expressed in his system networks were, and continue to be, reminiscent of structural aspects of the grammar (e.g. [clause], [indicative], [declarative], [interrogative], etc.). One characteristic of the Cardiff Grammar described here is the semantic perspicuity of the feature terms used in system networks (e.g. [situation] rather than [clause], [information] rather than [indicative], etc.).

Two major traditions have grown out of Halliday's theoretical formulation in respect of linguistic structure: a descriptive tradition (Sinclair 1972, Muir 1972, Scott *et al.* 1968, Halliday 1994, Downing and Locke 1992, Eggins 1994, etc.), and what can be described as a generative tradition (Fawcett 1974–6/81 and 1980, Hudson 1971 and 1974/81, Mann and Matthiessen 1983, 1985, Matthiessen and Bateman 1991, Fawcett *et al.* 1993, etc).[1]

The generative tradition developed in the late 1960s under the inevitable influence of the **transformational generative** approach to language, which began growing rapidly in the wake of Chomsky 1957 and 1965. As Hudson (1974: 5) explains,

> it became clear that the goal of writing generative grammars was feasible and interesting, so a number of us at University College London started developing the generative potential of our theory.

The history of the Cardiff Grammar starts at that period with the doctoral work of Fawcett at University College, London, under the influence of Halliday and Hudson and the 'goal of generativeness'. Also of considerable influence at that time – as can be seen from the computational linguistic orientation of Fawcett's current work – was Winograd's attempt (1972) to model language in a computer using systemic grammar.

The general theoretical orientation for the model is originally presented in Fawcett (1980) and a considerable number of modifications for the treatment of syntax are proposed in Fawcett (1974–6/81). Another significant contribution to the development of the model, with regard to systems of transitivity, is found in Fawcett (1987). The current model is most fully described in Fawcett *et al.* (1993).

With the exception of Davey's (1978) work on PROTEUS, using Hudson's (1971) syntax-oriented systemic grammar, the first real attempt to exploit the generative potential of systemic grammars for computational text generation came with the development of the NIGEL grammar in the PENMAN Project at ISI, University of Southern California (Mann and Matthiessen 1983, 1985). In 1987 the COMMUNAL Project began developing another large-scale computational implementation of a systemic functional grammar, with the goal of producing a fully interactive system – for natural language generation and understanding – rather than simply a text generator (Fawcett *et al.* 1993). The current Cardiff SFG provides the environment for the work reported here and it is this grammar that is described.

One important clarification is necessary. The Cardiff Grammar is 'computational' in the sense that it is computationally implemented and consequently expressed in programming language notation. In all other respects, it is a wholly independent systemic functional grammar, expressible in notation traditionally used in systemic description. The computational implementation of a model of language is as much concerned with the development of the linguistic theory *per se* as it is with building systems for exploitation in the field of artificial intelligence. The specific orientation of this book is therefore exclusively linguistic and is in no way dependent on theories or methodologies from within computer science. The cross-fertilization of linguistic theory and computer science informs both the linguist and the computer scientist about the nature of their respective domains. The necessary expression of a model of language as a computer program has given rise to the metaphor of 'language as program' (Fawcett 1992).

3.3 THE CARDIFF SYSTEMIC FUNCTIONAL GRAMMAR

3.3.1 Systemic functional grammar as a formalism

A systemic functional grammar is a formalism for representing the **meaning potential** of a language. This potential is expressed as a large **system network** of features, organized in such a way as to account for the choices that are available to speakers through the lexicogrammatical and intonational structure of the language. The structure is determined by a set of **realization rules** which apply as a consequence of the choices made.

3.3.2 System and system network

The term **systemic** is derived from the central concept of systemic functional grammars, i.e the **system**. A system is defined as a **choice point** between two or more **features** (or **terms**). For each system there is an **entry condition**. A simple system would be that given in Figure 3.1. This can be re-expressed as an 'if–then' statement: if *a* (the entry condition) then either feature *b* or feature *c*. In terms of choice, what it is saying is: if *a* is chosen, then either *b* or *c* must be chosen. A feature may also act as the entry condition to more than one system **in parallel**, (Figure 3.2). This can be re-expressed as: if *a* then either *c* or *d* and either *e* or *f*. The systemic relations of 'OR' are expressed graphically by the use of a square bracket ([ ) and those of 'AND' by a brace ({).

A feature in a given system may serve as the entry condition to another system of feature options. In this way, all systems may be connected up to produce a **system network**. The system network therefore shows the relationship between all systems and all features. Although only 'ORs' and 'ANDs' are necessary to express relations between features in the network, such relations in reality are often complex in two distinct ways. First, as was indicated above, a feature may

$$
a \left[\begin{array}{l} b \\ \\ c \end{array} \right.
$$

Figure 3.1. A simple 'either or' system

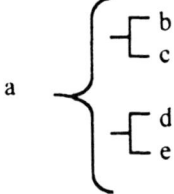

Figure 3.2. Parallel systems

lead to a number of systems in parallel (i.e. simultaneously entered). When this occurs, it gives rise to complexity on the right-hand side (RHS) of the expression. Second, the entry condition itself may be complex in that it may comprise more than one feature; this gives rise to complexity on the left-hand side (LHS) of the expression, to what is known as a **complex entry condition**. A complex entry condition may be satisfied by two or more features (Figure 3.3) This may be re-expressed as: if *a* **or** *b*, then either *c* or *d*. Two or more features in parallel may also comprise the entry condition (Figure 3.4). This may be re-expressed as: if *a* **and** *b* then either *c* or *d*. Finally, complex entry conditions may include features related in both ways (Figure 3.5). This may be re-expressed as: if *a* **and** (*b* **or** *c*), then either *d* or *e*. In developing the Cardiff Grammar, all RHS and LHS combinations of the two systemic relations have been found necessary for the expression of the meaning potential of English.

Figure 3.3. A system with a complex entry system

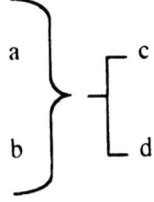

Figure 3.4. A complex entry condition with features in parallel

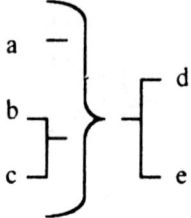

Figure 3.5. A complex entry system with both parallel and 'either or' feature arrangement

3.3.3 The meaning of systemic features

Halliday originally set up the category of **system** to account for 'the occurrence of one rather than another from among a number of like events' (Halliday 1961: 264). What early systems represented, therefore, were classifications of syntagmatic stretches of language operating in a given environment. Halliday's post-1966 work gives prominence to the paradigmatic relations which systems and system networks express. He describes the system as 'a representation of relations on the paradigmatic axis, a set of features contrastive in a given environment' (Halliday 1966b). This is at the same time a move towards seeing system networks as a kind of 'deep grammar'. It will be noted that this development came at a time when Hockett's original terms 'deep grammar' and 'surface grammar' were taken up and given central theoretical prominence in Chomsky's work (Chomsky 1965). As Butler (1985: 46) points out, this new direction is crucial in the development of Halliday's model, and quotes a statement of Halliday's (1966b: 62) which suggests this:

> it might be useful to consider some possible consequences of regarding systemic description as the underlying form of representation, if it turned out that the structural description could be shown to be derivable from it.

In Chomsky's 1965 theory, 'deep structure' is that which interfaces with the semantics in determining a semantic interpretation of the structure (16).[2] For Halliday (1966b: 62), underlying grammar is 'semantically significant grammar'.

Fawcett's position in this regard, and thus the position represented in the Cardiff Grammar, is that the system network **is** the semantics. The system network becomes the expression of what Halliday has termed the **meaning potential** of the language (Fawcett 1980: 55). This notion of semantics is what I would term 'linguistic semantics', in the sense that it is a statement of what meanings are expressible through the lexicogrammatical and intonational structure of a language.

The features in the Cardiff Grammar system network are therefore semantic features in the sense that they are those that are found necessary for the organization of meanings realized lexicogrammatically. This is less explicitly indicated in other systemic grammars, where the system networks bear labels which are ostensibly grammatical (see Fawcett *et al.* 1993 for some of the essential differences between the Halliday-influenced NIGEL grammar and the Cardiff Grammar). The semanticization of the system networks in the Cardiff Grammar can be observed in the names of the units for which the networks are designed. These are units of the **semantic rank scale**. Like the syntactic rank scale (which contains units such as clause, group, word, etc.), the semantic rank scale involves units such as **Situation, Thing, Quality**, etc. There is clearly a parallel between the two, in the sense that Situations are congruently realized syntactically as **clauses**, and Things as **nominal groups**. It is possible to realize a Situation incongruently, as if it were a Thing, using a different unit on the lexicogrammatical rank scale, in this case the **nominal group**, as is shown in examples (1) and (2). This phenomenon is generally treated as nominalization (cf. Chomsky 1970).

(1)   Howard frequently visits Cardiff
(2)   Howard's frequent visits to Cardiff

The semanticized system network is not, therefore, an expression of choices between formal items and syntactic constructions (which happen to express semantic features). The choice is now seen as being between the semantic features themselves. The relationship between meaning and form is expressed in two closely related ways: (1) by the 'reflex in form' that semantic features have in terms of their formal representations, and (2) by the realization rules that are attached to the semantic features. Features in system networks must be motivated, predominantly by the criterion that they should have 'some reflex in form' (see Fawcett 1974–6/81: 157, 1980: 101, 1987: 178–9 and Martin 1987: 16 for discussions on motivating features). Not all features bear realization rules, but those that do not are either (a) needed in the conditions on rules attached to other features, (b) in contrast with a feature that does, or (c) in an entry condition to a system containing such a feature.[3]

One final point needs to be made about the nature of semantic features. While semantic features, through their associated realization rules, determine the set of lexicogrammatical possibilities, the choice of such features is itself determined by other components in the overall model. A system network displays the **choices** in meaning which can be made, and which lead to a possible realization at the level of form. What they do not do, and cannot do, is provide the basis for these choices. Semantic features are selected on the basis of overall language planning, which involves **communicative goals, general and local beliefs, discourse knowledge**, etc. For any feature in a system to be selected, certain conditions must therefore hold at some other level of organization. The types of operations by which features may be selected range from simple **predetermination** (as in the case of a direct correspondence between an ontological object such as <TABLE> and the systemic feature [table] realized by the lexical item 'table') to the complex algorithms which are ultimately required for the selection of a pronoun, for example, rather than a full nominal group with a noun at its head. The nature of these operations is a matter of considerable interest, but it is not relevant to the work reported here. Any reference to the 'correlates' of semantic features outside the language system itself will be given in the form of general linguistic glosses.

3.3.4 System networks and generative grammar

A system network, together with its accompanying realization rules, is a generative device in the primary sense intended by Chomsky (1965). Unlike phrase structure grammars, however, the system network generates the semantic features that can co-occur in any linguistically well-formed structure. The syntactic structures are generated by the sets of co-occurring semantic features and the application of realization rules which are associated with these features. It is in this sense that a systemic functional grammar is a generative grammar of both the meaning potential and the form of a language. The extent to which an SFG is descriptively adequate, in Chomsky's (1965) terms, is ascertained by 'running' the grammar. This involves two stages: (1) **traversing** the system network along any permitted pathway, until the traversal is complete; (2) **executing** every **realization rule** that is found on the features involved in the traversal. The **output** of these two stages will 'generate' a **string** for which both a **structural** and a **semantic specification** will be given. The semantic specification, i.e the semantic features that constitute a given semantic unit (Situation, Thing, Quality, etc.), is represented by the list of features selected on the traversal of the network for that pass. This list is referred to as a **selection expression**. For an example of selection expressions generated in traversals of the network see Fawcett *et al.* (1993).

3.3.5 Recursiveness

Any generative grammar must consist of a finite set of terms. The linguistic output of such a grammar must, however, be potentially infinite, capable of generating an infinitely large set of sentences of a language, and sentences of potentially infinite length. This condition is as valid for a systemic functional grammar that claims to be generative as it is for the syntactically-oriented grammars of the generative tradition proper. Recursive devices in the Cardiff Grammar are of the following types:

1. **Co-ordination**: all units of lexicogrammatical description may be co-ordinated (e.g. *Two men, a woman and three children were strolling along the lane*).
2. **Embedding**: through the concept of embedding (or rank shift), elements of structure of one unit may be filled not only of units at the rank next below but by units of equivalent or higher rank. This accounts, for example, for recursive relative clauses in nominal group structure (e.g. *This is the man, who hit the child, who stole the dog . . .*).
3. **Reiteration**: certain elements of structure and the items that expound them may be repeated (e.g. *You're a very very very nice man*).

Types 1 and 2 require recursion at the system network level, given that they involve lexicogrammatical units. As is described in 3.4.3, a unit is generated by a traversal of (or 'pass' through) the system network. As there is one system network, even though it may be broken up into a number of individual **subnetworks**, recursion of the same unit or repeated embedding of a given unit (as in multiple embedding) requires **re-entry** into the network. Re-entry, therefore, is the construct which allows for what might be termed **semantic recursion** or more specifically **recursion of semantic units**, which in turn leads to structural recursion through the application of the relevant realization rules.

3.4 REALIZATION RULES

3.4.1 Syntactic relations

Realization rules relate semantic features to realization at the level of form. In this sense, they carry the burden of a systemic functional account of syntax. The rules build structures according to a specified set of syntactic categories and relations. Before describing the rules employed in the Cardiff Grammar, a short description is given of the model of syntax.

The general features of the Cardiff syntax (which are developed essentially from Fawcett 1974–6/81 and 1980) do not differ substantially from other systemic approaches. The major categories of **unit, class** and **structure** are present, as are the scales of **rank** and (to some extent) **delicacy**. Halliday's original scale of **exponence** is handled differently, and the term itself is used to reflect only one aspect included in its original formulation.

In brief, the Cardiff model recognizes units on the rank scale, but makes use of only two, **clause** and **group**. The category of **class** is found useful only at the rank of group, and even here classes of group, such as the **nominal group** and the **prepositional group**, are defined not with reference to the structure of the unit next above, as Halliday originally defined them, but according to their internal structure, i.e. their **componence**.

The essential modifications that Fawcett introduces are in the three relations of **componence, filling** and **exponence**. These relations allow the highest (or largest) unit to be related systematically to the individual items of which structure is composed. A unit of structure is composed (**componence**) of elements of structure. An element of structure, especially S (Subject), C (Complement) and A (Adjunct) in the clause (although not exclusively), is **filled** by a unit of the rank below or, in the case of rank shift (embedding), by a unit of the same or higher rank. Any element of structure which is not filled by another unit is expounded (**exponence**) by an item.[4]

The Cardiff Grammar syntax departs from other systemic approaches – notably those following Halliday – in several other important ways, two of which are given below. As they do not directly affect the discussion of lexis, they will simply be mentioned here. The first major difference involves the treatment of **hypotactic structures**. The Hallidayan notion of **clause complexes** involving subordinate (β) clauses and the relationships of **expansion** and **projection** (Halliday 1994: 274–91) are rejected in favour of the embedding of clauses in the structure of the main clause. The second important departure is the abolition of the **verbal group** in favour of the treatment of verbal elements M (Main verb), O (Operator) and X (Auxiliary) as elements of the structure of the clause itself.

Participant Roles (Agent, Affected, Carrier, etc.) are shown in syntactic representations. These are introduced by the process of **conflation**; that is, a given Participant Role is said to be **conflated** with an element of structure. The process of conflation is also employed at times between two elements of structure. A good example of this is the conflation of the element **X** (Auxiliary) with the element Operator (**O**) where one item (e.g. *has*) simultaneously carries the functions of the two elements. An example of a Clause structure showing the three relations and the representation of Participant Roles is given in Figure 3.6.

It is possible to describe the meaning potential of English either as a series of separate networks, each corresponding to a major unit in the semantics and its parallel in the lexicogrammar (e.g. Situation and clause), or as a large unitary network with individual subnetworks corresponding to the major semantic units. Both approaches have been explored in the Cardiff Grammar, with the latter being currently adopted.[5] It is important to note that the generation of a clause (and ultimately a **sentence**) involves the traversal of the network for each

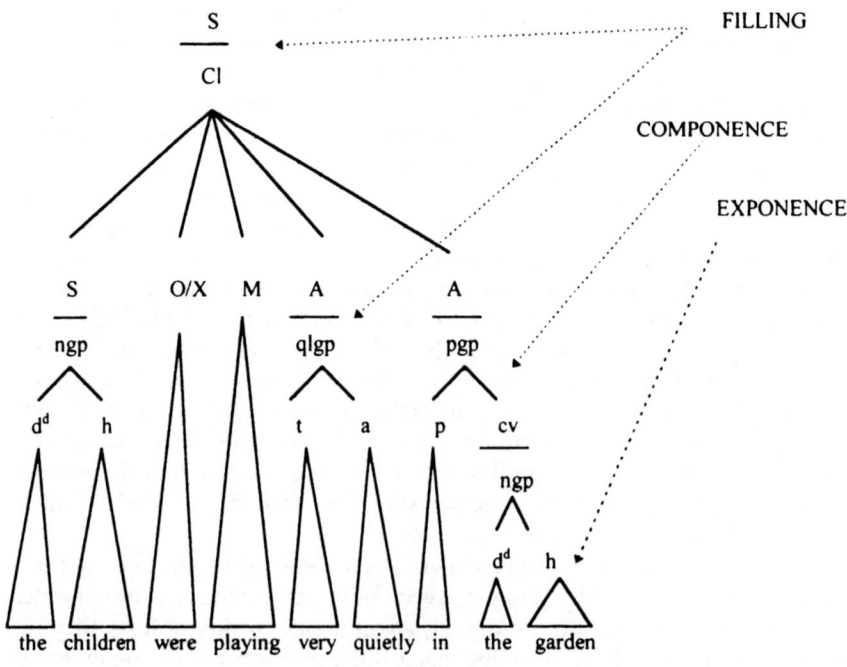

Figure 3.6. Syntactic analysis showing componence, filling and exponence

semantic unit (and therefore syntactic unit). Any traversal for a given unit will generate the set of semantic features and the lexicogrammatical structure for that unit alone. Thus, the traversal of the network for Situation will produce an output in terms of the elements of structure of the clause and any items that are directly expounded at this rank. Any unit which may fill an element of structure is generated by a subsequent traversal of the relevant subnetwork. For example, if the Subject of the clause expresses the Participant Role of Agent, and is to be filled by a nominal group, then the sub-network for Thing must be traversed.

The process of generation consists of an alternation of (1) system network traversal for each semantic unit and (2) specification of each unit of syntax and/or items and/or intonation. This process continues until each element of structure of every unit is expounded by items. As a system network is, in formal terms, a **directed acyclic graph**, and as such is not inherently **recursive**, the notion of recursion is introduced by the concept of **re-entry**.

In one sense, re-entry is fundamental to the whole process of generation. As a consequence of the role that lower units play in the structure of higher units, choices in the subnetworks which generate them are often highly constrained. This may be seen as limiting the systemic choices available in certain contexts, which entails, to some extent, re-defining what is available in the system network. A clear example of this is an embedded clause, such as a relative clause, which post-modifies a head in the nominal group. The structure of a relative clause is determined by its role in the nominal group. It will be generated by re-entry into the network for 'Situation', as are all types of clauses, but clearly, if the whole range of semantic (and therefore structural) options in this network is available, a main Clause could be the output, giving rise to the ungrammatical clause in (3).

(3)   *I saw the woman you were with the woman

The rules governing re-entry therefore include an important constraining device. They provide a way of **preselecting**, on re-entry, the necessary features in the traversal of the network, thereby ensuring the correct structure. Neither re-entry nor preselection can be modelled by network notation; they belong to the realization rule component of the model as described below.

3.4.2 Types of realization rule

The realization rules in the Cardiff Grammar are described below. They can usefully be divided into two types: **Type A rules**, which build structure and produce a structural description as in Figure 3.6; and **Type B rules**, which involve subsequent traversals of the system network.

Type A rules
These rules correspond to the structural relations described above; they are structure-building rules whose output is a syntactic string with its structural description (Figure 3.1).

- **Unit insertion** rules: these add a **unit** to the structure, e.g. the feature [situation] is realized by inserting the unit 'Cl' (for 'Clause'), and the feature [thing] by inserting 'ngp' (for 'nominal group').
- **Componence** rules: these locate the **elements of structure** of which a unit is **composed** at **places** (where 'places' are simply ordered 'slots'), e.g. 'S @ 35' means that the 'Subject' ('S') is located at Place 35.
- **Conflation** rules: these place a **Participant Role** (such as Agent) by an element of structure, e.g. 'Ag by S'.
- **Exponence** rules: these state that an element is **expounded** by an **item**, e.g. 'dd < *the*', which means 'the deictic determiner is expounded by the item *the*'. This is the relationship of **exponence**, and it takes us out of the abstract categories of **syntax** into **items**, i.e. to phenomena that have a phonological or graphological form.

Type B rules

These rules affect the traversal of the system networks. They concern re-entry into the network and specification of features and pathways upon re-entry, needed in order to ensure appropriate lexicogrammatical output.

- **Re-entry** rules, such as 'for Ag re-enter at [entity]'. In the current unified network, the feature [entity] is the initial entry condition. Thus all re-entry statements specify this point of re-entry. In order to generate a particular unit, e.g. a nominal group for the expression of the Agent, the preferences rules (as described below) must specify the preselection of [thing]. In this way only the traversal of the subnetwork for 'Thing' is permitted. Re-entry, together with the initial preselection of [thing], for example, generates a **unit** that will '**fill** the Agent'. This is the relationship of **filling**.
- **Preferences** (preselection) rules. These operate by specifying features that must be selected on re-entry to the network. The **preselection** of one feature from a system is equivalent to stating that in the relevant context there is no systemic choice, and consequently no choice in meaning or in structural realization. Feature preselection does not imply automatic selection of any feature; it simply means that **if** the pathway leading to that system is followed (i.e. its entry condition is met) **then** only that feature must be selected. If a given feature must be chosen, as a consequence of choices in previous traversals, then the complete pathway must be specified. This is expressed as a preselection expression containing every feature leading to the obligatory feature. Typically, this involves no more than half a dozen features and often far fewer.

In system networks containing probabilities, two types of preferences are possible. The first of these preselects a feature by assigning it a 100 per cent probability, consequently assigning all other features in the system 0 per cent. This is, of course, absolute preselection. The second type **resets** the relative probabilities on the features in the system (e.g 50–50 to 90–10). This type may therefore leave the original composition of the system in place, but redefine the probability of selection of the features, or cause the removal of one or more features, leaving the probability of occurrence to be defined for the remaining features.

3.4.3 The form of realization rules

Whereas, in general, different systemic approaches recognize a similar set of rule operations, they often use different rule formalisms to express them. It is therefore one thing to understand what rules do, yet another to understand what a given realization rule is in fact expressing. Our experience of presenting the Cardiff Grammar realization rules to those who have little familiarity with the formalism is that they often appear complex and at times indecipherable. No evaluation of the proposals made in this book can be complete, however, without reference to the realization rules. This section describes the form in which rules are expressed in the body of text in various later chapters, especially in Chapter 8, which describes the rules for the system network for Quality. The format for the rules derives from the way in which they are expressed in the computational implementation of the grammar, but with a number of modifications for the benefit of the reader.

The major influence on the form which rules take in this account is the Prolog representation used in the computational implementation of the Cardiff Grammar.[6] The formalization of rules is of course essential in computational linguistics, since they are part of a computer program. It consists of a number of operators (such as @, and →) which are defined within the program and which therefore act as instructions when the sentence generator program GENESYS is run.

Most rules have the following components:

(1)   {rule number:} (2) {network feature(s) to which rule is attached:}
(3)   {conditions on rule applications, if necessary}
(4)   {**rule operations.**}
       e.g.
       14.1: necessity:
       if [non conditional mod] **then O < "must"**.

As far as the GENESYS program is concerned, the network feature given after the rule number is not strictly necessary; it is the rule number itself which is responsible for invoking the rule.

Conditional statements are expressed as: **if [feature(s)] then** or **if not [feature(s)] then,** followed by the operation(s) to be executed. The meaning of the condition **if [feature x]** can be glossed as: **if [feature x] is in the selection expression.** This is a crucial factor. It is predominantly the **co-occurrence of features** in any traversal of the system network that is responsible for the final structural output.[7]

In the modified format used for realization rules in this chapter – and in other parts of the book where relevant – each subcomponent of a rule, where there is more than one, is labelled **(a), (b), (c),** etc. The operations which are to be executed are give in bold typeface, separating them from the conditions on the rule. Furthermore, features referred to in conditional statements are given in square brackets, e.g. [quality of thing], unlike in the computational version where no brackets are used.

A number of **subrules** are also employed through the system network. Subrules allow rules which apply in a large number of cases to be specified once only. An example of a subrule is the 'infl' subrule which is responsible for the inflecting morphology (+*er*) on adjectives. Subrules are referred to in the body of the operation statement of individual rules.

3.5   SUMMARY

This account of the Cardiff Grammar is necessarily brief and schematic. A much fuller account is found in Fawcett *et al.* (1993), which, set in the context of computational natural language generation, describes both the characteristics of the model and the process by which it generates sentences. Despite its brevity, however, the present account does indicate the specific model-theoretic principles upon which the entirety of the modelling of lexis presented here is based. If, in the account of lexis that follows, it turned out that problems were encountered to which solutions could not be found within this set of principles, this would severely weaken the descriptive and explanatory power of the model. As we shall see, the theory appears to be sufficiently powerful and flexible to handle the problems to be presented.

NOTES

1 Systemic linguistics embraces a much wider range of phenomena than may be suggested by this 'dual tradition'. This range includes work on discourse and generic structure (Berry, Fawcett, Hasan, Martin, Ventola) and on educational and ideological linguistics (Christie, Martin, Kress, Lemke, Thibault, etc.).

2 In Chomsky's Government and Binding Theory (Chomsky 1981) the deep structure (D–structure) level is no longer responsible for semantic interpretation. Chomsky posits an intermediate level, S–structure, derived from D–structure by transformations, which interfaces with the semantic component (LF rules). The original surface structure is now derived from the phonetic interpretation of S–structure by PF (Phonetic Form rules).

3 The only departure from the strong position on motivating features by reflex in form is found in the lexical subnetworks. This issue is discussed in Chapter 6.

4 'Items' include word base forms and inflectional morphemes. They correspond here mainly to the phonological or graphological sense of a word. The term **lexical item** as used in the literature is not always co-extensive with phonologically or graphologically defined words.

5 The adoption of a single unified system network has both theoretical and practical motivation. Halliday himself talks about a 'single network of lexicogrammatical options' (Halliday 1978: 43). If we think of the lexicogrammar of English as a device for allowing speakers to refer through language to certain aspects of their conceptual-semantic organization – in the Cardiff Grammar 'Situations', 'Things', 'Qualities' and

'Quantities' – then we can express the initial system in the network as choice between these four.

On the practical side, a single network facilitates the expression of **re-entry**, since the network is always re-entered at the very beginning, at [entity], which is thus the **initial entry condition** for all traversals of the network. In an even more practical sense, the initial choice of [situation], [thing], [quality], etc. allows each of the areas of the lexicogrammar to be tested separately: a necessary facility, given the overall size of grammar.

6 See Clocksin and Mellish (1987) for an account of Prolog.

7 If one considers the fact that many features in a selection expression contribute to the formal output through **co-occurrence**, the importance of associating a realization rule with one particular feature is reduced. It is, in theory, possible to have one complex realization rule per generation which, through a series of conditional statements and sub-components, specifies **all** the operations pertaining to a given selection expression.

4 Adjectives in English

4.1 OVERVIEW

This chapter provides an inventory of the principal areas in the lexicogrammar of English that are associated with adjectives as a word class, and an introductory discussion of these areas. Included in this inventory are aspects of the grammatical, morphological and semantic nature of the phenomena introduced here which will form the basis of later chapters. The purpose is to give a preliminary airing, in terms of general grammatical description, of the concepts to be fully explored from a systemic functional perspective in the ensuing chapters.

4.2 ADJECTIVES AND WORD CLASSES

4.2.1 Traditional classification

Adjectives constitute a major word class in English. They are members of an **open set**, which is characterized by Lyons as 'one of unrestricted, indeterminately large, membership' (Lyons 1968: 436). At any given time – and this is the dilemma of a synchronic approach to language – members of the class are under the threat of disappearance from general circulation, or are undergoing modification in their meaning and usage, while at the same time new members are being introduced. The adjective *gay*, for example, in the sense of 'lively and enjoyable to be with' or 'free from all worries and fears', is a feature of 'slightly more old-fashioned English', whereas the main sense has become that of 'a person who is homosexual' (COBUILD). The same dictionary lists an innovation of the 1960s, *fab*, but has not yet recorded another informal adjective of the 1980s and 1990s, *naff*, or a more formal contemporary term such as *proactive*.

Furthermore, the wide range of membership in open set classes lends itself to geographical and especially social variation. Thus, the range of adjectives and adjectival meanings used and understood by any one language user will be determined by his or her own social class membership. It is therefore not the case that any 'lexicon' of adjectives can simply list the whole range without some specification of membership in terms of variation.

Membership of an open set word class is established, however, through the distributional behaviour of an individual item. Indeed, it is on the basis of grammatical relations that a word is categorized as an adjective, noun, adverb, etc. This is especially apparent in a language such as English where inflectional morphology plays a minor role in distinguishing word classes. Moreover, as Starosta (1988: 55) argues:

Class membership is logically and temporally prior to the formation of inflectional paradigms. Words are inflected for a particular category because they are in the same syntactic class, and in fact that is one of the defining characteristics of inflection.

Although the decontextualized citation form *brave* is associated with an underlying meaning, as a 'content' word, its membership of the adjective class and of the verb class is primarily a matter of its grammatical distribution. In classifying a word as an adjective we are stating that its content (i.e. a 'quality' or 'attribute' of 'things') and its distributional characteristics are those shared by the general body of membership of that word class. Indeed, for the language user, the metalinguistic label 'adjective' has no part to play in using adjectives. It is the language user's knowledge of the item's overall properties and his or her use in this respect that allows the linguist or lexicographer to assign it to a word class. As will become clear in 4.2.2, word classes are less prominent in this approach than the functional element of structure at which the class typically appears.

It is not the case that all members of a particular word class share the same set of properties associated with that class. As Rosch's research (1978) into cognitive categories emphasizes, some members of a class ('prototypical members') are 'better' or more representative examples than others. The notion of prototypicality is as insightful for linguistic classification as it is for classification of any kind (cf. Lakoff 1987: 58–67). Certain adjectives are more 'adjective-like' than others; these are the prototypical adjectives. They comprise the set which has most or all of the properties which adjectives exhibit. If speakers are asked to give examples of adjectives, they are more likely to provide prototypical examples. Prototypical adjectives, corresponding to 'central' adjectives in Quirk *et al.* (1985: 402–4), are items like *big, happy, old*, etc. Quirk *et al.* refer to four criteria which traditionally characterize central adjectives:

(1)   their free occurrence in 'attributive' function, e.g. *a happy child*;
(2)   their free occurrence in 'predicative' function, e.g. *The child is happy*;
(3)   their potential to be premodified by the intensifier *very*, e.g. *very happy*;
(4)   their potential to appear in comparative and superlative constructions, e.g. *a happier child, the happiest child*.

Criteria (2) and (3) appear not to be individually significant, however, in that adjectives that accept premodification of the intensifier type are also found in comparative and superlative expressions. These properties are clearly connected with their classification as **gradable adjectives**. Adjectives with less prototypical behaviour ('peripheral adjectives' in Quirk *et al.*'s terminology) are those which do not satisfy all four criteria.

In distinguishing adjectives from 'manner' adverbs – since it is essentially this kind of adverb that corresponds to the adjective – the first two criteria are crucial. Whereas both central adjectives and adverbs satisfy the two criteria involving premodification, the predicative and attributive functions of adjectives relate to their syntactic distribution and function, which differs from that of adverbs. The differences and similarities between these two classes are more fully considered in Chapter 7, where it is shown how they can be incorporated into the same system network.

Much of the work in this book is concerned with the grammatical and functional properties that adjectives exhibit, both in their commonality and in their individual variation. It is the task of an explicit generative grammar to account for all such properties. A first step in the process is to provide a 'checklist' of them.

4.2.2 Feature-based approaches

In early transformational grammar (Chomsky 1970, Jackendoff 1977) feature systems were explored in an attempt to capture generalizations across lexical and phrasal categories. Such systems were based on the syntactic properties of the major categories: verb, noun, adjective and preposition. The similarities and differences between lexical categories and their phrasal projections (e.g. N and NP, ADJ and ADJP) are observable through their relative syntactic behaviour. As Horrocks (1987: 66) illustrates, in his modification of Jackendoff's 1977 proposals, the four major categories can be given a Boolean value in respect of whether, for example, they can have a subject, a determining element or an object. The conclusion that Chomsky reaches is that such categories may be expressed in terms of whether or not they are verbal in behaviour [+V, −V] or whether or not they are nominal [+N, −N]. Of the four categories, adjectives and adjective phrases are assumed to be [+N, −V], which distinguishes them from the others. This feature categorization is based on the observation that adjectives share syntactic properties with both nouns and verbs. Examples of this are (a), in terms of [+V], that verbs and adjectives share the property of verbal complementation (*wanted to help, happy to help*) and (b), in terms of [+N], that nouns and adjectives share (at least in some languages) nominal morphology (for example in Italian: masculine singular *un bravo ragazzo*, feminine singular *una brava ragazza*). The importance of this kind of classification, as Radford (1988: 149) points out, is that it allows the linguist to capture supercategorial generalizations.

This type of feature-based approach is of limited usefulness in the present framework, mainly because there is no separate lexicon, and furthermore, as is pointed out elsewhere, word class labels such as N, V, ADJ have no central part to play in the structural description. It does alert us, however, to the kinds of shared properties of lexical classes which must be modelled in any grammar. Furthermore, in some parts of the lexicogrammar of English, it appears that nouns, verbs **and** adjectives share certain distributional properties, as is the case in nominal premodification (e.g. *a London woman, a working woman, a happy woman*), and these facts too must be explained. A similar observation is made by Chomsky with reference to the suggestion that the verb and adjective are subcategories of a category 'predicator'. As he argues (1970: 198), 'The argument based on distributional similarities collapses when we recognize that nouns share the same distributional properties.'

The assignment of the category of 'adjective' is therefore not uniform across different theories of language. Starosta (1988: 223), for example, assigns the feature [+Adj] only when the 'adjective' is in its 'attributive' function; 'Adjectives are modifiers of nouns.' Thus, when adjectives appear in other syntactic contexts he assigns them to other categories, such as [+V] or [+N]. Adjectives in their 'predicative' function are considered to be [+V], e.g. *The* [+det] *book* [+N] *is red* [+V].

Differences in the treatment of adjectives are also found in systemic functional approaches. For Halliday (1994: 185), adjective is a subclass of 'nominal'. As a consequence, he does not recognize a separate 'adjectival group' alongside other groups that he sets up, such as 'nominal group', 'verbal group', 'preposition group', 'adverbial group' and 'conjunction group'.

It is not altogether clear why Halliday avoids positing an 'adjectival group'. His treatment of nominal group structure does include the embedding or 'rankshifting' of 'clauses' and 'prepositional phrases' at 'Qualifier' to account for expressions such as *the pobble who has no toes* and *the dong with the luminous tail* (Halliday 1994: 188). Expressions such as that indicated in bold typeface in the nominal expression *a rather more impressive figure* are treated as cases of 'submodification' (Halliday 1994: 192). Even adjectival expressions used 'predicatively', e.g. *the minister didn't seem sure of himself*, are still considered nominal group structures (Halliday 1994: 120). Yet, if Halliday considers such expressions to be group structures – albeit nominal group structures – why then are they not considered to be rankshifted when they occur within the structure of another nominal group?[1]

As will become evident in later chapters, the word class label 'adjective' – as with all word class labels – has no part to play in grammatical description within the Cardiff Grammar. The theoretical framework makes no overt generalization about word classes, and no unit at the rank of 'word' is introduced into the grammatical description. Words, in the traditional sense, are simply treated as **items,** which are grouped according to their potential to **expound** an element of structure of some unit, as was described in Chapter 3. The traditional word class 'adjective' comprises that set of items which expound the **a(pex)** element of structure in the quality group. Units are established by their internal **componence,** which is a functionally significant constellation of related elements of structure. The lexicogrammar also specifies the syntactic environments in which each class of unit may be found. (A full account of this is given in Chapter 5.) From a generative viewpoint, consequently, there is no need to specify whether a particular item is an adjective or not in a given environment.

4.3   STRUCTURAL PROPERTIES OF ADJECTIVES

4.3.1 Environment

Environment here is understood in both a structural and a functional sense. There is little to be gained by simply making statements about the syntactic environment of items or classes without at the same time stating what their function is in that environment. Clearly, a functional account may be more or less specific; it may refer to general functions such as 'complement of' or 'modifier of', or it may invoke more specific, semantically oriented functions, as is the case in the present approach.

Adjectives occur typically in four environments in English. They are found as:

(a) Pre-head modifiers in nominal structures (*a big parcel*)
(b) Complements of a copula in clause structure (*he is kind*)
(c) Complements expressing the result of the process denoted by the verb (*he shot him dead, he pulled the tooth loose*)[2]
(d) Postpositive modifiers of certain types of nominal expression (*something nice*)

As authors such as Quirk *et al.* (1985: 424ff) and Downing and Locke (1992: 518) observe, adjectives occasionally occur in other environments, namely as:[3]

(e) Complements of prepositions (*in short, for good, etc.*)
(f) Premodifiers of certain adjectives (*pale blue, red hot*)
(g) Adjuncts in Clauses (*I'm receiving you loud and clear*)
(h) Contingent adjective clauses (*Strange, I never suspected him*)
(i) Supplementive adjective clauses (*Soaking wet, he walked into the room*)

The central adjectival functions are those associated with environments (a) and (b) and are generally referred to as the **attributive** and the **predicative** functions respectively.[4] It is well known that individual adjectives differ in their potential to operate in attributive and predicative contexts. Prototypical adjectives are found in both environments. Smaller subsets are restricted to one or other of the two. Specification of any adjective must therefore include its behaviour in this respect. (This phenomenon is discussed in detail in Chapter 7.) In their attributive function, adjectives from different classes exhibit typical sequential ordering, e.g. *a lovely large red wooden box*, as compared to co-ordination, e.g. *an intelligent, courteous and thoughtful colleague.* In this approach adjectival sequences of this kind are handled through **modifier sequences** at the level of the nominal group and are fully discussed in Chapter 9. The relationship between the various environments listed above and the adjectival structures that realize them is also discussed in Chapter 9.

4.3.2 Adjectival structures

The class of adjectives, like all lexical classes, 'creates' its own environment. In constituent structure approaches, such as the widely accepted X-bar syntax of generative theory, they are said to stand as the **heads of phrases**. The other constituents of the phrase of which the adjective is the head have a close and direct relationship with the head. In dependency grammars, adjectives may be the **controller** or **controlling term** (Matthews 1981: 79) or **regent** (Starosta 1988: 21) in a sister relationship with other words. In the systemic functional approach adopted in this work, adjectives correspond to the principal element of structure in a class of unit composed of a number of elements, all of which are functionally related. Each element, in a flat representation, is labelled in

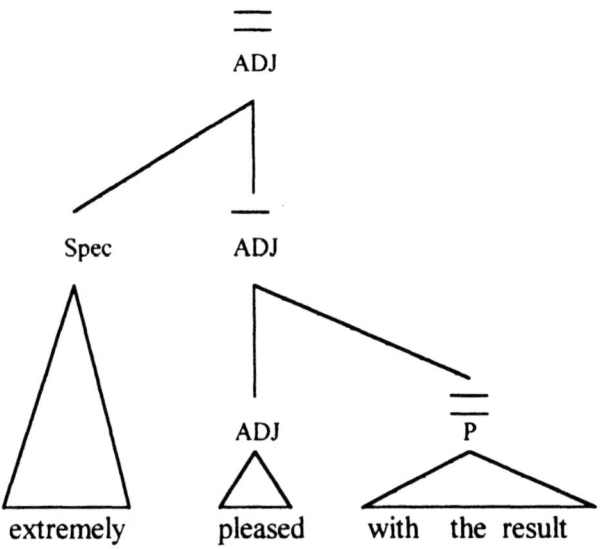

Figure 4.1. The adjective in a constituency approach (X-bar syntax)

functional terms. These three approaches are illustrated in Figures 4.1, 4.2 and 4.3.

There is general agreement that a grammar of English must therefore specify, either in constituency or in dependency terms, the local environment of adjectives as 'heads' or 'controllers'. This involves establishing which elements or constituents are present, their optionality, obligatoriness, potential for co-occurrence, and their ordering with respect to the adjective and (in a functional approach) the function of these elements. It will be noted that the SFG syntactic analysis shown in Figure 4.2 does not make explicit the dependency relations between the elements of structure of a unit. This is because such relations are expressed in the system network. The elements of structures and the relations between them are discussed fully in Chapters 5 and 7.

4.3.3 The modification and complementation of adjectives

As heads of structures, adjectives may be subject to modification and complementation. The potential for modification and complementation is not equally distributed across the full set of adjectives, however. Modification, in the form of **intensification** and **comparison**, is typically associated with **gradable** adjectives or **non-gradable** adjectives treated as if gradable (e.g. *more dead than alive*). Adjectives which take complements on a parallel with verbs (e.g. *fond of someone, angry about something*) constitute an even smaller set.

The 'modification' of adjectives is typically 'premodification', with the well-known exception of *enough*, as in *happy enough*. However, the 'completion' or

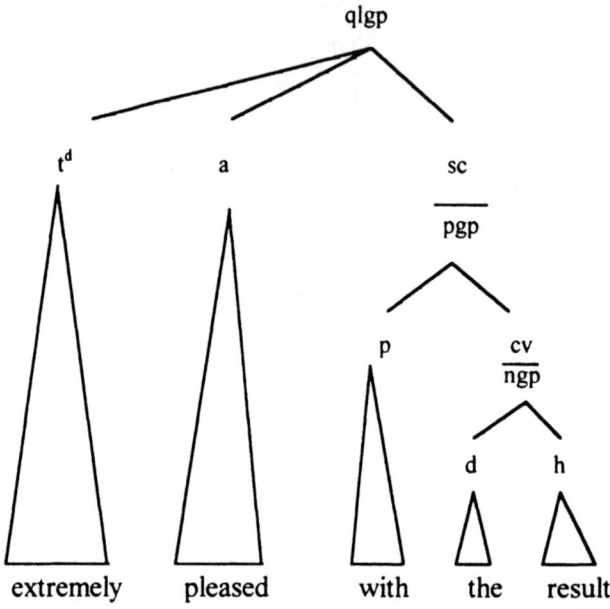

Figure 4.2. The adjective in a systemic functional approach (Cardiff Grammar)

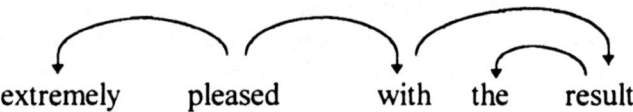

Figure 4.3. The adjective in a dependency approach

'extension' of meanings expressed in premodifying elements follow the adjectival head, especially in the case of comparative constructions, as can be seen in example (1).

(1)   much **more** beautiful **than I had imagined**

Premodifiers themselves may also be premodified, as (1) also shows. The elements of structure required to account for premodification and complementation of adjectives are discussed in Chapter 5; the system network for the meaning potential available through premodification is discussed in Chapter 10. Explicit comparatives, as examples of structures which carry the completion of meanings initiated in premodification, are also discussed in Chapter 10. The general interrelationship between adjectival senses and premodification potential is discussed in Chapter 9, as is adjective complementation. Explicitly functional labels for the elements of structure will be introduced, in the framework of the Cardiff Grammar, in Chapter 5.

4.3.4 The morphological properties of adjectives

Adjectives in English are not marked inflectionally for number, gender, case, etc., as in many other languages. However, a large subset of adjectives are inflected for comparative and superlative forms. They exhibit as a class a rich derivational morphology. Many adjectival suffixes are of neo-classical origin and are rarely found with native bases (e.g. -AL, -IC, -IV and -OUS). Other suffixes indicate the 'deverbal' or 'denominal' formation of the adjective, such as -ING, -ED, -FUL, -LESS, etc.

Adjectival word formation and the productivity of certain derivational affixes are not discussed in this work, since it is not the purpose of the model of a lexical resource presented here to make statements about derivational morphology. The question of comparative and superlative morphology is discussed in Chapter 9.

4.4 ADJECTIVES AND MEANING

4.4.1 The semantic function of adjectives

The semantic resource associated with adjectives is primarily concerned with **Qualities** of **Things**. One form of semantic classification of adjectives is therefore possible in terms of the classes of attributes or properties associated with Things. Dixon (1991: 78), amongst others, provides such a classification (discussed in Chapter 7). Adjectival senses are closely related to the Things they modify. Firstly, they are a function of the different classes of Thing that a culture recognizes. It is even arguable that our classification of Things is itself established by reference to the attributes with which they are associated. This association is important in the interpretation of adjectival senses; the sense of *green* in (2) and (3) is partly determined by the different nouns it modifies.

(2)   a green door
(3)   a green issue

It has been suggested that adjectives can either be directly 'ascribed' to the noun or indirectly 'associated' with it (Ferris 1993: 24). As Ferris claims, 'ascription' refers to the case 'where the adjective conveys a property which is valid for the entity instantiated by the noun', and association 'where it is valid for something else'. Examples of both types are:

(4)   a royal visitor
(5)   a royal hatmaker

In (4) the visitor is interpreted as directly having the property *royal* (i.e. someone born into a royal family), whereas in (5) the hatmaker is interpreted not as belonging to royalty him/herself but as making hats for members of the royal family. A semantic specification of adjectives must therefore take into account the relationship with the nouns or noun senses that they can modify.

Adjectives serve a number of functions. They are used to subclassify, identify or describe classes of Things. Here again, individual adjectives may serve more than one function; as Halliday notes, the adjective *long*, for example, has a different function in (6) from its function in (7), where it is identifying a particular train (Halliday 1994: 184).

(6)   a long train
(7)   the long train

Halliday's distinction above is made in the context of another functional aspect of adjectives, their contribution to the **ideational, interpersonal** and **textual** metafunctions of language. Classes of adjective also differ in their potential to be exploited for these functions. Halliday gives the example of the 'attitudinal epithet' *mighty*, which does not have the potential to identify as does *long* in (7).

4.4.2 Lexical semantic relations

Another semantic property of adjectives is **gradability**. This feature is itself related to the lexical semantic relations which hold between adjectives. Inherently gradable adjectives are typically involved in the relation of **antonymy**. The adjectives *large* and *small* are examples of antonyms, representing points on a scale of size. Degrees may be expressed by premodification of the adjective, e.g. *larger, very large, quite small*, etc. Any account of adjectival antonymy must also include the phenomenon of **unmarked terms** in measure expressions (see Quirk *et al.* 1985: 470), e.g. the use of *deep* in *six inches deep* rather than **six inches shallow*.

Opposites, of the **complementary** type (Cruse 1986: 198), such as *true* and *false*, are not typically gradable.[5] As can be seen from the examples above, the gradability of adjectives has important consequences for their grammatical behaviour. The modelling of antonymy (including the notion of unmarked terms, e.g. *how old are you?* rather than *how young are you?*) and complementarity is discussed in Chapter 7.

4.4.3 Collocation

Collocation is now clearly seen as an important aspect of the meaning of lexical items. The collocational behaviour of adjectives throws considerable light on the sense of the word. For example, the two frequently cited and quasi-synonymous adjectives *strong* and *powerful* can be teased apart through examination of their collocational patterning (see Halliday 1966a: 151ff). Not only does collocation provide important evidence for the semantic classification of adjectives, it also constrains possible output in many cases of lexical and grammatical structuring. For example, in the expression *I haven't the_____-est idea,* the range of adjectives available is considerably restricted. A full discussion of this is given in Tucker (1996). This example also raises questions of complex lexical patterning, fixed or semi-fixed expressions, etc.

The semantic characteristics of adjectives, including their collocational behaviour, are central to a functional model of grammar. It is a widely accepted principle of systemic linguistics that features in a system network (i.e. options in meaning) have some **reflex in form** (Fawcett 1980: 101, 1987: 178–9, Martin 1987: 16, but see also Chapter 6 for a fuller discussion of this). The system network is the formalism in which options in meaning, represented by features in systems, are related to lexicogrammatical structure through realization statements. It is in the design of the system network that the semantic characteristics which have reflexes in form must be modelled. Chapter 7 gives a fuller account of these characteristics in discussing the nature of the system network for Quality.

The consequences of the nature of the system network are found throughout this book, since the various aspects of adjectival behaviour derive, in the model, from the network and its realization rules.

4.5   ADJECTIVES AND ADVERBS

Although differing in form, function and syntactic distribution, adjectives and manner adverbs exhibit a number of similarities. First, they are formally related, differing – in purely formal terms – solely by the presence of inflectional morphology. That is, there is an *-ly* on adverbs (e.g. *careful – carefully, slow – slowly*, etc.). Second, they share predominantly the same dependent structure (e.g. *much more thoughtful/ly than before*). Finally, they share a semantic function, in that adjectives can be viewed as **Qualities of Thing** and adverbs as **Qualities of Situation**. It is because of the relatedness of the 'adjectival' and the 'adverbial', in terms of the semantic functions which are associated with them and the elements of structure required to express these functions, that they are treated as a single class of group in the Cardiff Grammar. This approach is further discussed in Chapter 7, as is the extent to which their respective meaning potential and structural potential can be modelled as one unified resource.

4.6   SUMMARY

In this chapter I have outlined the major characteristics of the members of the adjective as a word class or lexical category. Indeed, as I have pointed out, certain lexical items may be classified as adjectives precisely because they have such characteristics. Central among them is (a) the constituents or elements of structure which share a close syntagmatic relationship with adjectives and which modify and extend the meanings that they realize, and (b) the relationship between adjectives (and their dependent structures) and other structures in the clause. Here, also, adjectival structures contribute to the meanings realized by other structures. One example of this is the option of realizing the complement of certain verbs adjectivally as well as nominally, e.g. *he is happy* versus *he is a happy man*. A lexicogrammatical account of adjectives must therefore make explicit both the nature of adjectival structures and the relationships that they enter into with other structures. Given that an SFG such as the Cardiff Grammar has as its point of departure the choices in meanings which are available to speakers, it is necessary to account for both the organization of options in meaning and of the structure and items which realize the meanings. The challenge of modelling language in this way extends beyond simply capturing syntactic organization. The 'autonomy of syntax' is not a principle of systemic functional linguistics. A major assumption in SFG is that the structural potential is the way it is in order to reflect the meaning potential. Thus, for the semantic property of certain Qualities which allows them to be subject to modification by degree (e.g. *quite/very/extremely/happy*) there is a structural and further lexical resource to realize this.

The remaining chapters in this book explore the various characteristics of adjectives, their structures and the meanings they realize, and proposes an overall framework for modelling them. The next chapter embarks upon this task by considering the structure of adjectival expressions.

NOTES

1   Halliday distinguishes between 'rankshifted' structures which are 'those items which, in their own structure are of a rank higher than or at least equivalent to that of the nominal group' and 'ranking' structures, ones 'which function prototypically as constituents of the higher unit' (Halliday 1994: 188). Thus a nominal group, which functions as a constituent of the clause – a higher unit – should be rankshifted when it functions as a constituent of another nominal group. One can only conclude that, for Halliday, the nominal group cannot be rankshifted.

2   A number of different solutions for this type of construction have been proposed, including Halliday (1967), Fawcett (1987) and Ferris (1993). These are discussed, together with a further proposal, in Chapter 10.

3   I have retained the terminology used by the authors quoted. In the Cardiff Grammar they are described differently. The adjectival expressions in (h) and (i), for example, realize types of **Adjunct**.

4   Some confusion may unfortunately arise in this work over the terms **attributive** and **Attribute**. Whereas the generally accepted term for adjectives in their nominal premodifying function (e.g. *a hungry child*) is **attributive**, in the Cardiff Grammar the term **Attribute** is used in relation to the function of adjectives complementing copular and other verbs (e.g. *he is hungry*). The Cardiff Grammar use of the term derives from the fact that in such clauses the adjective or adjectival expression is associated with the Participant Role of **Attribute**, a characteristic of one kind of **Relational Process** in the transitivity system. *Caveat lector!* Thus the systemic feature [quality as attribute] introduced in Chapter 7 relates to the 'predicative function' of adjectives rather than to the 'attributive function', the latter being referred to in the system network by the feature [quality as modifier].

5   There is a notable tendency in contemporary English to use certain non-gradable adjectives as gradable, e.g. *you're very wrong*. Furthermore, the presence of intensifiers or comparative structure with a typically non-gradable adjective often indicates a different sense of the adjective, e.g. *a very wooden pupil.*

5 The syntax of adjectives: the quality group

5.1 OVERVIEW

This chapter examines the structure for the expression of meanings relating to Quality of Thing. This structure is traditionally labelled the Adjectival Phrase. Within the systemic functional framework, the term Adjectival Group is preferred, given the centrality of the unit group in grammatical description. In the Cardiff Grammar, the label **Quality Group (qlgp)** is adopted to reflect its role in expressing meanings relating to Qualities. A very full functional structure of the quality group is proposed and each of the elements of structure is discussed and illustrated in turn.

5.2 LEXICAL CLASSES AND PHRASAL PROJECTIONS

In constituent-based approaches to syntax it is widely accepted that the phrases that form constituents of sentences are essentially 'projections' of the major lexical classes. Thus there are constituents such as VP (verb phrase), NP (noun phrase), ADJP (adjective phrase), etc. The general characteristics of such phrases are central to many contemporary theories of syntax and are expressed in terms of X-bar theory (Chomsky 1970, 1981, Jackendoff 1977). X-bar syntax, which is widely accepted in contemporary generative theory in one formulation or another, is a way of generalizing across the structures that can accompany lexical (and functional) heads, providing both a set of constraints on possible phrase structures and a mechanism for projecting the properties of lexical entries into the structure of sentences.[1] Here, however, as we shall see, a different, though related, notion will be given priority: **functional elements of structure**, rather than word classes.

5.3 THE NOTION OF GROUP AS A UNIT IN HALLIDAY'S SYSTEMIC FUNCTIONAL GRAMMAR

In systemic functional grammar, structures which are broadly equivalent to phrasal categories are recognized, namely **verbal group, nominal group, adverbial group**, etc. According to Halliday's original formulation (Halliday 1961), these structures are classes of the category **unit**, which is 'set up to account for the stretches that carry grammatical patterns'. Grammatical units form a hierarchy and are related by a scale which is called the **rank scale**. Halliday first suggested that five units are required for the description of English: **sentence, clause, group, word** and **morpheme** (1961: 58). Now, however, the 'sentence' is dealt with as a 'clause complex' (1994: 215). Halliday sets up the category **class** to account for the relationship between places in the structure of one unit and occurrences of the unit next below.

Another aspect of linguistic patterning, as Halliday notes, is the 'fact that it is not true that anything can go anywhere in the structure of the unit above itself' (1961: 64). In Halliday's formulation 'a class is always defined with reference to the structure of the unit next above... A class is not a grouping of members of a given unit which are alike in their own structure' (1961).[2] While this is a concept that will shortly be challenged, early systemic descriptions of English, such as those of Sinclair (1972), Turner (1970) and Berry (1975), seem to have accepted the principle without question. The consequence of applying this principle is that the internal structure of a unit is considered secondary to the place of the unit in the structure of the unit next above. The problems inherent in this approach are illustrated by the treatment of one class of group, the **adverbial group**. On the basis of their relationship to the element Adjunct in the structure of the clause, structures with very different 'heads' are classified as adverbial groups. This includes, in Sinclair's (1972) description, adverb- and adjective-headed structures, the former including groups which are internally prepositional. Berry (1975) also includes prepositional structures in the class adverbial group.

There is an inherent paradox in this approach. On the one hand, groups are named after the lexical class at their head, while on the other, the main criterion that determines their classification is the function they have with regard to their place in the unit next above.

5.4 FAWCETT'S 'PROPOSALS FOR SYSTEMIC SYNTAX'

Fawcett (1974–6/81) proposes a reformulation of some of Halliday's original theoretical principles. Essentially, he rejects the principle according to which a class is not a grouping of members of a given unit which are alike in their own structure. Fawcett proposes that the internal structure of a unit should determine its class, and that the elements of structure (and therefore the class of unit) are functionally motivated. This proposal removes the deterministic relationship between a unit and its place in the structure of the unit next above, which 'class' was originally set up to account for. Fawcett replaces this relationship with that of **filling** which, along with **componence** and **exponence,** forms the theoretical basis for syntactic relations. Filling allows for the fact that a (functionally motivated) element of structure of one unit can be expressed by a number of different structures.

With this proposal, Fawcett is placing great emphasis on the functional nature of syntax. If different types of structure are used to realize major areas of meanings, such as those realized by elements in clause structure, then it follows that different meanings are involved. The range of structures available for the expression of time Adjuncts, for example, relate to the different ways of talking about time. They constitute the more 'delicate' options in meaning which the language resource makes available. In semantic terms, the time specification in the case above may be expressed to the addressee as (a) a **Quality of Situation** (adverbial expression, e.g. *currently*), (b) a **Minimal (time) Relationship with another Thing** (a prepositional expression, e.g. *on Sunday*), (c) a **Thing** (a nominal expression, e.g. *the day before yesterday*), or (d) as another **Situation** (a clause, e.g. *when he finishes*), which is related in some temporal way to the situation expressed in the main clause.[3] These choices are related to the need of speakers to express time meanings in a way that is relevant and clear to the addressee. The choice between them is an issue of the 'higher planning' of utterances, and it takes into account factors such as beliefs about the addressee's beliefs, the state of any ongoing discourse, co-operation between participants in the speech event, etc.

Fawcett's model of syntax, like phrasal approaches in generative theory, is based on the centrality of lexical heads, such as **noun**, **adjective**, **adverb** and **preposition**.[4] However, unlike approaches within the generative grammar paradigm, no generalizations are made about the nature of these structures, as they are in X-bar syntax, nor is the relationship of head to non-head elements expressed by means of daughter or sister dependencies. The structure of units in systemic functional grammar in general is represented as a flat, linear sequence.[5] Dependency relations between elements are expressed in the organization of the semantic system network and are represented in the syntax by the use of functional labelling. The notion of 'head', in syntactic terms at least, has no special significance in this approach, except that each unit has a 'pivotal' element of structure that is typically filled by an item which is a member of one of the word classes.

Fawcett even departs from otherwise similar functional approaches to syntax in the diversity of labelling of elements. With very few exceptions, elements associated with a particular class of unit are uniquely named for that class alone, on the basis again that it captures or signals their functional contribution. Here, Fawcett takes the notion of function one step further. Rather than a functional account of structure in terms of pre-head **m(odifier)**, **h(ead)** and post-head **q(ualifier)**, which can be generalized over different classes of unit, especially at the rank of **group**, Fawcett relates individual elements of structure to the specific **semantic functions** which they express in structure.

It is therefore difficult to understand the role of dependency in Fawcett's syntax without referring to the system networks and the realization rules which convert meanings into form. A formal syntax is only specified to the extent that a set of operations that build syntactic structures is contained in realization statements; structures are represented in terms of **componence, filling** and **exponence**, as described and illustrated in Chapter 3.

What is easily specifiable, however, for each unit, other than the clause, is its **potential structure**.[6] In the clause there is too much variation in sequence, with elements such as Adjuncts potentially appearing in up to three different places. A potential structure specifies all the elements that may be found in any instantiation of that unit in the order in which they may occur. It is thus an ordered inventory of functional elements. Ordering is achieved in a simple and economical way by assigning each potential element a place in structure as a serial number, e.g. **modifier at Place 3, head at Place 5, qualifier at Place 7**. Any element which is not fixed will be assigned two or more place numbers. The place actually occupied by an element in such cases will depend first on the semantic features selected in the system network, and second on the realization rule which is ultimately responsible for the insertion of that element into the structure. As a general principle, it is only at the rank of clause that multiple places are found necessary. Each type of Adjunct, for example, can be **thematized**, in which case it occupies an early place in structure. Most can also occur at places between the Subject and the Operator, the Operator and the first Auxiliary and so on, as well as at a place towards the end of the clause. At group rank this flexibility is minimal and elements of structure can generally, although not absolutely always, be assigned a single fixed place.

5.5 ADJECTIVE-HEADED GROUPS

An adjective, like any other lexical class, is a 'pivotal' element (or 'head') in its group. In terms of the Cardiff Grammar (and following Fawcett 1974–6/81), the class of adjective comprises those items that **expound** the pivotal element of structure of a unit at the rank of group. The other elements which are considered to compose this group are closely related in some way to this central element. Thus in example (1), the item *very* and the element that it expounds are a function of the element expounded by the adjective *serious*.

(1)   A very serious accident has happened

Somewhat surprisingly, the **adjectival group** is barely recognized in systemic descriptions. For Halliday (1994), Muir (1972) and Berry (1975), adjective-headed structures are treated as a subclass of the nominal group. As Butler (1985: 101) points out, this solution is based on the fact that adjectival structures, like nominal structures, can act as or occur at Complement in the clause. Once again, these descriptions invoke Halliday's principle of establishing classes on the basis of their relationship with 'the structure of the unit next above' (1961). Sinclair (1972) recognizes the term 'adjectival group', but like Halliday and others, he considers the modification of adjectives as a phenomenon within the nominal group.

Fawcett's adherence to the criterion of functionally motivated internal componence led him in 1980 to recognize the existence of the adjectival group. He later took the argument one step further by conflating adjective-headed groups with adverb-headed groups. This conflation into one group, **the quality group** (often henceforth simply **qlgp** for the sake of brevity), is motivated by the strong parallelism in structure between the two types.[7] This is illustrated by examples (2a) and (2b).

(2a)   far too quick for me to understand
(2b)   far too quickly for me to understand

Clearly, the conflation of adjective-headed and adverb-headed structures into a single unit weakens the explanatory power of the description in terms of the mutually exclusive functions that the two types have in respect of the environments in which they occur. The grammar can no longer state that the adjectival group relates typically to modification within the nominal group and to Complement in the clause, whereas the adverbial group performs an adjunctival function in the clause and occasionally an intensifying function within the adjectival group, e.g. *understandably upset.* What might be considered an overgeneralization at the structural level is counteracted in the following way. In the system network for Quality, as fully described in Chapter 7, the two functions of this group are separated by a system in which the options are either [quality of thing] or [quality of situation], referring to the adjectival expression and the adverbial expression respectively. Thus, when an adverb-headed group is required for an Adjunct, for example, the feature [quality of situation] will be preselected. The selection of one of these features within the system network for Quality will determine the morphology which distinguishes the adjectival form from the adverbial form. The characteristics of the system network for Quality and the realization statements which relate to it are fully explored in Chapters 7 and 8, and therefore will not be discussed here.

5.6 THE STRUCTURE OF THE QUALITY GROUP

5.6.1 Introduction

In the syntax of the Cardiff Grammar the elements of structure of the quality group are determined both formally and functionally. In formal terms, an element must be identifiable as a self-contained and coherent stretch of language. The need to make this a requirement is evident in establishing an element expounded by a single lexical item at the rank of word, but it is less evident in the case of an element which may comprise a number of items. In making decisions about how to isolate elements of structure, we appeal to our own intuitions as 'linguistically naive' informants. Constituents can also be determined by the application of a series of tests (cf. Radford 1988: 50–105, Cowper 1992: 19–47). I take this ability to recognize such constituents to be part of a speaker-listener's linguistic 'competence' in the sense intended by Chomsky (1965: 4). In functional terms, it will be expected that the elements recognized correspond to some function that relates to some aspect of meaning that is realized through the qlgp. In attempting to establish the structural elements necessary for the expression of meanings related to Quality there is a natural process of alternation between the semantics, as expressed in the system network, and the structure. It is ultimately the formal properties of the qlgp which reveal the meaning potential realized through it.

In the discussion of the qlgp which follows, each element of structure will be introduced separately, and we shall work towards the specification of a full potential structure. Constant reference will be made to the nature of the functions for which the elements are set up. As is by now clear, the point of departure for this description is Fawcett's (1974–76/81) account. I shall propose a number of modifications and additions to Fawcett's quality group (originally the 'quantity-quality group') to account for some complex aspect of the group's componence, but on the whole Fawcett's functional labels will be adopted. In any functional approach, the labels serve only to identify a set of elements, and in themselves have no theoretical significance. Fawcett's general philosophy when deciding on labels in his syntactic description is to retain Halliday's widely accepted labels wherever possible, and to propose alternatives only when there is a need to reflect as closely and as transparently as possible a difference from Halliday (1994).

As a preview, we can say that the componence of the qlgp is as follows: a pivotal element, **apex (a)**; a number of pre-apex elements **linker (&)**, **extent (ex)**, **emphasizing temperer (t^e)**, **quality deictic determiner (d^{qld})**, **quality quantifying determiner (d^{qlq})**, **degree temperer (t^d)**, **adjunctival temperer (t^a)**; a number of post-apex elements, **degree temperer (t^d)**, **first scope (sc1)**, **second scope (sc2)**, **finisher (f)**, and an **ender (e)**. The first and last elements, **&** and **e**, are present in both clause structure and the structure of the different classes of group. The first is necessary for overtly marked co-ordination, e.g. *very happy* **and** *very rich*. The last is expounded by intonational phenomena, or punctuation in the written language, whenever the group constitutes a separate information unit. The model of intonation drawn on in the Cardiff Grammar is based on Tench (1991). Here, however, nothing further will be said about intonation and punctuation.

5.6.2 Apex (a)

The **apex (a)** is the central element in the qlgp, and is expounded by adjectives, or by adverbs of manner. It is an obligatory element, and often the sole element present in the componence of the group. The term 'apex' is taken from Turner (1970) and is also adopted by Muir (1972). It is preferred to the term 'head', as proposed by Berry (1975) and Sinclair (1972), to avoid suggesting inappropriate parallels with the structure of the nominal group.

The function of the apex (when expounded by an adjective) is to provide a place in structure for the expression of the meaning of Quality that has been selected in order to classify, identify or describe a Thing (see Chapter 9 for a detailed account of Attribute functions). With the syllabically determined set of adjectives which inflect for comparative meanings (e.g. *sweet, pretty*, etc.), the apex inevitably subsumes the function associated with the element **temperer** (5.6.3). Unless the description allows the bound morpheme *-er* to expound a 'post-apex' temperer directly, this phenomenon can only be accounted for either by ignoring the morphology altogether or by positing the conflation of the apex with the temperer. This is further complicated by irregular comparative forms such as *better* and *worse*, which have no straightforward morphological segmentation. A parallel case of functional and elemental conflation is found in the structure of finite clauses, where the **Operator (O)** and one of a set of **Auxiliaries** (e.g. **Xr**) are conflated as **O/Xr**. The process of apex/temperer conflation is described in Chapter 8.

5.6.3 Temperer

Many adjectives, and in particular gradable adjectives, may be premodified. There are a number of word classes which serve this function; they are given in (a) to (g) below.

(a) 'De-adjectival' adverbs which retain the sense of the corresponding adjective (e.g. *inexplicably careless* = his carelessness was inexplicable)
(b) 'De-adjectival' adverbs which no longer reflect the sense of their corresponding adjective, and now serve the expressive function of 'intensification' (e.g. *extremely clever* = his cleverness is extreme)
(c) Morphologically simple items that have traditionally been classed as adverbs presumably on the grounds that they premodify adjectives (e.g. *so careful, very good, too easy*, etc.)
(d) Determiners (or 'determinatives' for Huddleston 1984: 304, 308) (e.g. *that careful, no good*)
(e) Adverbs which have no adjectival equivalent (e.g. *ever delightful*)
(f) Adjectives, usually in a strict collocational relationship with the adjective (e.g. *dead tired, dark blue*)
(g) Nouns, again usually in a strict collocational relationship with the adjective (e.g. *blood red, man crazy, stone cold*)
(h) Quantifying expressions based on 'measure nouns' (e.g. *three miles long, ten years old*)
(i) Verbal forms (which might be more appropriately considered to be adjectives) in a strict collocational relationship with the adjective (e.g. *raving mad, boiling hot*)

The single element of structure originally set up in the Cardiff Grammar for premodification – again following Turner (1970) – is the **temperer**.[8] In other descriptions (e.g. Berry 1975) the term **modifier** itself is used. One single pre-apex element of structure, however, is insufficient to capture the potential available within the quality group. Evidence for this is provided by (3).

(3)   So very politically aware

Example (3) suggests that a number of premodifying elements may co-occur before the adjectival apex. Setting aside the question of *so*, which is discussed separately in 5.6.4, the primary distinction that can be made is between the conventional degree adverbs (*very, quite, extremely, too* and the comparative and superlative items, *more, most, as, less*) and adverbs whose function is not that of expressing a degree. Thus, in (3) *politically* indicates the scope or domain of the awareness and parallels the function of the modifier *political* in the nominal group, as in (4).

(4)   He was chosen for his political awareness

Besides domain, such premodifiers express **manner**, as in (5).

(5)   She was noticeably silent on the matter

As degree is not signalled by such adverbs, it may also be expressed, as with *very* in example (3), or by other degree expressions such as *too, quite* and the comparatives and superlatives.

The potential to express degree in addition to domain and manner also serves to test and distinguish the precise functional status of members of the class of adverbs that, through the process of 'delexicalization', have themselves come to signal degree or are in the diachronic process of coming to do so. Typical adverbs in this class are *frightfully, extremely, awfully*, which no longer mean 'in a frightful/extreme/awful way'. As such, they are incompatible with common degree adverbs, as (6) shows.

(6)   *very awfully nice

The status of a number of such adverbs, given that the process of delexicalization is a gradual one, is not always clear. Does *amazingly*, as in *amazingly clever*, indicate that the person's cleverness amazes you, or does it signal a high degree of cleverness? The oddness of the co-occurrence of *very/extremely* and *amazingly* in (7) suggests the second of these two interpretations.

(7)   ?very/extremely amazingly clever

It is therefore possible and necessary to distinguish degree adverbs – including fully delexicalized adverbs – from the others, on the basis both of function and of potential co-occurrence. If we wish to retain the the term *temperer* for both sets, and also for *so*, as discussed below, it is necessary to distinguish the different subclasses with a second (superscript) letter. We shall therefore adopt the label *degree* temperer (t^d) and *adjunctival temperer* (t^a) accordingly.

Temperers are typically expounded by items classed traditionally as adverbs. There are a number of other word classes which expound temperers, as the list below indicates. It gives the various types in terms of word class rather than semantic function.

The relationship between the temperer and the apex is a complex one. Apexes expounded by fully non-gradable adjectives (e.g. *linguistic*) are typically not tempered. Where tempering is available it will be determined to a considerable extent by the semantic classification of the adjective expounding the apex. Temperers themselves can be semantically classified (cf. Downing and Locke 1992 for a classification within a systemic functional framework; Allerton 1987 and Johansson 1993 for recent studies). Finally, the temperer–apex relationship is subject to collocational patterning (Bäcklund 1973, Johansson 1993). Co-occurrence restrictions must ultimately be handled by the system network for Quality (discussed in Chapters 7 and 9), and are therefore not pursued further here.

The full potential at the temperer element, suggested by the range of structures in the list above, will not be explored here and is not currently included in the Cardiff Grammar. The network for tempering proposed in Chapter 9 is restricted to meanings expressed by (a), (b) and (c) in the list.

5.6.4 Emphasizing temperer (t^e): an arguable case

Temperers may also be preceded by other elements, as is shown in examples (8) and (9).

(8)   *so* very quick at tennis
(9)   *much* too intelligent to be a politician

The dilemma for the description lies in whether such expressions are to be considered as (a) premodifiers of the item expounding the temperer itself or (b) premodifiers of the apex.[9] One principle that might be applied is that, if an expression may be properly modified, a structure must be set up to account for the modifier–head relationship. Within the descriptive framework employed here, this would involve positing a **filling** relationship between the temperer and the structure which fills it. In this case – items at temperer which are adverbial in nature – the structure which fills the temperer would be a quality group. The premodifying elements would therefore themselves be temperers of an adverbial apex, and the whole of the quality group would be embedded at temperer in the matrix quality group. This solution is plausible in the case of **'de-adjectival'** adverbs such as *acutely*, since *so acutely* would automatically receive this analysis as a quality group filling an Adjunct in clause structure, e.g. *they felt it so acutely*. In 5.6.3, however, we set up an element of structure, the adjunctival temperer, to distinguish degree adverbs (expounding the temperer) from adverbs with a clearly different function. The co-occurrence of *so* and *acutely* is unproblematic both from a constituency point of view and from that of two independent elements of structure.

The analysis runs into difficulty, however, in the case of tempering items such as *very* and *too*. If it were universally applied, expressions such as *much too* and *so very* would have to be treated as quality group structures. The items *very* and *too* are exclusively tempering items (with the exception of *very* as in *the very person*); they are not exploited as clause Adjuncts and have no corresponding adjectival form. Consequently, the meanings which they express are not represented in the system network for Quality. In such cases, it would appear that some additional element of structure is required within the Quality group. Now if this solution is accepted, a further problem arises. As can be seen from example (11), the item *so* can clearly expound a temperer. It does this both in its function as an 'degree expression' and in its 'resultative' meaning as in *so ill that I couldn't attend*, which is treated as a separate meaning (see Chapter 9).

(10)   so very intelligent
(11)   so intelligent

Given the acceptability of *so*, both as a direct temperer of the apex, as in (11), and as a 'pre-temperer' element, before *very*, as in (10), where is this item to be attached? Is it to be analysed as a temperer of the higher qlgp, or as a temperer of the lower qlgp, whose apex is expounded by *very*? In the case of adjunctival temperers such as *acutely* or *noticeably*, it could be argued that two analyses of this expression are possible, as in Figures 5.1 and 5.2, and that the structural ambiguity is resolved in the spoken language by phonological distinctions. What I am suggesting here is that a speaker may indicate by intonation or pausing that, as in the Figure 5.1 analysis, *so* is considered to be separate from *acutely intelligent*, whereas in the Figure 5.2 analysis, the same phonological resources would indicate the grouping *so acutely*.

The analyses in Figures 5.1 and 5.2 are unproblematic, since *so* is treated either as a temperer of the apex *acutely* in the lower qlgp, or a temperer of the apex *intelligent* in the higher qlgp. However, in examples such as (10) *so* can combine neither with *very*, since *very* does not expound an apex in the quality

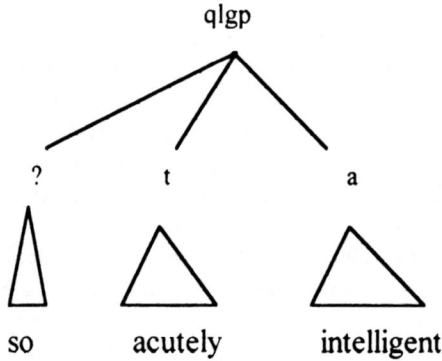

Figure 5.1. One analysis of *so acutely intelligent*

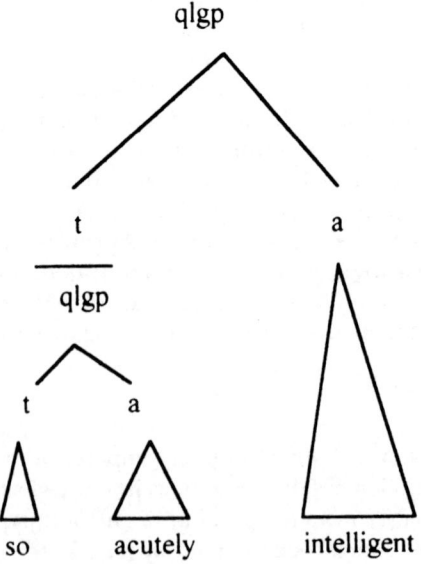

Figure 5.2. An alternative analysis of *so acutely intelligent*

group, nor with *very intelligent,* since the latter expression consists of two separate elements of structure.[10]

And it is not simply a question of the sole item *very.* Expletive degree temperers such as *bloody* and *fucking* may also be preceded by *so,* as in *so bloody/fucking clever!* Unless we recognize 'intermediate constituents' such as *very intelligent, acutely intelligent,* etc., as in X-bar approaches to syntax, there seems no alternative other than to posit an additional element of structure at the level of the higher qlgp. The label I propose to introduce for this element is t^e (**emphasizing temperer**).

This proposal may still seem unconvincing to readers who wish to analyse the item *so,* as in Figure 5.2, exclusively as a 'pre-modifier' of the temperer. Yet, as I emphasize again, there is no alternative solution to *so very,* since the item *very* (a) does not expound a pivotal element of structure in any group recognized by the Cardiff Grammar, and (b) does not realize a Quality or a Quantity meaning which can subsequently be elaborated through 'pre-modification'.

What remains to be established is whether each occurrence of *so* is an emphasizing temperer (t^e), or whether *so,* when it directly precedes the apex as in *so happy,* is straightforwardly a temperer (t). Here, I propose to distinguish *so* from all other forms of temperer by adopting the former analysis; that is, I am suggesting that *so* be treated as an emphasizing temperer whether it occurs alone with the adjective or adverb at apex or whether it precedes other kinds of temperers. This decision has consequences for the organization of the system network for **tempering.** Clearly, the option to have both a temperer and an emphasizing temperer depends on the class of temperer selected. If items such as *quite* and *too* are selected for tempering, or a comparative or superlative is selected, then *so* is excluded. Otherwise the network would allow expressions such as **so too big.* Emphasis tempering is therefore only permitted if it is (a) the only kind of tempering, or (b) one of the senses expressed by the 'de-adjectival' adverbs listed in 5.6.3. This is illustrated in the network for **tempering,** which is described and discussed in Chapter 9.

It is probable that the co-occurrence of *so* with *very* and the delexicalized degree adverbs such as *extremely, awfully, tremendously* derives from the fact that these adverbs (*very* included) were once restrictors, as described above, and therefore did not indicate degree. Nevertheless, as in Modern English these adverbs are clearly degree adverbs, the dilemma cannot be resolved by simply allowing them to expound the adjunctival temperer when preceded by *so.*

5.6.5 Extent (ex): another arguable case

The solution adopted above cannot, however, be extended to expressions such as *far,* which also precede the temperer. This element cannot be analysed as a temperer, however, given the ungrammaticality of (12).

(12)   *far intelligent

The item *far,* in fact, and other members of the paradigm, such as *much, considerably* and *a good deal,* only 'premodify' two temperers, namely *too* and *more.* It would appear that such modifiers have the function of indicating the degree or extent to which some Thing is, for example, *too important* or *more important*.

Fawcett (forthcoming) proposes the **quantity group (qtgp)** as a solution to this problem. His analysis rests firmly on the notion that a major function of the temperer is to provide a 'Quantity of Quality'. Thus, for Fawcett, Qualities, as realized in adjectives and adverbs, are subject to **quantification**. This is in itself a departure from the generally accepted notion that certain (gradable) adjectives and adverbs are subject to variation by **degree** (cf. Huddleston 1984: 308). On the basis of exemplification with the item *more*, Fawcett states that the qtgp expresses (a) 'Quantity of Thing' (e.g. *very many people*); (b) Quantity of Situation' (e.g. *Ike loves Ivy very much*); (c) 'Quantity of Quality' (e.g. *much more popular*); and (d) 'Quantity of a Quality (of either a 'Thing' or a 'Situation') (e.g. *well over two hundred people* and *he now loves her very much more than he did*). Whereas the item *more* is exploited by all the units expressing such meanings, the main types of 'quantity' meanings that Fawcett recognizes are not all available in each case. Cardinal quantification, for example, is not used for 'Quantity of Quality'.

Fawcett's use of the quantity group as a filler of the temperer element provides a neat solution in the case of expressions such as *much more intelligent* and *far more intelligent*, where *much more* and *far more* can be analysed as an **ad (adjuster)** and an **am (amount)**, the two elements of structure that are proposed for the quantity group. This will not, however, solve the problem posed by *much too intelligent* and *far too intelligent*, unless it is claimed that the item *too* expounds the element **am**.

It seems that such tempering expressions fall between two stools. There are parallels between 'degree of Quality' and 'Quantity of Thing', which is borne out by the use of items such as *more* for both. There are also considerable differences, however, which are obstacles to the complete transfer of the notion of 'Quantity' to 'Quality'.[11]

5.6.6 Post-apex elements

The qlgp exhibits a considerable degree of complexity in post-apex expressions. Most post-apex material has been accounted for in terms of a single element of structure (**qualifier** for Berry 1975, Sinclair 1972 and Downing and Locke 1992, or **limiter** for Turner 1970 and Muir 1972). In the present approach three post-apex elements are considered necessary. These are based on Fawcett's proposal for the two elements, **finisher (f)** and **scope (sc)**, to which we will argue here for the addition of a **second scope element**, giving **sc1** and **sc2**. The recognition of these three elements is discussed below.

What is generally missed by descriptions that propose a single post-apex element is the distinction made in other frameworks between 'modifier' and 'complement'. Admittedly, as Huddleston (1984: 309fn) points out, it is not always easy to make a sharp distinction between the two. However, there are clear cases where two separate elements are found in post-apex positions.

The motivation behind the notion of 'complement' is that some adjectives, like verbs, have an argument structure. A clear example of this is the adjective *fond*, which 'expresses a two-place semantic predicate (like the verb *love*)', to use Huddleston's words. In an expression like (13),

(13)   Howard is fond of Caroline

the prepositional expression *of Caroline* is considered to be a complement, as the nominal group would be in the expression in (14).

(14)   Howard loved Caroline

The similarity between adjective and verb complementation in such cases raises the question of whether or not the adjectival examples should be considered verbs. I shall return to this point shortly in 5.6.8. Before discussing this, however, we need to clarify the distinction between the complement-like elements that we have observed and what Huddleston refers to as modifiers.

If a single post-apex element is posited, it is difficult to account for the two functions that are expressed by the italicized structure following *eager* and *quick* in (15) and (16).

(15)   Howard was too eager *to please to be a manager*
(16)   He was so quick *to react that he fell over*

Both adjectives have recognizable complements, namely, *eager **to please*** and *quick **to react***. The remaining structure is explained not in terms of complementing the meaning of the adjective, but rather in terms of completing, or **finishing** – to make apparent the use of **finisher** as a label – the meaning which is introduced by the temperer.

In the case of (15), it is the meaning beginning in the temperer *too* that is completed by *to be a manager*. In (16) the temperer *so* (in its 'resultative' sense) requires obligatory completion, here expressed by *that he fell over*. It is generally the case that finishers occur only with a certain class of temperer. This class includes the 'telic' temperers *too* and *enough*, the comparative temperers *more*, *less*, *as* illustrated in (17) and (18), and the resultative temperer *so*. The analysis of (18) is given in Figure 5.3.

(17)   Howard was more/less eager to please than any other candidate
(18)   No candidate was as easy to please as Howard was

The potential in the structure to make explicit the degree of excessiveness or the standard of comparison suggests that a second post-apex element is required, in addition to the 'complement'. In many respects, this second element is more easily recognized than the first, and the label **finisher (f)** seems appropriate in functional terms. It is important to emphasize that finishers are dependent on the meanings of the temperers, rather than on the meaning of the adjective at apex. Finishers commonly occur as sole post-apex element, but in each case they co-occur with a temperer.

What remains to be accounted for is the first element, which until now we have referred to as the adjective 'complement'. Fawcett (1974–6/81), in positing a second post-apex element **scope (sc)**, provides a solution for this, which is discussed in the next section.

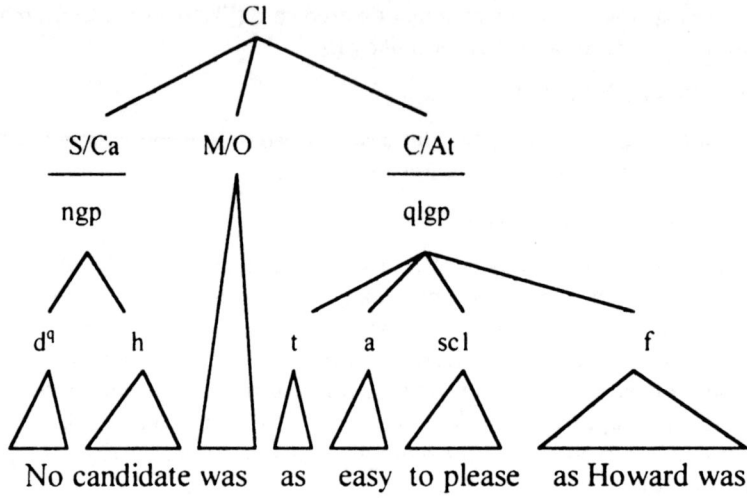

Figure 5.3. The quality group with both finisher and scope elements

5.6.7 Scope (sc)

Fawcett introduces the **scope** element to account for the presence of the italicized elements in examples (19)–(21) below. Although these examples appear, at first sight, to be different from what we have so far referred to as 'complements', we shall see that both kinds have much in common.

(19)   good *with children*
(20)   too good *at tennis* for me
(21)   too fat *around the waist* to get into his best trousers

The choice of **scope** as a label is intended to reflect the 'scope' or 'domain' of application of the Quality expressed at the apex. The examples above are evidence that, as was suggested in the last section, two functionally distinct post-apex elements are required. It is an interesting fact that the italicized elements qualify adjectives which do not take a 'verb-based' complement in terms of an underlying semantic argument structure. There are, however, striking similarities between the structures that Fawcett treats as scope, e.g. *good at tennis*, and those which are traditionally analysed as complements of adjectives, which were introduced in 5.6.6, e.g. *disappointed to hear it*. First, they both allow a finisher of the type introduced by the temperer *too* or comparative temperers. Second, when a finisher is present it tends to be the second element unless the 'endweight' principle applies, as in (22).

(22)   He's better than me at getting the children to bed in the evening

Finally, the two types, because they depend on different classes of adjective, appear to be mutually exclusive. Positing a typically early post-apex place in structure to cover both types therefore seems plausible and reasonable. What remains to be seen is whether Fawcett's label **scope** is a suitable one to cover both types.

However, Fawcett's proposals for the qlgp need to be supplemented. As Huddleston (1984: 307) points out, there is a possibility, with a small number of adjectives, of a 'double complement'. Huddleston's two examples are given here as (23) and (24) with the second complement italicized.

(23)   critical of Max *for his indecisiveness*
(24)   responsible to the directors *for implementing the proposal*

Among the adjectives which exhibit similar behaviour are *complimentary*, *answerable* and *accountable*. It is not the case that the second complement of such adjectives can be considered a **finisher**, since it may itself be a single complement as in (25) and (26) and is not 'finishing' any meaning whose expression begins with a temperer.

(25)   critical of Max's indecisiveness
(26)   responsible for implementing the proposal

Furthermore, both complements, or either one individually, can be accompanied by a finisher as in (27).

(27)   more critical of Max for his indecisiveness than his brother was

I therefore propose the introduction of a **second scope element (sc2)** into the structure of the quality group, which is shown in the analysis of (27) in Figure 5.4.

As a general rule, the realization of meanings associated with scope is optional. There are, however, a number of adjectives in a given sense which, as Quirk *et al.* (1985: 1221) point out, require a scope element. A prime example of this is *averse*, which must be complemented by a prepositional group. The 'given sense' condition applies to adjectives such as *conscious*. In the sense of

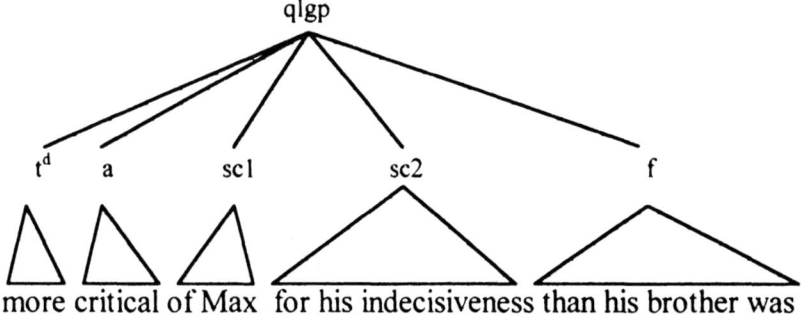

Figure 5.4. The quality group with two scope elements and a finisher

'noticing or realizing what is happening', the scope is obligatory, as shown in (28).

> (28)   she was conscious of the stranger staring at her

In other senses, and when it is used in the modifier function, *conscious* does not, or rather cannot, take a scope, since this would impose the interpretation of its sense as that intended in (28).

The notion of obligatory scope brings us back to the question of whether or not expressions such as *be conscious of, be fond of,* etc. are best treated as Processes. In the following section I return to this issue, which I briefly referred to in 5.6.6.

5.6.8 The case for adjectives as Processes

The danger of using adjectives such as *fond* and *conscious* as test cases for the existence of adjective complements, which I henceforth refer to **scope,** is that the argument can be turned on its head. In this sense of *fond*, firstly, the scope is obligatory, and secondly, *Caroline* can be 'raised' out of the prepositional group in 'cleft' clauses, as in (29), or arguably thematized as in (30).

> (29)   It's Caroline that Howard is fond of
> (30)   Caroline, John is fond of

The syntactic behaviour of *fond of* is so similar to that of a lexical verb that it could be argued that such expressions are indeed complex verbal items. On this view, (29) would be analysed as shown in Figure 5.5 below. The analysis introduces an element of structure, **Mex** (Main Verb extension), which, in this case, accounts for the adjectival particle following the verb *be.*

There is a drawback to this approach which I shall now explain and evaluate. This is that *fond* is an adjective, and is therefore, in the present approach, the apex in a qlgp. It may therefore be tempered, e.g. *very fond of Caroline, too fond of Caroline* and also conceivably *fonder (more fond) of Caroline.* And because temperers like *too* and *more* may be followed by finishers, we have expressions such as (31).

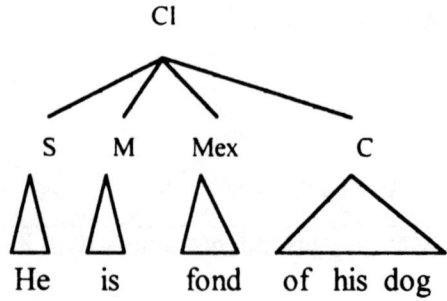

Figure 5.5. The analysis of *be fond of* as a complex verb

(31)   Howard was too fond of Caroline to be separated from her

The analysis of *be fond of* as a Process raises the problem of explaining the syntactic status of *too* and *to be separated from her*. It is difficult to see either of these two elements as direct elements of clause structure, which means positing a discontinuous qlgp, as is shown in Figure 5.6. The alternative is to treat the entire expression dependent on *fond* as the Complement of the Main Verb *be* (Figure 5.7).

Note that if the Process is expressed as a Main Verb, such as *love* in (32), the quality group fills the clause Adjunct and exhibits no discontinuity of structure.

(32)   Howard loved Caroline too intensely to be separated from her

The semantic parallelism of *be fond of* with *love* may well suggest a phrasal-prepositional verb analysis, but this leaves the problem of the discontinuity. Furthermore, the 'raising' phenomenon present in (29), repeated here, is common with many adjectival expressions, as illustrated in (33)–(35).

(29)   It's Caroline that Howard is fond of
(33)   It's the exam results that I'm happy about
(34)   It's the electric motor you have to be careful with
(35)   It's running that he's good at

A powerful argument in favour of the analysis of expressions such as *be fond of* as Processes is that it permits the expression, at Subject and Complement, of

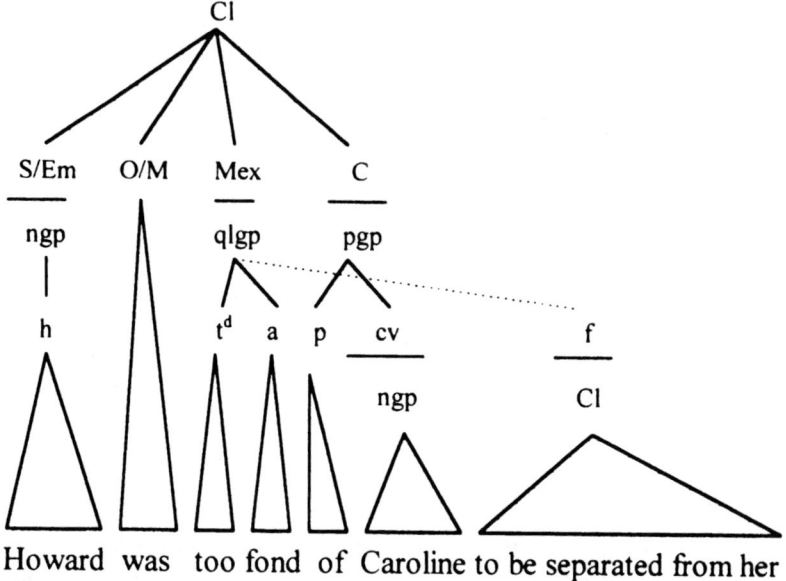

Figure 5.6. The expression *be fond of* analysed as a Process

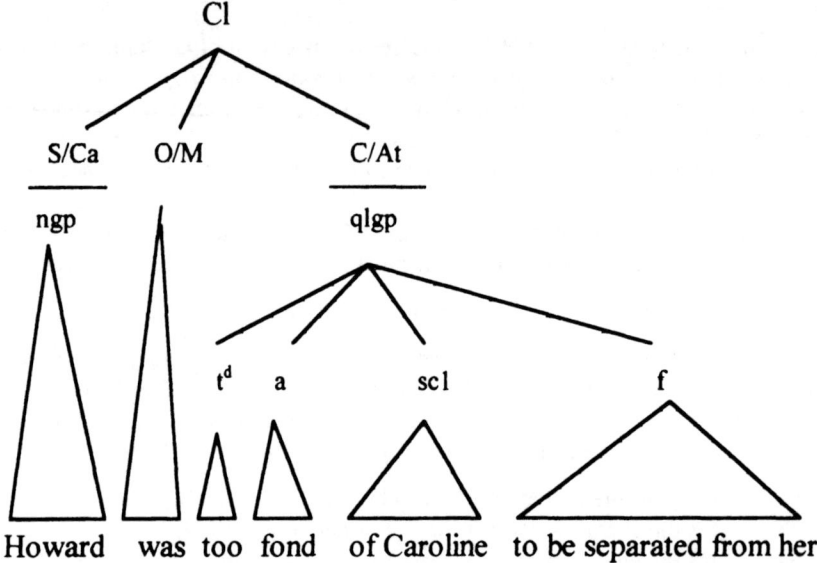

Figure 5.7. The quality group as Complement in a Relational Process

the Participant Roles which are associated with mental Process types. It is difficult to see *Howard* and *Caroline* as expressing any Role other than **Emoter** and
Phenomenon, precisely as they do with the mental Process *love*. If one treats
fond and its dependent structure as an **Attribute** of a Relational Process, the
relationship between *Howard* and *Caroline* is obscured. Yet, unlike the
Emoter/Phenomenon relationship in other mental Processes expressed
through Main Verbs such as *love* and *have*, adjectival expressions have no potential for passivization.

It is a matter of debate whether cases such as *be fond of* should be taken to be
verbal complements, but if they were, we would need to recognize a whole set
of Main Verb extensions, such as *be happy about, be careful with* and *be good at*. The
nature of the Cardiff Grammar as primarily a generative device does not allow
the luxury of dual interpretations of such structures. From the text-analytical
point of view, it is possible to see the process of 'grammatical metaphor at work'.
In the case discussed here, it is a question of an ostensibly mental Process being
realized by the structure associated with relational Processes.

5.6.9 Elements required for superlativization

Superlative meanings are marked by the affixes *-est* and *-er* or the items *most* and
more. The second of each pair is included since the 'dual superlatives' are no different in nature from 'multi-superlatives'. Moreover, there is clearly a different
function involved in (36) and (37) as shown in Figures 5.8 and 5.9.

(36)   a faster car
(37)   the faster car

The use of *most* as a superlative in (38), compared to its use in (39), must also be distinguished. The meaning of the first of these is something equivalent to *extremely*.[12]

(38)   a most intelligent person
(39)   the most intelligent person

   The function of the superlative has similarities to that realized by **deictic determiners**, i.e. it provides for the identification of a particular referent Thing by reference to its having a higher or lower degree of a Quality than any other Thing.

5.6.10 The quality deictic determiner (d^qld)

In terms of the structure of the qlgp, it is the status of the item *the* which concerns us here. Two alternative arguments may be proposed to account for it. In the first, *the* is treated as a deictic determiner in the structure of the nominal group and signals recoverability of the referent Thing, and the superlative form of the adjective stands as a clue to the addressee to how the referent is recoverable. This is similar to the use of nominal group qualifiers to support the recoverability signalled by *the* in expressions such as (40).

(40)   the book I have just bought

On this view, the deictic determiner is clearly **an element of structure in the nominal group**. Instances of superlative expressions such as *she is the most important*, with no apparent head, are considered to be 'headless' nominal constructions.

   The alternative approach, as proposed by Fawcett, posits the determiner in such cases as an obligatory function of the Quality at apex of the quality group. This position is given support by the use of superlative adjectives at Attribute, as in (41).

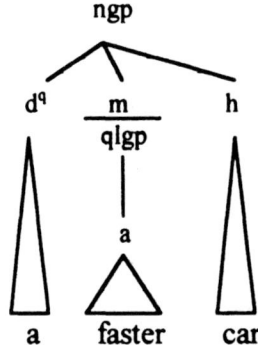

Figure 5.8. Analysis of *a faster car*

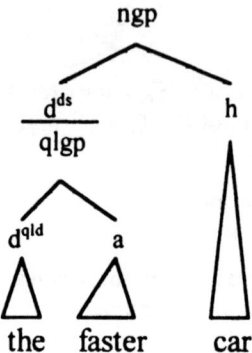

Figure 5.9. Analysis of *the faster car*

(41)   it's the biggest that I've seen

Here, the absence of a nominal head, which is typical in Attribute expressions, does not remove the need for the deictic determiner. On this view, the determiner is therefore **a necessary element of the quality group**, rather than an element of a 'headless' nominal group. The inclusion of the **d^{qld}** *the* as an element of structure of the quality group provides a neat solution to the role of superlativization in the nominal group. As Fawcett has proposed, an additional determiner element **d^s (superlative determiner)** is recognized, alongside other types of determiner. The **d^s** is then filled by a quality group containing its own determiner, as shown in Figure 5.10. It will be noted that such an analysis avoids the need to explain away the presence of two deictic determiners in the nominal group, both having the noun *ferrets* as their head.

 · There appears to be no convincing argument against the classification of superlativization amongst the set of 'determining' functions; it is clearly one of the ways in which speakers identify a referent in terms of 'which one(s)' they are talking about. However, a similar function is realized by the deictic determiner and a modifier, as in (42).

(42)   I'll have the big one

Here again, the clue to the recoverability signalled by *the* is in the attribute *big*. Superlativization only becomes important in this process when *big* alone is insufficient to identify a single Thing or a set of Things. Thus the difference between (43) and (44) is that in the former there is a recognizable difference between the apples that are big and those that are not, whereas in the latter all the apples from which some are to be selected may be 'biggish'.

(43)   Give me the big apples
(44)   Give me the biggest apples

If a quantifier is then added, as in *give me the three biggest apples*, a completely

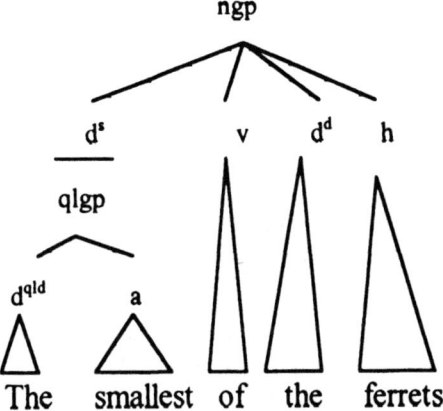

Figure 5.10. Fawcett's superlative determiner (dˢ) filled by a qlgp

defined set is specified, producing a more precisely determined selection from the whole.

If a superlativizing determiner (dˢ) were not posited, it would have to be replaced by a nominal group element expounded by *the*, and accompanied by a modifier selected from the range available, with the appropriate superlative morphology. The nominal group in Figure 5.10 would therefore be re-analysed as in Figure 5.11.

The analysis of the superlative structure in Figure 5.10 has repercussions on the structure of a superlative expression at Attribute in the clause, as in (46). If the Complement/Attribute is directly filled by a quality group, it is unclear how superlativization could be selected, given that the deictic determiner is a component of nominal group structure. Once again, the only analysis of the superlative in (46) would be as part of a headless nominal group.

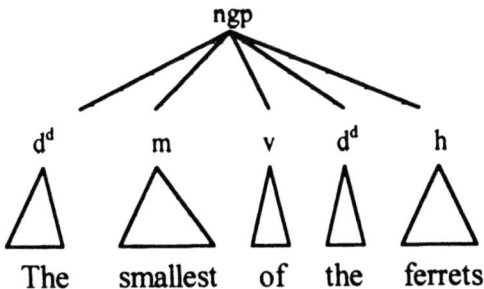

Figure 5.11. Superlativization without a quality group determiner

>   (45)   This ferret is big
>   (46)   This ferret is the biggest

In its relationship with the predicative form of adjectives, there is some evidence that the superlative is not presented as an identifying function to some 'Thing'. Consider the paradigm represented in (47)–(49).

>   (47)   I am happy when I'm alone
>   (48)   I am happier when I'm alone
>   (49)   I am happiest when I'm alone

These examples show that the basis of the comparison is not a referent Thing but a Quality. If the superlative form is possible with predicative adjectives, we need to ask what the function of the determiner *the* is.

Let us take another example, as in (50).

>   (50)   John's shirt is the whitest

Here, the function of *the whitest* is not to identify some referent but rather to compare the degree of the colour white over a range of 'referent Things'; it does not answer the question *Which shirt is John's?* Imagine a television advertisement in which a television personality has had three shirts washed in different brands of washing powder, with the aim of demonstrating the superiority of the advertised brand. The result of the 'experiment' might be expressed as '*and John's shirt is the whitest*'. If we were to supply a head to the Complement, as in (51), thereby positing a nominal group, the clause would now be ambiguous, in the sense that the Subject or the Complement may be understood as the 'identified' or 'identifying element' (cf. Halliday 1994: 122ff) in the two readings respectively.

>   (51)   John's shirt is the whitest one

There is then good reason for claiming that the presence of *the* in superlatives does not indicate the presence of a 'headless' nominal group. For Complements at least, this supports Fawcett's decision to include *the* as an element of the quality group.

Let us now consider comparison at Subject with a similar paradigm. In this function it is necessary to invoke a nominal group, given the unlikelihood of a quality group alone filling the Subject. We can, however, use an 'indefinite' (or 'unparticularized' in the Cardiff Grammar) nominal group for the paradigm as given in (52)–(54).

>   (52)   Rich people usually go abroad for their holidays
>   (53)   Richer people go to another continent
>   (54)   The richest people go on luxury world cruises

The process of **selection** (Fawcett 1974–76/1981: 22) is operating here, purely in terms of class membership, or more precisely in terms of membership of subclasses of a Quality *rich* based upon comparative degrees of the Quality. There is no formal means of distinguishing the superlative in (51) from its use in an equivalent paradigm of definite expressions, as in (55)–(57)

(55)   The rich people usually go abroad for their holidays
(56)   The richer people go to another continent
(57)   The richest people go on luxury world cruises

In this set, the deictic determiner signals recoverability, which is established by reference not only to the set of people who are rich, but to some other selected set recoverable anaphorically from previous discourse. The utterances may be referring, for example, to *the people who live in Liverpool*. Thus, to take up the example in (44) again, if I ask to be given *the biggest apple*, I intend the biggest from a set already specified in the co-text and signalled by the presence of *the*. The same would hold for *the big apple*.

It is then almost impossible to establish a single role for *the* in superlatives, since, in Subject position at least, it is required whether or not there is some selection other than from the class of Things indicated by the addition of an adjective. The only instance of its absence is in examples such as (58).

(58)   My most expensive possessions

Here, the initial selection from the class denoted by the item *possession* is by the deictic determiner *my*. A further selection is made by singling out *expensive possessions* and finally a further selection of *most expensive*.

Note that quantification, before or after the superlative, is also possible in this environment, giving nominal groups like (59) and (60).

(59)   My three largest shirts
(60)   My largest three shirts

The possessive determiner *my* in these examples appears to be in a paradigmatic relationship with the determiner *the*, at least at the level of structure, if not at the semantic level of the system network. If this is the case, Fawcett's solution of including the latter determiner in the qlgp is problematic. The status of *my* is further discussed in 5.6.11.

Let us sum up the arguments in the treatment of superlative constructions. It can be argued that in the context of the nominal group all determiners require heads, either overt or elliptied. Furthermore, they must be **nominal** heads. If this principle holds, then the presence of a determiner entails the presence of a nominal group with an appropriate head. If the item *the* preceding a superlative adjective is taken to be a determiner in the nominal group, then, according to the principle above, it belongs to a nominal group at all times. It can be argued on the same grounds that **quantifying determiners** also require an overt or covert head, and that **quantification** is a function of Things.

There are two problems with the above argument. Firstly, the deictic determiner *the* can appear twice before a single head, as in (61), and can signal deictic recoverability with reference to both a singular and a plural Thing. In languages which have determiner–head agreement for gender and number, the two determiners would be morphologically different (as in the French equiv-lent: *la plus belle des* (*= de + les*) *chemises*).

(61)   *the* largest of *the* shirts is far too large

The only explanation possible, according to the principle that requires that 'there always be a head', is that the first occurrence of *the* is a determiner of some covert head different from *shirts*. This explanation would be supported by the requirement of the verb to agree in number to the putative covert head of the first determiner, as in (62).

(62)   the largest (covert head) of the shirts *is* being washed

The very apparent difficulty that is encountered with this solution is that it creates two nominal groups, or rather a nominal group with a prepositional group as the postmodifier or **qualifier** in which the second nominal group is embedded. This runs contrary to Fawcett's notion of selection, in which the rightmost nominal in a group is always the head and any determiner or string of determiners to the left **selects out** from that head as in (63).

(63)   a few of the largest of my shirts

Although the application of Fawcett's selection principle is questionable when it includes cases such as (64) and (65), it is difficult to argue that superlatives are not in fact constituents of the larger nominal group.[13]

(64)   a portrait of the artist as a young man
(65)   a photograph of his girlfriend

Fawcett, as we have seen, sets up the element of structure **d**[s] (superlative determiner) to reflect the function of superlative structures in the process of selection. The fact that it is not expounded directly by a single item need not be a distraction. Complex genitive constructions such as *the Queen of England's* and quantifying expressions such as *a lot of* or *a good few of* are clearly 'complex determiners', and are paradigmatically related to simple exponents such as *her* and *some* respectively.

The second problem with the 'nominal head requirement principle' is that there are occurrences of the item *the* in expressions which are in no sense nominal. Most obvious amongst these are Manner Adjunct superlatives such as (66).

(66)   In the tests, Fords were found to run *the most smoothly*

This use of the determiner in such cases provides strong support for Fawcett's position. It clearly cannot be argued here that in (66) *the* is a determiner in some nominal group that might follow the superlative (e.g. *the most smoothly of all the cars tested*), or that the superlative modifies some 'headless' nominal group, since this is uncontroversially an adverb-headed group (i.e. a quality group). Thus, in dealing with the structure of adverbial expressions a determiner-like element, *the,* is necessary. Its function is clearly associated with the 'uniquifying' function of superlatives which it has in some sense 'inherited' from its use with nominals.

As a consequence, it is not implausible to posit this same element of structure for the adjectival-type quality group, thereby also retaining complete parallelism of adjectival and adverbial structures within the group.

5.6.11 The case of possessives

Having argued the case for *the*, it is necessary to see whether a similar analysis can be extended to possessives. A number of observations suggest that, at first sight, it cannot. Firstly, there is no parallel in adverbial expressions. Second, possessives are not found with the superlative, as is *the*, when the superlative represents a further selecting out; the possessive and superlative functions do not combine in *of*-expressions. Structures like (67), unlike (68), are accordingly ungrammatical.

(67) *My cleanest of the shirts
(68) The cleanest of my shirts

At Complement in the clause, possessive superlatives are reasonably common, however, as in (69) and (70), although it could be argued that in such cases they are in fact part of a headless nominal structure.

(69) This is my cleanest
(70) John is my eldest

The inclusion of the possessive determiner within the quality group is therefore more problematic than the inclusion of the determiner *the*. Nevertheless, without convincing arguments one way or the other, it will, for the present, be treated in the same way. Its inclusion, however, will require a further constraint on the selection of superlative meaning, in order to avoid the ungrammaticality of (67) above. The choice of possessive rather than deictic must only be available if superlativization is the sole definite selecting process present. Superlativization may of course be used for a second definite selection, but must be *the* superlativization, as in (71).

(71) The most expensive of his five most famous paintings

5.6.12 Quantifiers

It was noted above that cardinal quantification can co-occur with superlatives either before or after the adjective as illustrated in (72) and (73) below. Fawcett also includes a quality quantifying determiner $\mathbf{d}^{ql q}$ in the quality group, and allows for its dual position by positing two potential places in the structure of the group. This is again in contrast with the view according to which quantifiers are always elements proper of the nominal group. It is difficult to reconcile these two views, especially when the quantifier precedes the superlative. Attributing nominal group status to the quantifier in this case would lead to discontinuity between the determiner within the quality group and the superlative adjective, thereby weakening the case which has been argued for inclusion of deictic and possessive determiners.

It is already difficult to tease apart the difference in meaning between (72) and (73).

(72)   The three largest shirts
(73)   The largest three shirts

One plausible explanation is suggested by the relative ordering itself, in the sense that there is a tendency for the first of two elements to be seen as modifying the second. Thus in (72), *three* is understood as a temperer of *largest*, whereas in (73) the numeral more directly premodifies the nominal head. A second function related to alternative ordering of this kind is that of indicating **new information**, which is typically associated with later positions in structure.

What is also important here is the function of the quantifier itself. Quantifiers involved in nominal groups which have an initial deictic determiner function differently from those which have quantification alone. In (74), for example, *two* is recoverable, in association with the function of the deictic; it gives no new information in terms of quantification, but acts as a marker of cohesion. In (75), on the other hand, *two* is providing new information with regard to quantification.

(74)   The two boys started fighting
(75)   Two boys started fighting

In superlative constructions, the presence of a cardinal number is quantificationally relevant. Superlatives, unless singular, indicate a quantified subset only indirectly, in the sense that in any set *some* members are larger, taller, faster, etc. than others. The co-selection of a cardinal specifies the exact quantity which is included in the subset.

There is therefore a conflation of functions between superlativization and quantification; the quantity can only be related to the head **through** the superlative. Given the strict association between superlative and quantifier, Fawcett's position of allowing for a **d$^{q|q}$** (quality quantifying determiner) in the qlgp is tenable in the case of pre-apex cardinals. Wherever the cardinal follows the apex, the quantification will be deemed to be outside the scope of the superlative and to be an element proper of the nominal group.[14]

5.6.13 Superlatives and finishers

Superlatives, like comparatives, associate with meanings realized through the **finisher** element of structure. The main option available involves the specification of the set from which the superlative members are drawn. In a sense it parallels the finisher with comparative, as is shown in (76) and (77).

(76)   The most beautiful of all
(77)   More beautiful than all the others

The descriptive dilemma lies in the similarity between these apparent finishers and what might be seen as the rest of the nominal group. Clearly, in (78) the material after the superlative contains the head to which the superlative applies.

The function of *of the lot* in (79) is less clear.

(78)   The most beautiful of the girls
(79)   The most beautiful of the lot

The status of the *of*-expression can be tested by attempting to add a noun after the superlative. With the examples above, this would prove successful for (79), i.e. *the most beautiful girl of the lot*, but not for (78), e.g *the most beautiful girl of the girls*. This test rests on Fawcett's **selection** principle, which was introduced in the last section. In (78) the superlative determiner constitutes a further selection from *the girls*. In (79), it is a selection from some referent Thing, either **covert** when the superlative is in the nominal group at Subject, or **recoverable anaphorically** when the superlative is a quality group at Attribute in the clause. In the second instance, the expression *of the lot* is an aid to the recoverability of the referent Thing.

The test also differentiates between the closely related expressions *of them* and *of them all* as illustrated in (80) and (81), and would indicate that the latter is a finisher, whereas the former contains the head of the nominal group.

(80)   *The biggest liar of them
(81)   The biggest liar of them all

Unavoidably, the superlative–finisher structure involves discontinuity wherever a nominal head is realized. This is also the case with comparative adjectives and *than*–expressions. The only way of avoiding this discontinuity would be to claim implausibly that such post-head expressions are in fact **qualifiers** of the nominal head.

5.7   A FULL POTENTIAL STRUCTURE

It is now possible to specify a full potential structure for the quality group. We should remember, however, that this is a potential structure in the sense that it states what places in structure are available for potential use. As was explained in Section 5.5, a potential structure specification does not tell us what a 'well-formed' quality group is, as is the case of a phrase structure rule or X-bar theory in generative grammar. Questions of obligatory and optional elements or co-occurrence restrictions are the responsibility of the system network and associated realization rules. The presence or absence of elements in any given structure will, in large measure, be dependent on the individual or class behaviour of the adjectives themselves. The potential for gradability of an adjective will determine its potential for tempering and finishing. Thus, only in some exceptional interpretation of (82) will this group be acceptable.

(82)   *he is more retired than I am

The potential structure for the quality group is therefore:

& @ 1, ex @ 2, t^e @ 3, d^{qld} @ 4, t^d @ 6, t^a@ 7, d^{qlq} @ 8, a @ 10, t^d @ 12, f @ 16, sc1 @ 18, sc2 @ 20, f @ 22, e @ 24.

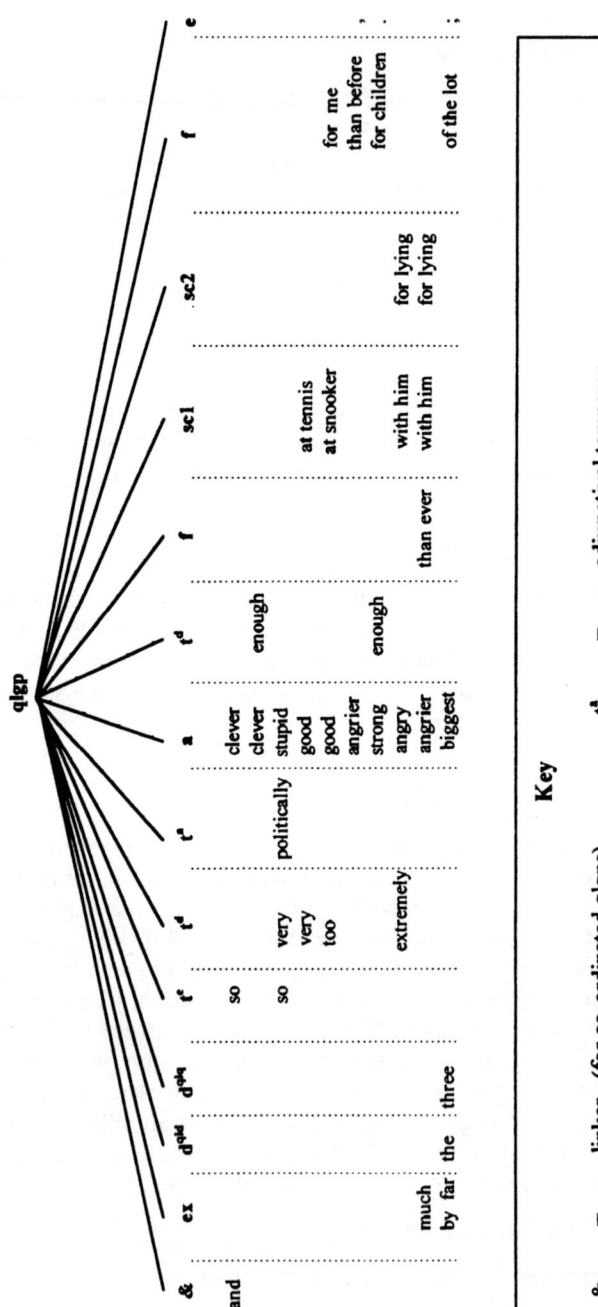

Figure 5.12. The structure of the quality group (with adjectival apex only)

Two places in structure are posited for the **degree temperer**, to account for the item *enough,* and for the **finisher (f)** which may precede the **scope** element(s). The finisher must be placed each time that it is required, since the exact place cannot be known in advance. With the temperer, the position is different. Given that all temperers expounded by any item other than *enough* will be at Place 6, it is sufficient to state this with a single rule, which can be informally expressed as: 'if the feature [sufficiency of quality] has been selected, place the temperer at 12, otherwise place it at 6'. This avoids having to place the temperer each time it is present. Only elements which have a fixed place in structure can there-fore be specified in advance by a general placement or insertion statement as shown in the potential structure given above. Figure 5.12 provides a represen-tative sample of quality group structures.

5.8 CONCLUSION

As I emphasized in Section 5.7, the potential structure of the quality group, as of any unit, does not constitute an independent rule-governed syntactic specifi-cation. The structures in the Cardiff Grammar are generated by the set of real-ization rules as described in Chapter 4. But these rules depend on the set of semantic features (**selection expression**) which are co-selected in a traversal of the system network. Realization rules simply generate units, place elements of structure, fill certain elements of structure by generating other units, and expound 'terminal' elements of structure in items. Any grammatical structure generated by the grammar depends initially on the co-selection of semantic fea-tures and the application of the realization rules. In systemic grammar, the gen-eration of 'all and only all of the sentences of a language' is secondary to the generation of those meanings which the linguistic structure (including intona-tion) can express. Few syntactic constraints are expressed by the realization rules alone. One of the few independent constraints is the placement of elements of structure. Thus, for example, the potential structure specification for the qlgp places the **apex** at Place 10, with respect to other elements. Yet, even in terms of placement, any element which **potentially** occupies two places in structure can-not have its **actual** place specified independently of system network feature selec-tion. The placement of the **finisher** element depends crucially on a textually motivated decision taken in selecting the appropriate feature(s) in the network.

The functional syntactic description in this chapter is independently useful, however, for **textual analysis.** In analysing text, the analyst is interested in under-standing the meanings which have been realized by the creator of the text, rather than producing new text. Once the functional motivation has been understood, the syntagmatic and paradigmatic relations will be evident, albeit in a more informal way than is specified by system networks and realization rules. An explicit model of language such as the Cardiff Grammar is **only** a model. It would be a dangerously strong claim to suggest that our brains contain system networks and realization rules of the kind employed by the Cardiff Grammar.

NOTES

1 Recent X-bar syntax includes functional categories, such as I (for INFLECTION), which also have phrasal projections, e.g. I' I".

2 Halliday introduces the notion of 'type' to account for the internal organization of groups. This is discussed in Butler (1985: 24–5). Berry (1975: 76–7) also introduces 'type' into her description. For Berry, 'types' are groupings on the basis of similarity of structure, e.g. those which exhibit an **m,h,q** structure. Berry's 'types' generalize across 'classes' in Halliday's sense, or 'groups' in the sense used here. The structures *quite quickly enough* and *the boys next door* are therefore considered to be of the same type because they share the same m,h,q structure.

3 Expressions such as *the day before yesterday, next week*, are considered to be realizations of nominal groups. It should be noted that they are not prepositional groups with an ellipted prepositional element.

4 Fawcett departs radically from approaches both in the systemic tradition and outside in not recognizing a **verbal group** or **verb phrase**. Instead, he 'promotes' the verbal elements **Auxiliary**, **Operator** and **Main Verb** to function as direct elements of clause structure. The motivation for this is found in Fawcett (1974–6/81).

5 Flat tree structures are criticized for their inability to identify intermediate phrasal projections such as single bar projections in X-bar approaches. Dependency, it is claimed, is necessary to capture the fact that in the phrase *the old wooden box* there is an intermediate phrasal projection *wooden box*. Evidence to support this is provided by the possibility of substituting *one* for *wooden box*, as in *I don't want the old wooden box. I want the new **one***.

6 The term **potential structure** is now preferred to the earlier **starting structure** to avoid the suggestion that such a representation in any way specifies actual group structures.

7 I have no real preference between the individually labelled classes **adjectival group** and **adverbial group** and the conflated class **quality group**. In one sense, Fawcett's label is inconsistent with the general labelling of groups according to their lexical head. Furthermore, for descriptive purposes, the original word class based labels may be felt to be more appropriate. Whilst a return to separate labels would in no way affect the grammar as a generative device, it should be remembered that there is **only one system network**, the **network for Quality**.

8 The one exception to the pre-apex place in structure for temperers is the item *enough* which immediately follows the apex. There is no real doubt that this item is anything but a temperer. It is clearly in a systemic relationship with other temperers such as *too, more, very*, etc. and co-occurs with scope and finisher elements as in:

(a) eager enough to please
(b) good enough at cricket to be in the school team

There seems no alternative but to allocate a place in the structure of the group, immediately following the apex.

Interestingly, equivalents of *enough* in the Romance languages have pre-apex positions: *bastante importante* (Sp), *abbastanza importante* (It), *assez important* (Fr), etc.

9 This problem can be avoided – rather than addressed – by using the notion of 'sub-modification'. This approach is adopted by Downing and Locke (1992), who introduce 'submodifiers' (sm), 'subsubmodifiers' (ssm) and 'subsubsubmodifiers' (sssm)

to account for such adjectival expressions as *she was really quite the most stunningly handsome woman*. In the Cardiff Grammar framework, which allows elements of structure of whatever unit to be filled, the submodification approach would simply mean 'unfinished business'.

10 If we were to take *so* as a temperer of *very*, then *very* must expound an apex, and as such must be a Quality sense. In its original sense, related to the French *vrai*, it did, and still does in expressions such as *the very thing*. In contemporary English, it does not have this sense when modifying another Quality sense, either an adjective or an adverb. Historical linguistics will not therefore provide a plausible 'escape clause' for this item.

11 It is possible to overcome the problem of *too* by claiming that it is a variant realization of the meaning 'excessive Quantity' which must be selected when this meaning applies to a 'quality'. The 'Quantity of Thing' realization is then *too much/many*. Note that in Romance languages the same item is used in both cases, e.g. (It) *troppo zucchero* [too much sugar] and *troppo dolce* [too sweet]. This would entail positing *too much* as a single item. In Fawcett's current analysis *too much* is further analysed into **ad** and **am**. The same solution would also apply to *very* and *very much*.

12 Interestingly, Italian has a morphological form to indicate the non-superlative *most*, i.e. *una bellissima serata* (a most beautiful evening), which is distinguished from the superlative construction, *la serata la più bella* (the most beautiful evening).

13 While I accept Fawcett's interpretation of *the roof* in *the roof of the house* as a further 'selecting out' – in this case involving a 'part–whole' relationship – I have difficulty in accepting the inclusion of 'representations', such as *a photograph of* or *a painting of*, in this process. Selection typically involves the narrowing down of a class of Thing into smaller and smaller groups, each of which is a part of the previously specified group. Once one has reached a single Thing, one can select further on the basis of parts of the Thing. I cannot see, however, how a representation can be thus considered. Is *the idea of a fight* a similar candidate for selection?

14 Fawcett's latest position on quantifying expressions is that they are realized by the **quantity group (qtgp)**. This group is composed of two elements of structure: an **amount (am)** and an **adjuster (ad)** which accounts for structures such as *about ten*. It also accounts for complex quantifiers such as *a pair of*. We note here that in the case of superlatives such complex quantifying structures cannot precede the superlative, thus producing an ungrammatical utterance in the second example below.

    (f1)   the smartest pair of thieves I've met
    (f2)   *the pair of smartest thieves I've met

6. System networks and lexically-oriented meaning

6.1 INTRODUCTION

In the previous chapter I set up a quality group structure which is found necessary to express the range of meanings which are associated with adjectives. In the following chapters I shall examine the way in which system networks and their associated realization rules can be used to model meanings pertaining to Quality. First, however, I shall discuss the system network modelling of lexis in general. Then in Chapters 7, 8, 9 and 10 I shall make specific proposals for the modelling of Quality. This chapter, therefore, concerns the organization of those sections of the system network in which realization in open set lexis is predominant. Approaches to lexis within systemic linguistics have already been surveyed and discussed in Chapter 2. Here, the problems of the organization of the 'lexical areas' of the system network are discussed and the solutions proposed within the Cardiff Grammar are presented.

The assumption on which the Cardiff Grammar is based is that there is one network of lexicogrammatical options, as originally suggested by Halliday (1978: 43). The system network must therefore contain all options which lead to exponence in lexis. There is no separate 'lexicon' as a repository for lexical entries and the information which is needed to express their relationship with structure, their semantics, and any idiosyncratic behaviour that they may exhibit.

If this assumption is valid, then extensive parts of the system network will be concerned with meanings which are expressed, at least in part, by items from open set word classes, etc. One (optimistic) estimate of the 'mental lexicon' of college students is of up to 250,000 words (Diller 1978). Even conceding that this may be an exaggeration, it is not unreasonable to assume that a full lexicogrammatical description should account for tens of thousands of items.

6.2 THE INEVITABILITY OF THE SYSTEM NETWORK SOLUTION TO LEXIS

In a number of places in the full system network there must appear systems of features responsible for the choices among Processes, Things and Qualities, which will ultimately be realized as items. The extension of such systems constitutes the resource which organizes the meanings associated with items from the open set word classes. In most views of linguistic organization, as we saw in Chapter 1, this is the transition point from 'grammar' to 'lexis'. For example, in the Nigel Grammar (Matthiessen and Bateman 1991), the system network specifies the structurally realized options, and the choice of lexical item is the responsibility of the lexicon, rather as in generative grammars, as described in

Chapter 1. The relevant features would therefore have to specify exit from system network and entry to the lexicon, where the process of lexical selection and 'insertion' would take place. There are, however, a number of factors which make this solution problematic.

First, the features in the Cardiff Grammar are semantic in nature; they do not directly specify grammatical features such as [clause], [declarative], etc. They do, of course, specify meanings which are expressed through structural configurations as well as through lexical items, such as [situation], [information], [giver], etc.

Second, much of the specification required for lexical items is already contained in the system network. This includes:

(a) Specification of the syntactic environment of the lexical item. In the case of adjectives, for example, earlier systems in the network will have already specified the function it is to serve: an **Attribute** conflated with a **Complement** in clause structure, **modifier** in nominal group structure, etc.

(b) Specification of the relations between the item and other items expounding the elements of some unit, in terms of the componence relations associated with the unit. In the case of adjectives, the internal componence in terms of syntagmatic relations is already specified. The adjective will expound the apex element and will have the potential to be accompanied by other elements, such as temperer and finisher.

(c) Specification of the general semantic function of word classes. The network is subdivided into semantic areas, e.g. 'Situation', 'Thing', 'Quality'. In the case of adjectives, their semantic function of 'Quality of Thing' in relationship to the other semantic functions such as 'Thing' is specified. Moreover, the contingent functions of 'Tempering', 'Superlativization', etc. are also specified.

All syntactic and semantic generalizations about lexical items must, therefore, be built into the system network in the form of initial systems. Any feature which directly leads to exponence in lexis **inherits** all the features in the system network which have been selected as a result of following a particular route through the network. The syntactic and semantic information which is represented by these features would closely parallel much of the content of a lexical entry in a standard lexicon.[1]

Third, important areas of the lexicogrammar are dependent on, or closely linked to, the selection of a lexical sense/item pair. It is only by selecting a feature corresponding to a lexical item that its dependent lexicogrammar is brought into play. A good example of this is the **complementation potential** of verbs and, more relevantly here, the **scope potential** of adjectives. Once the choice of an adjective such as *angry* has been made, a range of further meanings are introduced (see Chapter 9). And given the nature of systemic grammar in general, and the Cardiff Grammar in particular, these dependent choices are modelled **systemically**. It is difficult to envisage how the system network could be 'exited', in order to select an item from the lexicon, and then 're-entered', to express the dependent meaning potential. This is a crucial point. In a model that integrates meanings realized in lexis and syntax, however, there is no need to leave the system network. As was indicated above, the general properties of the lexical item are already contained in the system network, up to the point where a feature specifies the item by means of an exponence statement. If, as a consequence of the choice of a given item, further options arise, the system network is extended to express this potential. Again this is fully discussed for the dependent lexicogrammar of the sense [angry] in Chapter 9.

The important task that remains is to account for the organization of the whole range of features which lead to exponence by items from the open set word classes. How can a system network formalism account for differences which, *prima facie*, appear to be between one lexical item and another?

6.3   MOTIVATING SYSTEMIC FEATURES

If meanings associated with lexical items are to be expressed as features in systems, and systems arranged in system networks, then we must be clear about what the features represent and how they are motivated. Yet again, we need to return to what the lexicogrammar itself sets out to do. The lexicogrammar is, in part, a principled account of those meanings which are formally expressible through language. And this implies meanings which are distinguished through linguistic form (including intonation). The potential of language structure to allow the expression of different meanings derives from the possibility of formal opposition in a given context. The **system** of systemic functional grammar is an expression of the paradigmatic relations between two or more features which are in opposition in a given context. The context is expressed by the **entry condition** to the system. Extant systemic descriptions demonstrate that systems comprise relatively few features. Systems are characterized as 'closed sets' rather than 'open sets'.

Features are motivated in some way which relates to the formal output of the lexicogrammar. Systems which do not give rise to distinctions expressed formally in the language may thus be considered suspect or superfluous. A relevant point of departure for the motivation of features in such areas of the system network is the detailed discussion of the meaning of features provided by Martin (1987: 37). He presents a useful set of six criteria for defining the **formal** meaning of features:

    (a)   having a reflex in form;
    (b)   being an entry condition for simultaneous systems;
    (c)   being a disjunctive entry condition for a more delicate system;
    (d)   being a conjunctive entry condition for a more delicate system;
    (e)   being associated with a markedness convention;
    (f)   being terminal, with all other terms in the system motivated by (a) through (e).

Martin also distinguishes, on the basis of these criteria, three types of system network:

First level networks: essentially grammatical networks with features justified by his six criteria;

Second level networks: essentially semantic networks using features that encode non-formal meaning (i.e. meanings not covered by the six criteria);

Mediated networks: where non-formally motivated features are used to make generalizations about more delicate formally motivated features.

Martin suggests that it is legitimate to motivate features either formally, in terms of his six criteria, or informally, in the light of the semantic generalizations they involve. His main concern is the lack of interpretability of system networks which results from using both types of feature, without at least notationally distinguishing between them.

In order to maintain a strictly tristratal (three-level) approach to linguistic description, he recommends as much a separation as possible between first- and second-level networks, thereby distinguishing the semantic from the formal. If our aim is to relate meanings and form in some close way, it may well be that the two networks can be conflated. The Cardiff Systemic Grammar, following Fawcett's semantic approach to system networks, is a model which does not set up parallel first- and second-level networks. Martin (1987: 33) recommends the use of stratification(-al separation) as a heuristic. An alternative approach is to adopt features which express semantic choice and at the same time are realizable through realization rules at the level of form. Even when such features and their organization in a system network do not at first appear to be formally motivated, it often happens that future investigation and fuller, more delicate description may reveal some formal evidence for ostensibly semantic feature classification. One is reminded here of Whorf's 'cryptoypes' (Whorf 1956: 90), the cryptic or covert categories of the language system, compared with his 'phenotypes' or overt categories.

The evident problem with lexis, and in particular nominal and adjectival lexis, is that open set classes are involved. Clearly, features in a system which lead to exponence in items have a reflex in form. But this only shows that possible features such as [table], [cow], [wheel] and [tree] are formally distinguished from each other by having the forms *table, cow, wheel* and *tree* respectively. It says nothing about how these particular forms are distinguished from any others, such as *pen, river, road* and *writer*. Given the internal morphological coherence of words, there are no structural patterns to provide the basis for formal systemic distinction. All the features above do, however, constitute a set (albeit an open set) which is distinguished from other lexical sets on the basis of form. They are part of the set of **nouns** which can be formally identified by their syntagmatic relations and distribution, and to some extent by their inflectional morphology (in terms of number marking, for example). This is very different from the set of adjective forms; members of the adjective class distribute differently, and have different inflectional morphology.

So far little more has been achieved beyond establishing two large open set classes. If we are to end up with systems as closed sets, further distinctions must be established. Within both sets, further subcategorization can be made on the basis of formal criteria. There are formal distinctions between **mass** nouns and **count** nouns, for example, which manifest themselves in the relationship of the noun to structures realizing quantification. With a handful of exceptions (such as **pair only**: *trousers* and **plural only**: *police*, etc.), all nouns fall into the count/mass distinction.

But where do we go from here in terms of formally motivated distinctions? There are, of course, formal distinctions of traditional grammars between **proper nouns** and **common nouns**, but little else beyond this. Other types of sub-categorization also seem promising, in terms of representation as a system, such as the distinction between **concrete nouns** and **abstract nouns**. But can this distinction, if represented as a two-feature system, be motivated by formal criteria, or are we at this point embarking upon a purely semantic classification?

6.4   LEXICAL SEMANTIC RELATIONS

Semantic subclassification into progressively smaller classes can be attempted until one reaches the senses represented by individual items. 'Concrete' may be subcategorized as 'living' or 'non-living', 'non-living' as 'natural' or 'artefact', etc. The outcome will be a classification of the Things which are represented in a given language by the lexis of nouns. What it fails to account for is any formal motivation for the numerous intermediate features, many of which (e.g. 'living thing') do not even correspond to a lexical item.[2] The further the system network extends to the right-hand side, the more overtly semantic the nature of the distinctions appears to be. If categories such as 'mass', 'count', 'concrete' and 'abstract' have a grammatical feel about them, as well as a semantic sense, 'robin', 'starling' and 'blackbird' do not.

That each lexical item possesses its individual grammar, its unique set of collocates – as is forcefully argued by Sinclairian corpus linguists – is incontrovertible. If this is the only feature of a lexical item that can be established, then it provides us with no other basis for systemic organization than can be accounted for with a simple listing of all open set items in a lexicon. Clearly, we have to account for the lexicogrammar of individual items; or otherwise we cannot explain how words are used. Yet by the same token, our knowledge of a word, its behaviour and its sense, is bound up in its paradigmatic relationship with other words. The sense of *hot*, for example, is closely related to *cold*. It is impossible to explain or interpret one without the other. These are the sense relations, such as **hyponymy, meronymy, synonymy**, etc., which have traditionally formed the basis for the study of lexical meaning, and which have been discussed in depth, notably by Lyons (1977) and Cruse (1986).

It is important to point out that the 'systems' of systemic linguistics have always been based on relations of this kind. This applies as much to the structure-oriented concept of system in Halliday (1961) as it does to semantically-oriented systems, such as those which constitute the Cardiff Grammar. The grammatical classes of 'interrogative clause' and 'declarative' clause', for example, are related to the superordinate class 'clause' in the same way as 'robin' and 'blackbird' are related to 'bird'. In both cases, an organizational principle of 'class inclusiveness' and 'delicacy of description' is in operation. An obvious example of the relation of oppositeness at the grammatical level is that between 'positive' and 'negative' in the POLARITY system. Synonymy manifests itself in the relationship of 'active' to 'passive' in the VOICE system. Finally, there is a part–whole relationship between units at group level and the clause, which is paralleled at the level of semantics by the relationship between Situation (whole) and Thing (part), Process (part), etc.

Much depends here on what any such lexical semantic classification contributes to the lexicogrammar. Is it the claim that this classification is grammatically motivated, that all the features that are recognized in the network correspond to some formal distinction in grammatical structure? On the whole, the answer is 'Yes', at least in terms of general expectations, and especially if we extend our sense of 'formal' to cover less overtly grammatical co-occurrence phenomena such as collocation. Indeed, much of the challenge of observing and describing 'lexicogrammar' rather than 'grammar' is in the discovery or uncovering of less overt 'behavioural' patterns of linguistic entities. As Dixon (1982: 9) argues, by giving priority to semantic types, and examining their syntactic implications, one is likely to greatly reduce the number of words which have to be admitted to show *ad hoc* syntactic properties. I would wish to claim that the priority of semantic classification is at the base of the working hypothesis behind the construction of a model of a language. As with theories and models in the 'hard sciences', one cannot always observe the facts. And despite the warning of corpus linguists, we cannot put our models on hold until the behaviour of every lexical item has been described and understood.

The dilemma of the quest for absolute formal motivation arises from the study and systemic description of the 'grammatical end' of lexicogrammar. Here, the point of departure has always been the recognition of formal oppositions carried by structural configurations. The systems and features which are posited derive from clear grammatical paradigms such as [declarative] versus [interrogative] or the different arrays of verbs and their argument structure. The debate on the motivation of features has largely been a consequence of this area of description. Wherever systemic descriptions have been extended into the area of lexis, with the exception of verbs (Process types), little consideration has been given to the motivation of features. The relevant question becomes: 'How do lexical senses pattern?' It is this consideration which has led to other solutions, or at least to the conclusion that lexis is best seen as a different level of linguistic organization (e.g. Halliday 1961).

With lexis it is necessary to look beyond the generalized and easily observed patterns of language structure. Put from another angle, it is important to reintroduce lexical difference into the observation of structure. A survey of most literature on syntactic structure reveals the lack of attention given to lexical differentiation. Indeed, lexis is introduced, at the whim of the syntactician, often simply to put the flesh on the bones of syntactic structure. This accounts for the long and eventful lives of John and Mary, or closer to home, *pace* Fawcett, of Ike and Ivy. Once the interaction of individual lexis with linguistic structure is observed, a different picture emerges.

It must be assumed that lexical relations do not simply allow us to account for semantic well- and ill-formedness, but that they influence the syntactic structures which carry them. One small illustrative case in point is the relationship between certain antonym pairs (e.g. *tall/short, old/young,* etc.) and the syntagm *how X is he?* This is a clear example of the co-occurrence of an overtly structurally realized option, which we may call [new content seeker], where what is sought is a degree of some Quality, and an overtly lexical semantic option in terms of the unmarked pair of height or age Quality.

The developing hypothesis is, then, that lexical semantic relations, in terms of the relative semantic similarity and difference between word senses, correlate with structural differences in terms of co-occurrence.

The shape of the 'lexical' network and the presence of features is therefore motivated in large part by a theory of lexical semantic relations. It resembles a **thesaurus** rather than a dictionary, since the former foregrounds meanings, whereas the latter foregrounds forms. Indeed, systemicists (e.g. Matthiessen 1990, Martin 1992) have always followed Halliday (1961) in claiming that the thesaurus, rather than the dictionary, is the preferred model for lexical organization within the lexicogrammar. Yet at the same time, as I indicated in Chapter 2, Matthiessen specifies the ways in which the thesaurus model differs from a systemic network approach. One such difference is that unlike Roget's thesaurus, where the organization reflects 'fields of experience', in systemic lexis 'fields like these are organized in terms of the categories of the grammar' (Matthiessen 1990: 259). The examples that he gives are – as so often in discussions of lexis – verbal, i.e. **mental, material, verbal** and **relational Process types.** Implicit in Matthiessen's assumption must be that ultimately all Processes can be accounted for in terms of categories of the grammar, down to the degree of delicacy which distinguishes one verb sense from another. If Matthiessen is right – and there is reasonable evidence from the work on TRANSITIVITY of Fawcett (1987) and Hasan (1987) to suggest that this is a plausible hypothesis – we need to ask what the categories of the grammar might be for nominal and adjectival lexis. This is a more difficult exercise. Processes are at the centre of the 'structural universe'. The consequences of differences between them are manifest in the structure of the clause itself and in the other units which realize their Participant Roles. The structural domains of nouns and adjectives are the nominal group and the quality group respectively. Complex as these groups are, one feels intuitively that they do not have the same resource for grammatical categorization as does the clause. Nevertheless, I shall suggest answers to the question, in relation to adjectives, in Chapters 7, 9 and 10.

For the present, I shall continue to explore the means of modelling lexis as system networks which make available, through feature organization, those aspects of the semantics of words which have lexicogrammatical importance. The question of semantic features and lexical semantic relations was introduced in Chapter 1. We shall now see how the question is addressed in terms of lexical system networks, beginning with the phenomenon of cross-classification.

6.5   CROSS-CLASSIFICATION

Another distinction that Matthiessen (1990) makes between a thesaurus and a system network is that the former is organized as a **strict taxonomy** or **discrimination network**, whereas the latter is organized according to **cross-classification** through **simultaneous systems** (Figure 6.1).

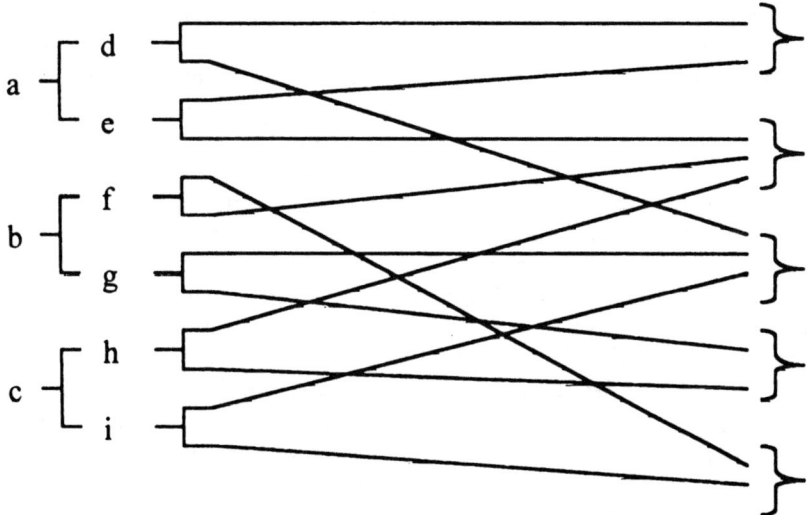

Figure 6.1. Cross-classification through simultaneous systems in a system network

The association of cross-classification with system networks has developed out of the history of systemic descriptions, especially those centred on the clause. This association has been further reinforced by the concept of **'meta-functions'** in **grammatical systems**, in that the major systems that reflect the three metafunctions (TRANSITIVITY, MOOD and THEME) are modelled as largely independent simultaneous systems in the lexicogrammar of English. The effect of selection in these parallel systems is to configure the clause in a number of ways. Thus, options in TRANSITIVITY concern the ideational elements (Participant Roles, Processes and Circumstances) whilst mood options concern the syntagmatic relations between a Subject and finite verbal element. The final product is one clause configured by the contribution of different, simultaneously entered areas of the lexicogrammar.

However, if one gives cross-classification the status of **necessary condition** in system network organization, there is the risk of introducing it compulsorily, irrespective of whether it has reasonable justification or not.

As discussed and illustrated in 2.4.2, Berry's early attempt at an illustrative part of a lexical system network incorporates cross-classification (Berry 1977: 62). In modelling the lexis of 'animate' things, she introduces three parallel systems: '(sexually) differentiated versus 'undifferentiated', 'human' versus 'non-human' and 'adult' versus 'youthful'. Such cross-classification allows us to account for *cow bull calf, man woman child.* But as Butler (1985: 135) points out, this is little more than a 'formalization of the familiar componential approach to lexical meaning'. A more recent attempt to model areas of noun lexis in this way is found in Cross (1991), who makes substantial use of initial parallel features (see Chapter 2). Once again I would emphasize the need to motivate the inclusion of categories used in cross-classification, and to do so in terms of lexicogrammatical description.

I want to suggest that there is a fundamental difference, in this respect, between the system networks for which cross-classificatory features enable us to account for structural configurations and those which lead essentially to individual lexical items. When we are building structure, the relevance of the various features is manifested in structural difference. The range of features will influence how the structure is put together. This is patently not the case with lexical items. If I wish to express a Thing, say *table,* I can use a taxonomic classification which will take me along a pathway through a system network and will produce a list of features such as [concrete], [non-living], [artefact], [furniture], [with flat surface], etc. Such a list will not exhaust all the possible ways in which a table may be characterized, such as [wooden] versus [metal], [movable] versus [immovable], [heavy] versus [light], etc. But if such systems are placed in parallel at the beginning of a network then, according to systemic convention, each system must be entered and features selected from all of them. If the network is correctly wired, we will of course end up with a lexical item which expresses the combination of all such features. And naturally the selection expression will specify the classificatory features of the item selected.

Furthermore, what we learn from Rosch's investigation of prototypes is, as Lakoff (1987: 51) puts it, that

> the relevant notion of a 'property' is not something objectively in the world independent of any being; it is rather what we will refer to as an *interactional property* – the result of our interactions as part of our physical and cultural environments given our bodies and our cognitive apparatus. (emphasis in original)

In other words, the suggestion is that we do not have sets of independent classification systems out of which we create entities or, in respect of language, lexical items such as nouns. If we were to take a large set of putative systems, not all of them would be relevant to classifying the entities for which our language has words. As Dahlgren (1988: 69) illustrates, we do not have a concept such as 'THORK' (i.e. a 'bird with wheels'). Because of what Lakoff refers to a 'interactional properties', only certain systems can be combined in cross-classification. There would be no lexical output, for example, in cross-classifying [abstract] with [movable] versus [immovable] since the latter features are dependent on [concrete]. Even if we are able to motivate this feature approach in the first place, the network must be designed in such a way as not to vitiate the dependency principle.

The difficulty of designing such a network is seen in Berry's illustration (Figure 2.1). In terms of the feature specification [animate], the two systems SEXUAL DIFFERENTIATION, [differentiated] versus [undifferentiated], and MATURITY, [adult] versus [youthful], do not consistently interact. There is no set of lexical items which corresponds to options selected from each in the case of, for example, [mouse]. The choice of [mouse] does not involve options in sexual differentiation or maturity. In the case of [equine] they do interact, producing *stallion, mare* and *foal.* Berry's network, as it is represented, would therefore require extensive additional **wiring** necessary to prevent entry to systems which do not influence the outcome.[3] Without such wiring, certain paths through the network have no realization; they indicate the presence of a lexical gap. I would emphasize again that certain systems are dependent on others.

A system network can of course be designed in such a way as to show dependent systems only when they are required, at the expense of repeating systems. Such a network takes the form of what Fawcett (1988: 14) has called a 'displayed' network, rather than a 'consolidated network'. Thus, as Figure 6.2 illustrates, we can have such a network configuration, albeit expensive in repetition, that makes a precise statement of the relevance of certain systems in specifying the lexis of animals.

Let us suppose, then, that we can use cross-classification in this way and exhaust the lexical potential of the language in question. This is of course a language-specific issue, since other languages may in fact have lesser or greater degrees of specification for phenomena such as maturity and sexual

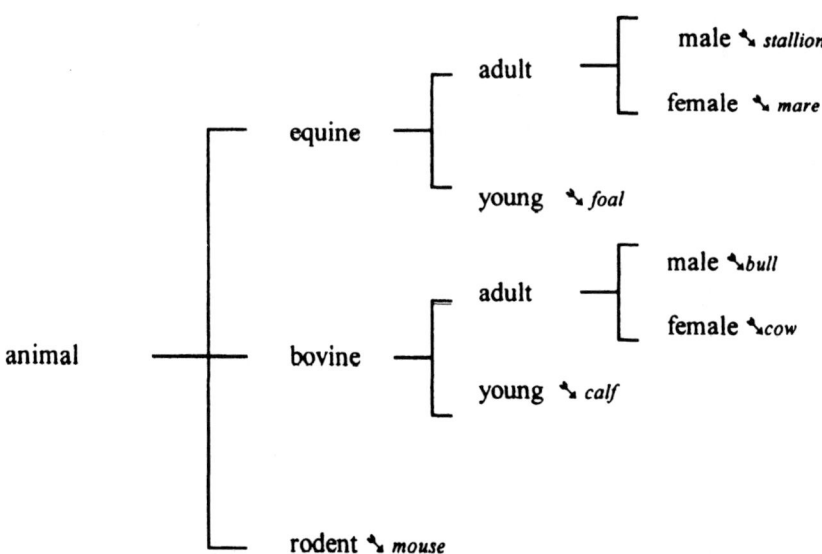

Figure 6.2. A displayed system network modification of Berry's 1977 network

differentiation. What we must turn to now is the relevance of such features, whether in strict formal terms or in terms of capturing patterns of co-occurrence. I shall begin by exploring co-occurrence constraints – traditionally discussed under the label of 'selectional restrictions'.

6.6 SEMANTIC RESTRICTIONS

6.6.1 Selectional restrictions in generative grammar

The specification of semantic features associated with lexis was introduced into transformational-generative grammar by Chomsky (1965: 95). He refers to them as 'selectional restrictions' or 'restrictions on co-occurrence'. They are in contrast with 'strict subcategorization statements', which specified co-occurrence in terms of lexical categories such as [+NP], [+PP], etc. Selectional restrictions were expressed as [+animate], [+abstract], etc. and their function was to specify, for example, the type of NP which co-occurred as Subjects and Objects with certain verbs. Thus, for example, the lexical entry for *frighten* would have a subcategorization frame such as [— +NP], with the selectional restriction [+animate]. This would account for the well-formedness of (1) and the ill-formedness of (2).

(1)   he frightened the man
(2)   *he frightened the table

The inclusion of selectional restrictions such as [+animate] is, however, no longer current practice in contemporary generative theory. As Horrocks (1987: 36) observes:

> The features in terms of which the selectional restrictions are stated seem to have more to do with semantics than syntax, and indeed could only be regarded as having syntactic import in a theory which required the syntax and lexicon together to generate all the grammatical sentences of a language, and no non-sentences, without assistance from other components.

Generative theory is essentially a theory of syntax. Chomskyan generative theory is primarily concerned with the discovery of universal syntactic features of human language. Since the short-lived appearance of generative semantics (e.g. Katz and Postal 1964), the general position within the theory has been that the semantic component is **interpretative** rather than **generative**. The type of ill-formedness found in (2) is therefore considered to be **semantic** rather **grammatical** (see Radford 1988: 9ff). A separate semantic theory of the kind proposed by Jackendoff (1985, 1990) is required to account for semantic ill-formedness. Syntactically relevant 'semantic information' included in the lexicon is reduced to the specification of semantic roles and is covered by Theta Theory within the general theory of Government and Binding (Chomsky 1981: 34–48). Yet even with Theta-roles, the ultimate goal is still, as Levin (1985: 2) points out, to arrive at a classification (of syntactically relevant semantic classes of predicates) on purely syntactic grounds, with the hope that this classification would receive semantic support.

Systemic grammar is not concerned with a purely syntactic account of language, as I have emphasized in a number of places. System network features are semantic and have a central place in the theory. As this is the case, the notion of 'selection restrictions' or its systemic counterpart merits further consideration, and I turn to this in the following section.

6.6.2 Subcategorization and preferences in systemic grammar

The features that are proposed and used in 'lexical' system networks in systemic grammar appear to be 'of the kind originally proposed in terms of 'selectional restrictions'. In an important contribution to the modelling of lexis in systemic theory, Hasan (1987: 185) clarifies the difference between such features in her description and in Chomsky's selectional restrictions (see 2.4.4). For Hasan, they are features of 'subcategorization', in the sense that the presence of some feature in a network (e.g. [disposal] in the network for TRANSITIVITY) may subcategorize the Participant Roles and Processes involved (e.g. the option [disposal] subcategorizes the Event as /(material action) of disposal involving change in location of Medium, the Medium Thing as /alienable object/ and Agent Thing as /human, person(s) or institutions/). Thus this subcategorization, if followed, would correspond to an output such as (3).

(3)   Susan collected a lot of leaves

Hasan emphasizes, however, that such statements are not to be confused with selectional restrictions, since the latter 'operate on items; possess directionality, e.g. assign features of the Subject and Object to the Verb; and their non-observance leads to linguistic malaise'. In the case of Hasan's subcategorization statements, apparent non-observance would simply indicate 'a different semantics from that of a clause whose underlying selection expression contains [disposal]'. Thus, a clause such as (4) does not have a systemic description which involves [disposal], since the Agent is not [human].

(4)   The roof collected a lot of leaves

Hasan's use of features in subcategorization statements therefore has an important function in accounting for the range of TRANSITIVITY options involving the Verb *collect*, such as the examples above and others, such as those in (5) and (6).

(5)   She collected her thoughts
(6)   I collected the parcel

The lack of linguistic *malaise* results, however, from the fact that one could write subcategorization statements to cover all these different senses of *collect*. This approach accounts for the '*malaise*' which is found in (7).

(7)   The idea collected a bunch of grapes

It is the non-observance, in this instance, of any of the subcategorization statements appertaining to the senses of *collect* which accounts for its oddness.

The inclusion of features of this kind, whether in a formal linguistic approach or in an SFG framework, raises fundamental issues of what grammars or linguistic descriptions are supposed to explain. The goals of linguistic theory have been massively influenced by those established by Chomsky (1965: 3), and developed over the course of three decades. They are also influenced by the seemingly rigid division between syntax and semantics, and within semantics itself, between 'conceptual' semantics and what might be termed 'linguistic semantics'. Linguistic theory has become as compartmentalized as other areas of scientific investigation. The task of modelling human communicative activity is such a formidably holistic endeavour that little would be gained by trying to accomplish it. On the whole, linguistics has eschewed the relationships between conceptual organization, semantics and form. One can simply define the domain of linguistics by excluding phenomena which one does not want to investigate – thus the emphasis of formal, grammatical phenomena and the exclusion or separation of semantic and conceptual organization. What is not included in a theory of language is committed to other areas of enquiry or assigned to non-linguistic components of an overall model of a communication system.

There seems to me to be a choice to be made in this respect. One can either extend the scope of the theory to incorporate phenomena which may be perceived conventionally as outside the scope of linguistic investigation, or one can simply exclude such phenomena and account for them in terms of some other 'component'. What is intended by the former alternative is seeing how much the theory can account for. Taking this course, one might ultimately conclude that certain phenomena, after all, are best handled elsewhere, but at least the exploration will have thrown some light on what needs to be accounted for in the relationship between form and meaning.

Let us return to the analysis of the type of features that we have been discussing. Their incorporation derives from a decision to extend the scope of lexicogrammatical description. In terms of lexical organization, there still appears to be little to say about traditional grammatical organization, without incorporating features of their lexical semantic organization. Compartmentalization helps define operationally notions like 'grammaticality'. We are thus in a position to specify 'what is in' and 'what is out', to distinguish between sentences and non-sentences. This seems to be too strong a concession to a strict classical theory of categories (cf. Lakoff 1987: 5ff). Unlike Rosch's prototype theory of categories, it has little to say about the difference between central and peripheral members of categories. Communication does not necessarily break down if our utterances are not always categorizable in such black-and-white terms; linguistic categories are as fuzzy as those posited for other observable phenomena.

It flourishes and develops because of variation and consequent change. As much as we might like to have as the object of investigation the 'idealized speaker-listener in a homogeneous speech community' (Chomsky 1965: 3), this could not be further from reality.

There is a sense in which the principle behind Hasan's subcategorization statements highlights one aspect of linguistic knowledge: we are not always bound rigidly by a set of rules which keep us within, or take us outside, linguistic possibility. Rather we have a set of expectations about structure and co-occurrence by which we can create and interpret the central and the peripheral. The question is: 'How can we best model these expectations?' This question is addressed in the following section.

6.6.3 Preselection, preferences statements and probabilities in the Cardiff Grammar

Another way of viewing Hasan's notion of subcategorization and preselection is through the application of **preferences statements** and **probabilities**, which were described, in the context of the Cardiff Grammar, in Chapter 3. One aspect of our linguistic knowledge is that certain co-occurrences are more probable than others. Thus, when faced with the improbable, we must adjust our interpretation in order to allow the communication to be effective. It has been increasingly observed that much of our everyday language use involves metaphor, including Halliday's notion (1994: 342) of 'grammatical metaphor'. Metaphor is, by nature, in conflict with our expectations, with what we understand to be congruent realizations of our meaning. Without the flexibility of probability, our capacity to interpret utterances would be less versatile.

It is only because we expect the Participant Role at Complement in (8) to be [alienable object] that we can arrive at a satisfactory interpretation of its meaning. Our expectation, in terms of congruence, invites us to interpret some property of *houses* as such, and therefore understand the apparently incongruent.

(8)   The wealthy woman collected houses

What is important, as Hasan emphasizes, is that such specification is not a condition on well-formedness, but expresses expectations of the co-occurrence of features. The association of probabilities to features in the Cardiff Grammar allows the expression of co-occurrence relationships in terms of relative expectations (see Fawcett *et al.* 1993: 127 for a fuller justification of probabilities). The equivalent in the Cardiff Grammar to Hasan's (1987) 'subcategorization statement' is a **preferences statement**. A feature or combination of features may be associated with a preferences statement, which has the following form:

for Agent prefer [features a, b, c, d, n]

Its purpose is to **preselect** features on subsequent re-entry into the system network, such as re-entry into the network for Thing, in order to generate the nominal group which realizes a Participant Role.[4] As explained in Chapter 4, features may be accompanied by absolute or relative probabilities (e.g.

100%/0% or **90%/10%**). Probabilities are expressed on the features of relevant systems. Thus in a neutral or context-free situation the features in a given system may be considered to have equal weighting, with each feature receiving a probability equal to 100 per cent, divided by the number of features in the system. Any feature on which this system is dependent may bring about a resetting of the probabilities. The full set of preferences will therefore specify preferred traversals of the network which is entered as a consequence of the original determining feature.

The difference between absolute and relative resetting allows the lexicogrammar to express obligatory and expectational consequences. The absolute type is needed to express predominantly syntactic constraints. Thus if a given syntactic structure is required as a consequence of some selection, then the features required to generate this structure will be reset to 100 per cent, specifying an obligatory pathway through the relevant network. Such is the case for the restricted types of complementation that are permitted with mental Processes in the TRANSITIVITY system. Features that lead to the exponence of the verb *know*, for example, must specify features in dependent systems which will lead, in the case of clausal complementation, to clauses of the 'proposition' kind, e.g. *that he is lying*. Features which express a relationship between a Process type and subcategories of Things which realize its Participant Roles will be of the relative kind.

Semantic feature specification thus provides a means of modelling co-occurrence phenomena. As the following two sections illustrate, this gives us a way into the modelling of collocations and 'fixed' and 'semi-fixed' expressions.

6.7 TOWARDS THE MODELLING OR EXPLOITATION OF COLLOCATIONAL PHENOMENA

It will be observed that the relationship between Processes and their Participant Roles, in terms of such feature specification, suggests a way forward to the modelling of some of the phenomena which come under the general heading of **collocation**, introduced in Chapter 3. Any strong collocates of a lexical item may be specified in terms of their high probability of co-occurrence. Unless we are dealing with strict collocation, where two lexical items must co-occur, relative probabilities capture statistically strong relationships, without ruling out the possibility of other lexical items that would not normally be included in the collocational set in question.

The statistical nature of collocational relationships is, however, a phenomenon in need of an explanation that goes beyond the statistics. Collocational relationships provide powerful evidence of the senses of items in showing that certain items prefer the 'company' of other items. As Carter (1987: 53) importantly points out, 'the description of restrictions on the range of collocability of particular items can provide a way of differentiating words from each other'. Let us briefly examine that of the collocations of *strong* and *powerful*, a favourite example of Halliday's (1966a), and also used by Butler (1985: 129–30). The difference between the senses of the two roughly synonymous adjectives is revealed in the different set of collocates which each associates with. The respective sets, when examined, suggest that *powerful* collocates with Things that **generate** force, whereas *strong* collocates with Things that **resist** force. This generalization allows us to interpret in different ways the use of either with *argument*, as in *a powerful argument* and *a strong argument*. A powerful argument is one that convinces, whereas a strong argument is one that resists attack.

It is consequently not a question of simply modelling collocational phenomena, but rather of exploiting them to provide further motivation for the organization of the features in the system network. The relevant features which account for collocational preferences can therefore be incorporated into the system network. And once they are there, their selection, in terms of co-occurrence, can be expressed through **preferences**.

6.8   FIXED AND SEMI-FIXED EXPRESSIONS

Preselection and probabilities within the Cardiff Grammar also provide a powerful device for the modelling of 'fixed' and 'semi-fixed' expressions, such as *pull someone's leg, haven't the faintest idea, kick the bucket,* etc.[5] Such expressions, especially the fixed variety, may be handled in two ways: (1) by considering them non-decomposable complex lexical items or (2) by considering them to be obligatory choices. The first approach would require that the system network feature responsible for their sense specifies the whole phrase through an exponence rule, e.g. the combination of [informal] and [die] would lead to a realization rule:

die: if [informal] then (**M < "kick", Mex < "the bucket"**).

This would allow for the appropriate morphology to be generated for *kick* as a Main verb, and expound the Main verb extension (Mex) as the unanalysed compound item *the bucket*. The second approach would generate the Main verb extension by re-entry into the network for Thing and preselection of the necessary features leading to the obligatory exponence of the determiner by *the* and of the head by *bucket*.

The extent to which it is necessary to include lengthy preselection statements of this kind depends crucially on the need to have further structural and semantic information about the expression in question. The idiom *kick the bucket* is perhaps not the best example of this, since it is clearly a 'dead metaphor', and the association between dying and physically kicking a bucket has been lost to all but the etymologist. However, many other expressions contain metaphorical meaning much closer to the surface, e.g. *see the light, burn the candle at both ends,* etc., and their generation, through the process indicated above, may well contribute to the interpretation and understanding of the metaphor.

Semi-fixed expressions, on the other hand, require the preselection approach. In an idiom such as *pull someone's leg*, the network for Thing must be re-entered in order to ensure that the possessive deictic determiner reflects appropriately the referent of whom the expression is used (e.g. *pull my/his/her/leg*).

6.9   THE INCLUSION OF NECESSARY FEATURES

The investigation of individual Process types, or classes into which they fall, should reveal categories of their Participant Roles which need to be incorporated into the network for Thing. Likewise, the investigation of nouns and adjectives, which realize Things and Qualities, should reveal, through their collocational behaviour, semantic aspects of the items with which they collocate. This, however, brings us back to the dilemma discussed above: which types of feature should be included. There would appear to be a conflict between categories such as 'alienability' and the more prevalent categories of the taxonomy. If we do not include 'alienability' as a major cross-classifying category, yet we find, as does Hasan (1987), that it is needed for Processes involving [disposal], we would have no way of generalizing over the very large range of Things which are 'alienable' objects. Since I have argued against indiscriminate and unconstrained cross-classification, as is found in Berry's 1977 network and in the networks proposed by Cross (1991), another solution must be found to ensure that the required feature is available.

It is at this point that one might decide that the network is not the right place to express other types of classification. They could be expressed, for example, in terms of features in the **ontology** in the **belief system,** or in some kind of **conceptual net**. In terms of belief systems, we may express a whole set of properties of individual entities, ranging from those which are central to the entity, such as [human], [male], etc., to those such as [carnivore] or [not dangerous] which may be considered 'encyclopaedic knowledge or beliefs'. We do have rough criteria, however, for deciding that something like 'alienability' is linguistically motivated (i.e required by a Process type) whereas [dangerous] is a feature which is necessary for **pragmatic interpretation**. Thus the well-worn example in (9) can be interpreted pragmatically as a warning, on the basis of our understanding that *bull* has the property [potentially hostile].

(9)   there's a bull in that field

In the following section, I shall describe the use of an unusual type of system which is known as a **gate**.

6.10   GATES

One possible solution to incorporating peripheral categories without massive cross-classification is to adopt the **gate** convention (Mann and Matthiessen 1985: 87, Martin 1987: 28), and to adapt it to the need of lexical system networks. Let us explore this possibility.

Essentially, a gate is a system which has one feature on the right-hand side. It represents the statement **if x then only y**. Such single-feature systems can, I maintain, be the consequence of a simple or a complex entry condition, of which the latter is the more widely used. A gate which results from a complex entry condition, as in Figure 6.3, states that if a certain combination of features is selected, then the only outcome is a single feature. In the case of a simple (i.e.

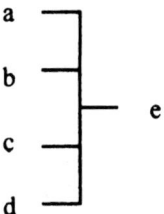

Figure 6.3. A gate with a complex entry condition

a single-feature) entry condition, the gate states that if *a* is chosen so must *b* be. It may appear contradictory, in terms of systemic convention, to introduce a further feature for which there is no choice, since it can be seen as unmotivated according to any established criterion. Yet, if the extra feature is necessary to express a preference on some previously selected feature, then it is motivated. Applying the gate principle to the problem of alienability we may now wire the network as in Figure 6.4. Each feature otherwise classified and motivated which also entails [alienable object] or [inalienable object] may lead the appropriate feature.

In this way, one of the two features will appear in the selection expression, allowing the relationship with [disposal] to be made or suppressed. This is clearly not a notational variant of systemic cross-classification, since there is no

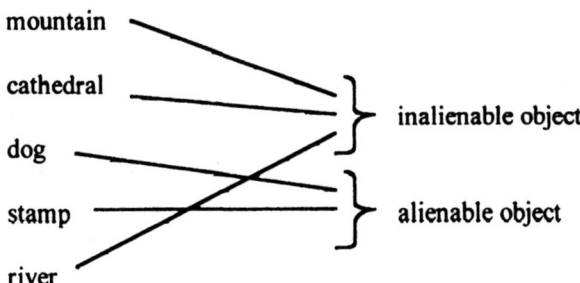

Figure 6.4. Gates for [alienable object] and [inalienable object]

system of 'alienability' in the network. However, it does express the inseparability of the two features, suggesting that in no real sense is *stamp* a realization of (at least) the features [stamp] and [alienable object].

6.11   SYSTEM NETWORKS AND INTERPERSONAL AND TEXTUAL MEANING

In discussing lexical organization, it is easy to overlook the contribution of the interpersonal and textual functions in lexical choice. I emphasize in various places, as does Matthiessen (1990), that lexical choice is related to all three metafunctions, not solely to the ideational metafunction. And even if, as I suggested in Chapter 2, lexical system networks have a predominantly ideational orientation, they must provide for choice deriving from the other metafunctions.

I shall take two instances of interpersonal and textual lexis, and illustrate how a system network approach, and specifically the network in the Cardiff Grammar, can provide for them.

6.11.1 Lexical cohesion

One aspect of textuality is the signalling of co-referentiality. An 'object', for example, introduced into a text may subsequently be mentioned a number of times. The producer of the text must therefore ensure (a) that any subsequent realization of the object is understood as co-referential with the original expression and (b) that some co-operative principle on the lines of Grice's maxim of quantity (1975: 46) is respected. The latter consideration is important in cases where the referent is introduced in the form of a complex nominal group such as *a large black dog with hungry eyes and extremely sharp teeth*.

As Halliday and Hasan (1976: 288) and Martin (1992: 294ff) point out, the lexical semantic relations between word senses provide a major resource for expressing co-referentiality and, therefore, achieving textual cohesion. Producers of text exploit relations of synonymy, hyponymy, meronymy, etc. in order to express co-referentiality.

We have already seen that such relations are expressed in the organization of the lexical system network for Thing. Selection of the item *Alsatian*, for example, will be the consequence of a path through the network involving [thing], [living thing], [animal], [dog] and [alsatian]. Each of these features are related through the relation of hyponymy, and the lowest hyponym [alsatian] **inherits** the superordinate features; they are all included in its selection expression. What the system network must provide for, however, is the possibility of selecting a superordinate of [alsatian] for the purpose of textual cohesion, as in (10).

(10)   A large **Alsatian** appeared from nowhere. The **animal** was at least three feet high.

At any place in the network path where a superordinate may be realized by a lexical item, the choice must be offered to 'discontinue' the traversal and select the superordinate item. All features in such a network which correspond to a lexical item have an exponence realization rule, e.g. **animal < "animal", dog < "dog"**. Clearly, however, only one lexical item per Thing is possible, which means that if *animal* is selected, then *dog* or *Alsatian* cannot be. It is therefore not simply a question of representing such relations as they might be in a conceptual taxonomy or ontology. This problem is solved by the use of the features [x-as such] and [x-specified]. Essentially, they provide the above-mentioned choice of continuing or not along the network path in terms of **specificity**, ultimately towards realization by the most specific lexical item. A fragment of such a network is given in Figure 6.5. Notice that the feature [dog] itself in this network has no realization. It will consequently be included in the selection expression for [alsatian] without leading to the realization of the item *dog*.

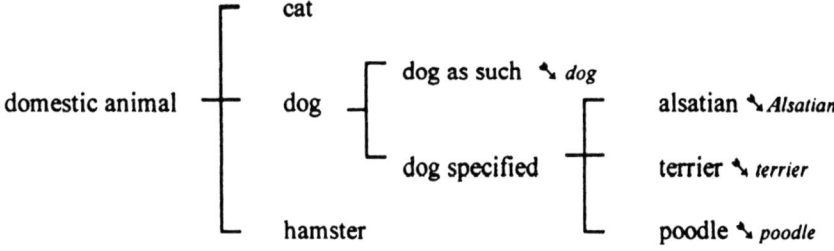

Figure 6.5. The 'as such' and 'specified' provision for lexical choice

The type of network organization in Figure 6.5 does not, however, determine the generality or specificity of lexical choice; it only provides for it. The choice of *Alsatian, dog* or *animal* must ultimately be made, in line with the demands of textuality, through interaction with systems that reflect such textual considerations.

The demands of the kind of lexical choice discussed above provide further formal supporting evidence for the proposal that a system network is an appropriate formalism for modelling lexis.

6.11.2 Providing for interpersonally motivated lexis

I shall briefly illustrate provision in the lexical system network for the interpersonally motivated choice between items such as *friend, mate, chum, pal,* etc. Ideationally, these terms are, to all intents and purposes, synonymous. Interpersonally, they differ in at least two ways. Firstly, *friend* is opposed to the others in the set in terms of degree of formality/informality. Secondly, the informal options, e.g. *mate, chum, pal,* etc., reflect personal and social lexical variation. I do not personally use the terms *chum* or *pal* to refer informally to my own friends. On the other hand, I fully understand their meanings when they are used by others, and indeed might be tempted to use them exceptionally in accommodating to the language use of others, typically children.[6]

How can such matters be modelled in an explicit model of language? The Cardiff Grammar has two ways of incorporating interpersonal lexical choice of this kind. Both involve interaction between the 'lexical' systems and the system for TENOR. This latter system contains the features [frozen], [formal], [consultative], [informal], [casual] and [intimate], borrowed from Joos (1961). The selection of one of these features may affect lexical choice wherever lexis allows the reflection of the choice. The simultaneous selection of [friend] and of [informal], [casual] or [intimate] rather than [formal] or [consultative] will be realized by *mate, chum, pal*, etc. rather than by *friend*. The first way to model this would be to represent these as systemic cross-classification as shown in Figure 6.6.

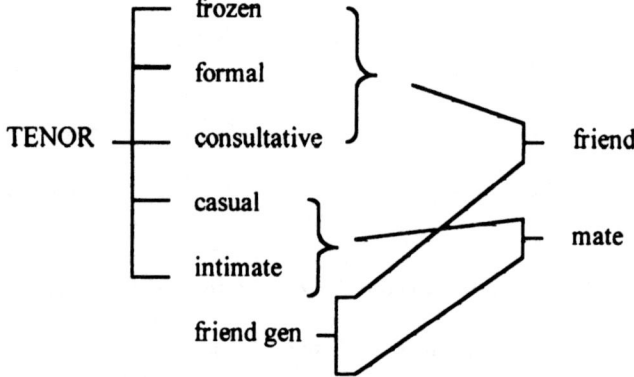

Figure 6.6. The interaction of TENOR and features in the 'lexical' network

The alternative solution is to express the choice by means of a realization rule. Features from the TENOR system constitute **conditions** which determine how the feature [friend] is to be realized. Such a rule would be of the form:

friend: (1) if [frozen] or [formal] or [consultative] **then h < "friend"**,
      (2) if [casual] or [intimate] **then h < "mate"**.

6.12 SUMMARY

All approaches to modelling lexical difference in a system network notation to date have been based on lexical semantic classification. There is therefore no strong claim that, whatever semantic classification is adopted, it is formally motivated throughout. However, semantic classification (in terms of taxonomy, meronymy, synonymy, antonymy, complementarity, etc.) does interact with structure in many parts of the lexicogrammar. And, as we have observed, it is also instrumental in textual lexical selection.

If we were to disregard this formal motivation for non-terminal features, we might conclude that such lexical system networks do not constitute 'lexis as most delicate grammar'. If indeed this were to be the conclusion, then either we must find an alternative model, or we must simply refute Halliday's original claim. I shall return to this debate in Chapter 11, 'Conclusions'.

What is important here is that the lexical system network proves to be a powerful formalism for representing the types of meaning **and** formal consequences involved in lexical opposition. If these aspects of lexis are not all currently modelled it is mainly because, as linguists, we are not yet fully aware of them (and indeed may never be) and, we do not have the resources to undertake the enterprise.

Now that we have explored the nature of 'lexical' system networks, we can address the problem of modelling the lexicogrammar of Quality as a system network. This I undertake in the following, somewhat lengthy chapter.

NOTES

1   The Cardiff Grammar is clearly generation-oriented. In the complementary process of interpretation, information about items is needed for parsing (see Weeransinghe 1994). Such information should be therefore recoverable from the system network representation and represented in terms of an item list which the parser uses in parsing and interpretation.

2   In the computationally implemented Cardiff Grammar, use is also made of absolute preferences for this kind of relationship. The purpose of this is to test the generative capacity of the grammar in random generation, and also, for the sake of public relations when demonstrating, to ensure that the grammar produces 'reasonable' sentences!

3   The term **wiring** refers to the way in which systems are related in terms of dependency. It is a metaphor clearly derived from its use in describing electric circuitry.

4   Hasan's approach to exponence or expression by actual items, such as *collect*, differs from the Cardiff approach. For Hasan, it is the whole selection expression which requires that the Event be expressed by a lexical item, e.g. *collect*. There is no realization statement among those she uses which specifies an exponent; it is the completion of the network traversal and the consequent total selection expression which will specify some formal structure(s) known as 'lexical item'. In the Cardiff Grammar, exponence by any item is associated with a given feature in the network (which may of course involve specification of other features selected in terms of conditions). There is thus an exponence rule of the form

M < "collect"

which is a result of the process type feature [collect].

5   Gross (1993) offers an interesting solution to the problems of fixed and semi-fixed expressions in a finite state grammar approach.

6   I am using the term 'accommodate' roughly in the sense as understood in 'accommodation theory' associated with Giles (1973). For an account of accommodating language see Giles and Coupland (1991: 60–93).

7. The system network for Quality

7.1   INTRODUCTION

Earlier chapters have spelled out the range of syntactic and semantic considerations that need to be taken into account in modelling lexis. It is now time to
explore the lexical 'core' of the lexicogrammar of Quality.

The current system network for Quality in the Cardiff Grammar contains
approximately 200 senses, which corresponds to a slightly lower number of
items expounded as adjectives. This allows for homonymous and polysemous
senses sharing the same item, e.g. the two senses of *light*, contrasting with *dark*
and *heavy* respectively. There is a significantly lower number of adverb items,
given that many senses in the network have no adverbial form, e.g. **bigly*, **yellowly*, etc. The coverage was initially based on three sources: the adjectives listed
in the 2000-word defining vocabulary of the *Longman Dictionary of Contemporary
English* (LDOCE) (Proctor 1987), the *Cambridge English Lexicon* (Hindmarsh
1980) and the *General Service List of English Words* compiled by West (1953). This
initial choice, especially with reference to the LDOCE, was motivated by the perceived usefulness of having a 'core vocabulary' with which all other lexical
senses could be defined and ultimately included in the lexical resource.
Hindmarsh provided a cross-reference on the senses of the lexical items
included (see Tucker 1988 for a discussion of this). West's *Service List* provided further information about the frequency of the senses of certain items.
Another important source of lexicographical information, which has increasingly become the primary source, is the *Collins COBUILD Dictionary*
(Sinclair 1987a).

The appeal of COBUILD, whose publication corresponded with the start of
the COMMUNAL Project, was that it represented the onset of a new era in lexicography. As Sinclair (1987a: xv) claims in the introduction to the dictionary,
'for the first time, a dictionary has been compiled by the thorough examination
of a representative group of English texts, spoken and written, running to many
millions of words'. Furthermore, the word senses in the dictionary are based on
frequency of occurrence, and the dictionary gives special attention to the most
common words used in contemporary English.

The addition of further senses has come about for two main reasons: (1) the
need to complete paradigms in systems where they did not appear in the
LDOCE, and (2) the goal of a constantly expanding lexical resource. Unlike
many other computationally implemented grammars and lexicons, the Cardiff
Grammar has not been subject to restrictions on lexis in terms of register
domain. The COMMUNAL Project itself has explored language generation and
understanding in two specific domains – Personnel Management, and latterly
Telephonic Route Planning Services (Browning 1992) – but any domain-specific

lexis has been added as a supplement to the 'core' lexis, rather than determining its overall shape.

Some parts of the system network have been developed in greater detail than others. It is not therefore claimed that the network represents the full lexicogrammar of all the senses that are included in it, or of all the senses of any lexical item that are specified by the realization rules. The parts which are more fully developed are intended to be representative of the complexity of modelling the lexicogrammar of Quality. Thus, for example, the range of options realized through the scope element in the case of a good number of adjectival Quality senses is illustrated by the network for a particular sense, i.e. *angry*, as will be discussed fully in Chapter 9.

In representing the lexicogrammar of Quality, the network contains senses realized through adjectives and adverbs at apex in a group structure that is common to both, i.e. the quality group, described in Chapter 6. Although this book is primarily concerned with adjectival lexis, the relationship between the two classes, as exponents of different types of Quality, is an integral part of the network organization, and will therefore be discussed, wherever relevant, in the course of this chapter. What follows is therefore an 'itemized' account of the network, system by system.

7.2   THE SYSTEM NETWORK FOR QUALITY

7.2.1 The initial entry condition [quality]

The initial entry condition to this network is the feature [quality]. Whenever an element or Participant Role in a higher unit is to be filled by a quality group, it will **re-enter** the system network and **prefer** (preselect) the feature [quality]. The specification of this feature will therefore be found in **preferences statements** (a) on features that generate modifiers in the nominal group; (b) on features realized in relational clauses that introduce the Participant Role of Attribute (when this is to be expressed as a Quality); and (c) on features that generate clause Adjuncts (realized adverbially) and copular Complements (realized adjectivally).

7.2.2 Initial systems

The feature [quality] is an option in the initial system for **ENTITY TYPE**, together with [situation], [thing] and [quantity]. These features correspond to major semantic units stereotypically realized through the clause (for Situation), the nominal group (for Thing), the quality group (for Quality) and the quantity group (for Quantity). It is assumed here that sentences are 'generated' in a 'top-down' process, beginning with the Situation. On a first traversal of the system network the feature [situation], with a 100 per cent probability of selection, is obligatorily selected. On subsequent **re-entries,** other features in this system will be assigned a 100 per cent probability by a **preferences statement** attached to a feature chosen on the preceding pass through the network (see Chapter 4).

Thus, at some point in the generation of a clause or nominal group, where a meaning is to be realized through a quality group structure, a preferences statement will specify the selection of the feature [quality] in the ENTITY TYPE system.

In the simplified network in Figure 7.1, two other systems, MODE and TENOR, are entered simultaneously. Features selected from both these systems have consequences for selection and realization in the network for Quality. Some of these are discussed below.

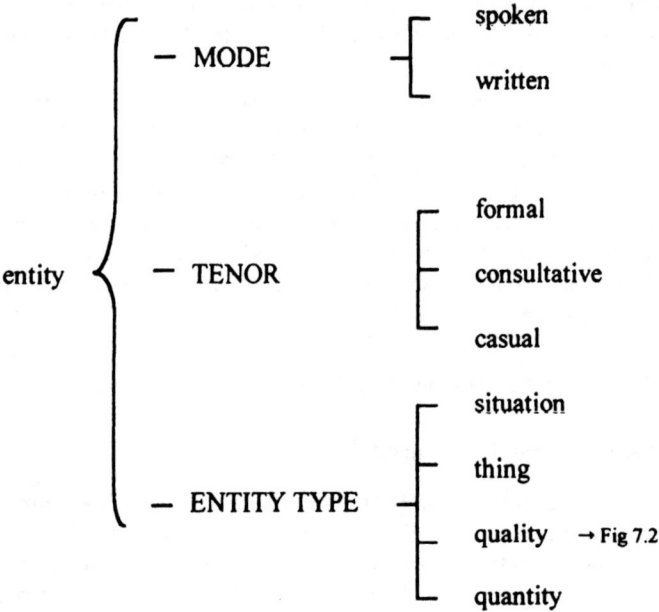

Figure 7.1. The initial systems in the full network

7.2.3 MODE and Quality

The MODE features [spoken] and [written] concern the choice of presenting the message as a spoken or a written one. Essentially, MODE options determine the output of the message in terms of a phonological or graphological representation. Besides the segmental phonology and orthography, the MODE system will determine phenomena such as intonation and punctuation, with regard to co-ordination, and co-ordination occurs with all units, including Qualities realized in quality groups.

7.2.4 TENOR and Quality

The TENOR system, located in the network for Situation, also provides conditions for entering systems and for realization in the network for Quality, as with

116

other lexically-oriented networks. In the Cardiff Grammar, TENOR concerns the degree of 'formality' to be expressed. It provides for choice in interpersonal, rather than experiential, terms (cf. Matthiessen 1990). The item *daft*, rather than *foolish* for example, would result from the interaction of a TENOR feature [intimate] or [casual] with the feature [foolish].

7.2.5 Initial systems in the Quality network

The initial system in the network for Quality given in Figure 7.2 contains the two options [quality presented] and [quality sought]. These features express the potential for Qualities to be **presented** or **sought**. If the speaker presents it, she or he is able to specify the Quality with lexical content. If it is sought, the speaker's utterance will indicate this through the choice of interrogative clause structure, in conjunction with some form of WH–expression. As a consequence, decisions to seek a Quality originate in the system network for Situation. However, not all choices relating to this kind of 'seeking' are realized through the Quality network itself. Commonly used for this purpose is the nominal expression *what kind of X...* as illustrated in (1), or the expression *what was X like?*, as illustrated in (2).[1]

(1)   What kind of shoes did he have on?
(2)   What was the party like?

In terms of the network for Quality, the item *how* is used, commonly in the case of Quality of Situation, and in restricted senses of Quality of Thing, as illustrated by (3) and (4).

(3)   How did you get in?
(4)   How was the meeting?

The selection of [quality sought] represents an extremely brief incursion into the network for Quality. It has a realization rule which expounds the apex element of structure with the item *how*. The feature is always preselected from a previous network traversal for Situation, which will reflect the 'seeking' through interrogative structure. No other simultaneous or subsequent system within the Quality network is associated with the generation of this item, although it could be argued that examples such as (5) require the addition of a limited potential for tempering.

(5)   Exactly how did you get in?

Options for this tempering role are limited to a set which contains *exactly, precisely* and *just*.

A further option in meaning lies in the possibility of requesting the addressee to provide only the **degree of Quality**. Questions such as those in (6) and (7) invite the addressee to indicate the degree or extent to which something was done politely or to which someone was happy.

(6)   How politely did he ask?

117

(7)   How happy was he?

In the formally similar case of Quality of Thing, as in (8), the speaker may be concerned with Quality along a given scale of meaning, and may use the 'unmarked' term to indicate this.

(8)   How old is it?

The speaker is presenting *old*, not in terms of suggesting some degree of *old* itself, but rather as some degree of **age**. The use of unmarked Qualities such as *old, tall, big*, etc. is discussed more fully in 7.3.6.2.

As with [quality sought], the feature [tempering sought] is preselected on a previous traversal of the network for Situation. It is the selection of the MOOD option [information seeker] which determines the interrogative structure of the clause. Seeking the **degree** of a Quality is treated here as an option in 'presenting' Quality rather than 'seeking' it, since the Quality itself is presented. What is being sought is the degree of Quality, which is typically realized through **tempering**. The item *how* therefore expounds the temperer element of structure in the qlgp, as do items such as *very, extremely*, etc., which present the degree of Quality.

7.2.6   QUALITY ROLE (1): Quality of Thing, Situation and Quality

As Figure 7.2 shows, the feature [quality presented] is an entry condition to four simultaneously entered systems. We shall begin with the system of QUALITY ROLE. This system reflects the function that the quality group assumes in the structure of other units. It could be argued that, as these functions are determined by choices made in the generation of the clause, nominal group, etc., they have no place in the network for Quality. The lexicogrammatical resource for Quality senses varies, however, according to the Quality role selected, as discussed below and in Section 7.2.7. A system of this kind is therefore necessary in order to provide features which act as entry conditions to the systems of Quality senses themselves. Each of the features in the QUALITY ROLE system will be preselected by rules on features in other networks (for Situation, Thing, etc.). The selection of some class of modifier in the nominal group will invoke a rule which preselects [quality of thing] and [quality as modifier] upon re-entry into the Quality network. Irrespective of the generation-oriented procedures of the Cardiff Grammar, any explicit account of the lexicogrammar of English must be able to express the constraints imposed on the adjectival and adverbial resource in terms of their various roles in the structure of sentences.

We return now to the QUALITY ROLE system itself. It reflects the function of Quality senses in either adjectival or adverbial structures. The structural environment of adjectives is, by and large, the same as that of adverbs. What differs is (1) the structural and functional environment in which the two subclasses of quality group operate and (2) the selection of members of the two lexical classes for their respective environments. The parallelism observed in the componence

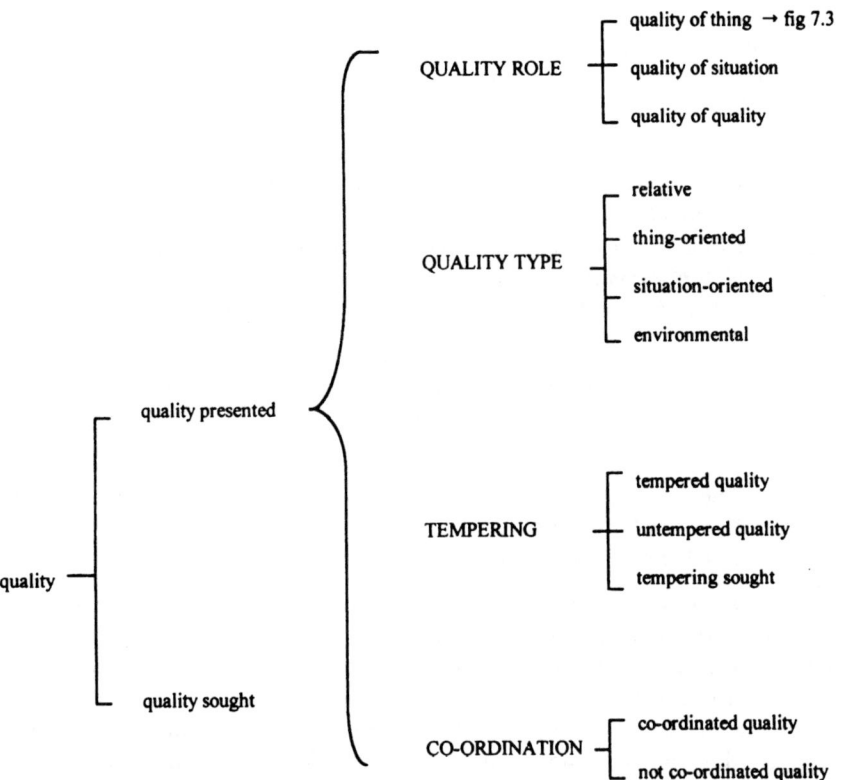

Figure 7.2. The initial system for Quality

of the two subclasses of the quality group is therefore reflected in the subnetwork which specifies the meaning potential and, through the realization rules, generates the structure.

A third manifestation of this parallelism is in the forms that the adjectives and adverbs themselves take. Most adverbs are derived from an adjectival base by a regular morpheme realized by the phonemes /ll/ and the orthographical form *ly*. In the case of the orthography, minor adjustments are made to the adjectival base when it has its adverbial suffix: an example of this is the replacement of the letter *y* with the letter *i* as in *happy – happily*.

It is therefore possible to cover all such cases with an 'adverb production rule' which attaches the morpheme to the adjectival base, and a number of 'graphological adjustment rules' which adjust the word-final orthography. Graphological adjustment rules are also needed for certain plural nouns and third person singular verb forms, e.g. *party – parties, carry – carries*. The 'adverb production rule' is triggered by the selection of the features **[quality of situation]** or **[quality of quality]**. The features themselves are preselected from previous passes through the network. For example, if an **Adjunct of Manner** is to be

119

realized 'adverbially', the realization rules will specify re-entry into the network for Quality and the preselection of the feature [quality of situation].

Clearly, however, an 'adverb production rule' is not universally applicable in English. There are three cases where it cannot apply:

1. With whole classes of Quality senses that are used adjectivally but have no adverbial equivalent (e.g. *big* – **bigly*, *plastic* – **plasticly*, *Victorian* – **Victorianly*).
2. With a small class of senses which have special adverbial forms (e.g. *good* – *well* (not **goodly*).
3. With classes of Quality senses which have no adjectival equivalent (e.g. *often, seldom*).

Moreover, in the classes under the first case, the adverbial forms are typically derived from adjectival forms, but with a different or extended sense. So for example, we find:

(9)   The fire was **hot**
(10)   *The fire burned **hotly**
(11)   The bill was **hotly** disputed in parliament

COBUILD, for example, lists *hotly* as a separate lexical entry, and defines one of its senses in the following way: *if you do something **hotly**, you do it angrily and with determination*. In such cases, there may be a corresponding sense of *hot*, or the adverb may not be directly related to any adjectival senses.

The main criterion for the 'adverbialization' of a Quality sense is whether or not it may indicate the manner of some Process. We can construct the equivalence relation below to test for this:

to do something x-ly = to do something in an x way or manner

This test works well for many Quality senses, especially those which refer typically to attributes of human beings, e.g.

(12)   He works intelligently (= He works in an intelligent manner)

It also allows us to recognize metaphorical uses of some adjectives, e.g. *warm*, which apart from its primary sense as a **physical Quality** is used as a Quality of human behaviour (COBUILD: *a warm person is friendly and shows a lot of affection and enthusiasm in their behaviour*). Thus, we have:

(13)   He greeted us warmly (= He greeted us in a warm manner)

The test will exclude **colour adjectives**, as the second half of the equivalence cannot be construed:

(14)   *he painted it yellowly (= *he painted it in a yellow manner)

It is not however the case that we can simply derive an adverbial expression from the second half of the equivalence; the test is only interpretative, not productive. Thus, for example, the equivalence in (15) is invalid.

(15)   *he dressed old-fashionedly (= he dressed in an old-fashioned manner)

Such cases are instance of the problem of **expressibility**, and emphasize the nature of language as 'resource'.[2] In seeking a suitable expression for the intended sense *in an old-fashioned way* a speaker must 'interrogate' his or her lexical resource in order to ascertain whether 'adverbialization' is possible, and if it is not, as in the example above, some form of alternative expression must be found. Clearly, knowledge of this resource involves knowledge of which 'Quality' senses can be 'adverbialized' and which cannot. Again, it is difficult to generalize across even clear classes of Quality senses. Take for example the different behaviour of the temperature senses in (16) and (17).

(16)   The fire glowed warmly
(17)   *The fire blazed hotly

In respect of 'adverbialization' and the applicability of the 'adverb production rule', the network must specify which senses have 'adverbial' potential and which do not. As we have seen, this is not simply a question of adjective/adverb formation; it is determined in large part by the particular senses which the adjective has. Once this is established in the network, the selection of an 'adverbial' Manner Adjunct, and consequently the application of the 'adverb production rule' may be properly 'blocked' by an **entry condition**. Thus 'adjective-only' senses will have only [quality of thing] as an entry condition. There are also a number of adjective forms for which 'adverbialization' is similarly blocked, but on the basis of their phonology, as Katamba (1993: 75) points out. These are the adjective forms ending in *ly*, such as *silly*, *brotherly*, *miserly*, which, if 'adverbialized', would give rise to the 'dispreferred' /lIlI/.

The third feature in the system [quality of quality] refers to the use of adverbs to temper adjectives and other adverbs. These include an constantly increasing number of 'intensifying' adverbs, e.g. *terribly important*, and those referred to by Quirk *et al.* (1985: 448) as Adjunct adverbs converted into premodifiers, e.g. *a quietly assertive manner*, and viewpoint adverbs, e.g. *theoretically sound*. Because all such adverb senses constitute part of the resource for Quality, selection of the feature [quality of quality] must give access to them, thus involving re-entry to the Quality network. Adverbs used as temperers typically occur as single lexical items, although they may themselves be tempered. But they may not be 'postmodified' through scope and finisher elements, so that the selection of [quality of quality] therefore imposes considerable constraints on choice within the network for Quality. The role of Quality temperers is more fully discussed in Chapter 9.

7.2.7 QUALITY ROLE (2): Quality as Attribute and Quality as modifier

The feature [quality of thing] leads to a further specification of the qlgp to be generated, in terms of whether it is to realize the Participant Role of Attribute at clause rank ([quality as attribute]) or the role of modifier in the nominal group ([quality as modifier]). This specification is important in two ways. First, it constrains the distribution of Quality senses as Attribute or modifier, ensuring that no sense is selected for a function which it cannot serve. Thus, for example, if [quality as modifier] is selected, senses expounded by items such as *afraid, asleep, alight,* etc. will not be available since they function only as Attributes. The grammar will not therefore generate a nominal group such as (18) below.[3]

    (18)   *An asleep child

Second, it allows the distinction between certain senses in terms of their ability to take a scope. Note, for instance, the behaviour of *disappointed* in examples (19)–(21).

    (19)   She is disappointed with her children
    (20)   A disappointed mother
    (21)   *A disappointed mother with her children

Thus, while (19) illustrates the possibility of scope with *disappointed* at Attribute, and (20) the possibility of the adjective at modifier, (21) illustrates the unacceptability of the scope with *disappointed* at modifier. The two features [quality as attribute] and [quality as modifier] therefore serve as entry conditions to later systems, thereby imposing the constraints outlined above. (See, for example, 7.3.6, on **scope** in respect of *angry*, where the scope options are available only if [quality as attribute] has been selected.)

The behaviour of *disappointed* and *angry* is typical of the whole class of Quality senses which regularly take the 'adjective complementation' type of scope. With the other type of scope expression, e.g. *clever **with words***, the occurrence of scope in the qlgp at modifier is acceptable in certain cases, as in (22), yet questionable in (23). The system for [quality of thing] is shown in Figure 7.3.

    (22)   a clever man with words
    (23)   ?too tight a pair of trousers around the waist

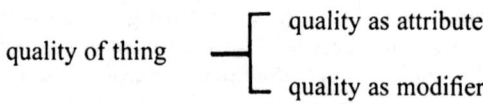

Figure 7.3. The system for [quality of thing]

7.2.8 Overview of the other 'Quality presented' systems

The part of the network dependent on [quality presented], given in Figure 7.2, had four simultaneous systems. We have considered **QUALITY ROLE**, and, of the other three, it is the system of **QUALITY TYPE** that constitutes the core of the network for Quality. It is here that the Quality senses expounded in adjectives and adverbs are specified. Section 7.3 fully describes this central area of the network. The system of **TEMPERING** represents the potential for premodification of adjectives and adverbs (e.g *very/so/blissfully happy*). It is briefly discussed in 7.2.9 and is more fully described in Chapter 9. The system of **QUALITY CO-ORDINATION** represents the potential for co-ordinated qlgps (e.g. *an intelligent and thoughtful person*) and is discussed in 7.2.10.

7.2.9 TEMPERING

The potential for pre-modification of (especially gradable) adjectives is specified by the system of TEMPERING. An account of the complex structural potential for such senses was given in Chapter 6. The network in Figure 7.2 represents an over-simplification of the role of tempering, since it suggests open simultaneity with other systems. In reality, tempering is a function only of those Qualities or classes of Qualities which can be premodified. The set of **classifying Qualities**, in general, is not typically tempered, as examples (24)–(26) illustrate.

(24)   *a very retired colonel
(25)   *an extremely metal box
(26)   *a splendidly economic question

If the TEMPERING system were entered simultaneously with other systems, as Figure 7.2 suggests, all Quality senses would be open to premodification, giving rise to the inclusion of the structures in (24)–(26). In order to prevent such over-generation, the TEMPERING system does **not** appear, as shown in Figure 7.2, in the full network, but at those points in the QUALITY TYPE subnetwork where it is needed to provide an entry condition to selected subnetworks. Furthermore, certain classes of Quality senses have modifiers that are exclusive to them, with colour Qualities providing a clear example of this. The range of TEMPERING senses and how they are to be modelled is discussed fully in Chapter 9.

7.2.10 The CO-ORDINATION of quality groups

Qualities, like Things and Situations, can be related through structural co-ordination. This includes the co-ordination of qlgps with an adjectival apex at both modifier and qlgps at Adjunct of Manner, as illustrated in (27a)–(27c) below. It is assumed that whole units are the subject of co-ordination, rather than elements of structure.

(27a)   A charming and courteous fellow
(27b)   They were dull and uninteresting
(27c)   The plaster was removed painlessly and quickly

With qlgp structures at Attribute and at Adjunct of Manner, co-ordination is obligatory if two groups are in sequence. In the case of qlgp structures at modifier, the situation is different. Here, co-ordination is distinguished from

modifier sequence, which is described in detail in Chapter 10. Essentially, in modifier sequences, a single qlgp fills a different class of modifier, as in (28).

(28)   The dirty old brown plastic bag

Co-ordination is found under two conditions. First, when the Quality senses selected are subsumed under the same modifier function. A typical example of this is (29), where clearly all three senses are colour Qualities and are realized by an **m**^{col} (colour modifier).

(29)   A red, white and blue flag

Second, it is found where two Qualities realizing different modifier functions contradict some implicature, as in (30).

(30)   a young yet retired army officer

The default implicature relates the status of 'being retired' to age, and under normal circumstances we would find a modifier sequence rather than co-ordination, as in (31).

(31)   an old retired army officer

The **linker** element, (**&**), which introduces the second co-ordinated qlgp, is typically of the concessive type, expounded by items such as *yet, although, albeit*, etc.[4] The Quality co-ordination network is not further discussed or described here.

7.3   QUALITY SENSES

Figure 7.4 gives a general overview of the system network for QUALITY TYPE. An initial system of four features is recognized: **Relative, Thing-oriented, Situation-oriented** and **Environmental**. Relative Qualities (7.3.1) correspond, in general terms, to what Halliday (1994) labels with the structural label 'post-deictic'. They identify a subset of the class of Thing, as Halliday (1994: 183) points out, 'by referring to its fame or familiarity, its status in the text, or its similarity/dissimilarity to some other designated subset'.

Situation-oriented Qualities and **Thing-oriented Qualities** (7.3.2) are distinguished on the basis of whether they are considered primarily attributes of Things or of Situations. Most of the lexical resource for Quality is Thing-oriented, which in itself is unsurprising, given the strong association between Qualities and Things.

Environmental Qualities, discussed in 7.4.5, are associated neither with Things nor with Situations, and typically occur with the 'non-referential' (dummy) pronoun *it*. It is on this basis that they are considered to represent a separate class, much in the same way as their Process counterparts in the system for TRANSITIVITY (e.g. *rain, snow*), which are not associated with a Participant Role.

The remaining 'broad cut' in the early part of this network is between **epithetic** and **classifying** in the system for Thing-oriented Quality, discussed in 7.3.2.

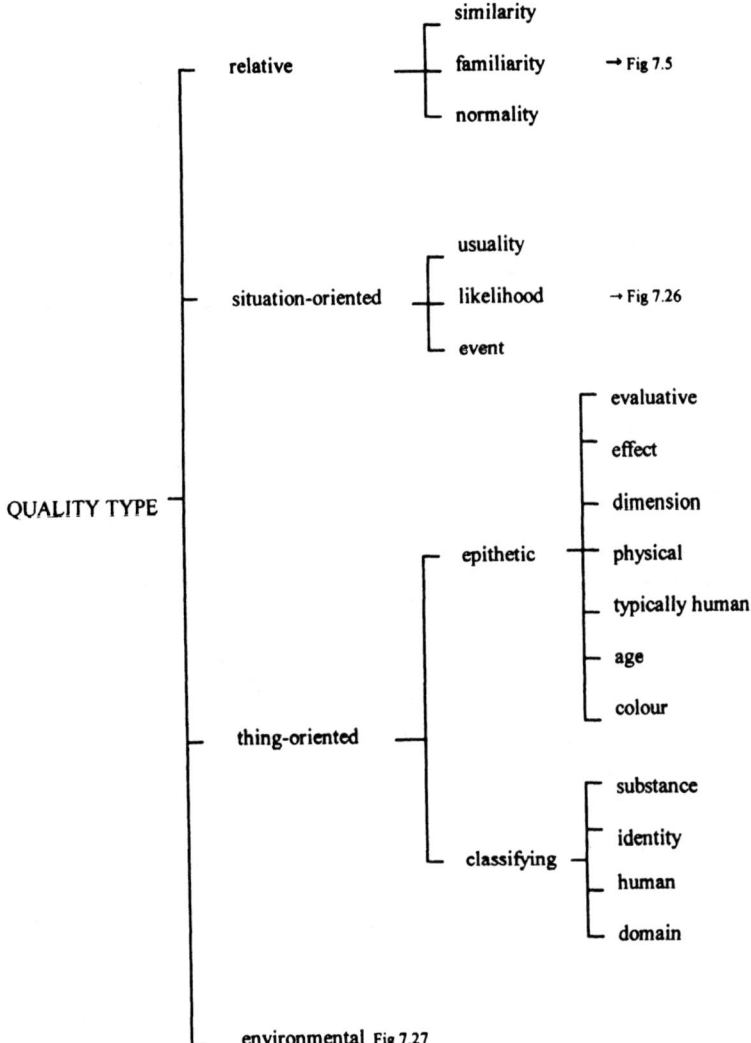

Figure 7.4. An overview of the network for QUALITY TYPE

Of all the criteria for Quality classification, it is the relationship which holds between a Quality and a Thing and/or a Situation which lies at the heart of the whole system. This relationship is twofold. First, certain classes of Quality stand as properties of certain classes of Thing. Weight, for example, is a property of concrete Things, but not of event or abstract Things. Secondly, Qualities relate to Things in different ways. Both *people* and *reception* can be modified by *enthusiastic*, but the latter is an indirect or secondary association which is dependent

125

on the former. This difference has been characterized by Ferris (1993: 24) as 'ascription' versus 'association' respectively, and by Quirk *et al.* (1985: 436) as 'inherent' versus 'noninherent'.

The particular relationships between adjectives and nouns also find an explanation in the observation (made by a number of scholars) that adjectives represent single properties, whereas nouns represent complexes of properties (cf. Bhat 1994: 24–5, Frawley 1992: 441, Jespersen 1924: 79 and Wierzbicka 1980b: 468). Ascription, in Ferris's sense, therefore refers to a value of one of the properties which is associated with a given Thing, as denoted by a noun.

It is a predominantly semantic criterion, but one which is ultimately reflected in the lexicogrammar of English. Foremost among the lexicogrammatical correlates of semantic distinctions is the order in which Qualities are presented in **modifier sequences** (discussed in Chapter 10). Relative Qualities, which serve to establish similarities and differences between members of any class, rather than being 'properties' of them, occur very early in modifier sequence. The **epithetic** versus **classifying** distinction of Thing-oriented Qualities is also reflected in modifier sequence; classifying Qualities typically follow epithetic Qualities. Furthermore, these two types of Quality differ in their potential to be tempered; this is almost exclusively a characteristic of epithetic Qualities.

The more delicate systems (e.g. colour, age, dimension) represent more familiar classes of Quality. Most of them correspond to Dixon's semantic classification of adjectives. Dixon is concerned with those 'monomorphemic forms which have basic membership of the part of speech Adjective' (Dixon 1982: 15); he excludes discussion of forms which do not have '"basic" (or "deep") association with a single part of speech' (1982: 12). In his 1982 account, Dixon initially recognizes seven semantic classes of adjectives: 'dimension', 'physical property', 'colour', 'age', 'value', 'speed' and 'human propensity'. He increases the number to ten in his 1991 account, and includes, in addition to the original seven, 'qualification' (e.g. *probable, sure, usual*), 'similarity' and 'difficulty' (Dixon 1991: 80). The main syntactic and semantic correlates which Dixon identifies for his seven types are discussed, in respect of the equivalent classes recognized in the present framework, in the following sections of this chapter. These include properties such as 'derived adverb' and 'kind of semantic opposition', as well as morphological properties, such as 'derivations with *un-*'. The central correlate of order of modifiers within the nominal group is given in Chapter 10.

It would be mistaken and presumptuous to claim definitiveness for the systemic classification I propose here. Even the most well-motivated classes 'leak', and we are reminded of the lessons that have been learnt from Wittgenstein's notion (1953) of 'family resemblances' and Rosch's 'prototypes' (1978). As more evidence is gathered – and I refer here essentially to corpus linguistic evidence – one will need to adjust, refine or increase the classes recognized. Such evidence may well reveal what Whorf (1956: 70) calls 'cryptotypes', 'covert linguistic classes' which may have 'no overt mark other than certain distinctive "reactances" with certain overtly marked forms'.

We should also remember that, irrespective of an apparent primary classificatory criterion, system networks build in cross-classification, as discussed in

Chapter 6. In modelling 'meaning potential', it is a reasonable hypothesis that semantic classification is a valid starting point. It is Dixon's belief (1982: fn9) that,

> if semantic types are taken as prior, and their syntactic implications examined in detail, the number of words which have to be admitted to show ad hoc syntactic properties will be greatly reduced.

This is, in general terms, a view that is espoused in the present work. Yet, as Dixon (1982: fn9) points out, 'the division into semantic types can be justified in terms of the syntactic/morphological properties of the member of each type'. It is ultimately through fuller investigation of the formal behaviour of any 'semantic type' that one can posit its existence.

In the following sections I shall provide brief discussions of the salient characteristics of the major systems for QUALITY TYPE. The richness and variety of the network is something that it is difficult to appreciate without providing at least this kind of discussion. Each area of the network has its points of interest, as we shall see.

7.3.1 Relative Quality

Relative Qualities (Figure 7.5) classify a Thing or Process not in terms of some inherent property that it possesses, but rather according to how it is perceived in relation to others. They are typically concerned, therefore, with **similarity** and **difference, normality** and **abnormality**, or with some degree of **familiarity** with a Thing or Process. In an attributive role at modifier in the nominal group, they occupy the first modifier element (**m^{rel}**) in modifier sequence (Chapter 10). This place in structure is signalled in Halliday's (1994: 183) treatment by terming these as 'post-deictics', clearly because they immediately follow determiners in the syntagmatic organization of the nominal group.

The rules on [similar] and [different] must specify the potential for scope of these Qualities, in both adjectival and adverbial expressions, and specify the prepositions which introduce the completive. The question of the range of prepositions following *different* in contemporary English (i.e. *from, to* and *than*) can be resolved through attaching probabilities to each, which can be changed according to the dialect of the speaker.

7.3.2 Thing-oriented Quality

Most Quality senses tend to be attributes of concrete Things. There are, however, a number of senses whose direct association is with **Situations**, and consequently with nouns which express Processes as Things (reified Processes), which are referred to, in the Cardiff Grammar, as **event Things** realized as nouns. Situation-oriented Qualities include those expressing **likelihood of occurrence** through 'modal' adjectives and adverbs, such as *probable/probably* and *possible/possibly*; those involving **usuality of events** through items such as *usual* and *frequent*; and those involving **relative time of occurrence** such as *late* and *early*. The

127

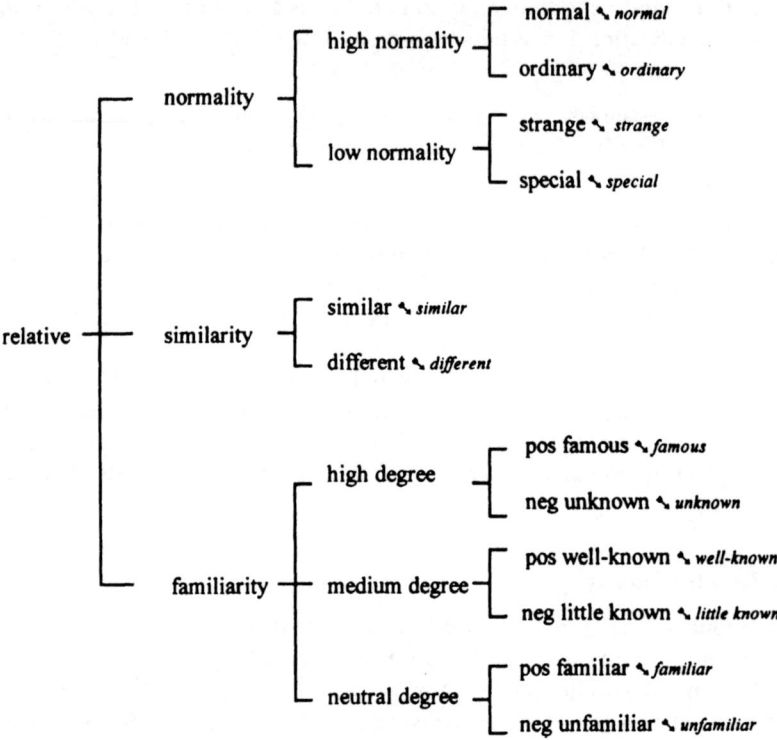

Figure 7.5. The system for relative Quality

nouns they typically modify are, not unsurprisingly, nouns such as *encounter, victory, arrival,* etc. They usually modify only concrete or abstract Things where the sense of the Thing is related in some way to a Process or event. Thus we have examples such as (32), which means *someone who visits frequently,* and (33), which means *someone who will possibly win.*

(32)   a frequent visitor
(33)   a possible winner

7.3.3 Epithetic Quality

The subclassification of Thing-oriented Quality into **epithetic Quality** and **classifying Quality** reflects a general functional difference, especially in the use of adjectives, and this is equivalent to the distinction made, using similar terms, in Halliday (1994: 184–6). Epithetic Qualities are generally used to describe a Thing either in terms of (1) identifying it (e.g. *I want the red book*), (2) expressing subjective orientation towards it (e.g. *It's a beautiful house*) or (3) pointing out some aspect of it which is contextually relevant (e.g. *She's an intelligent person*). Classifying Qualities are generally used to reflect the significant sociocultural subclassification of Things (e.g. *she's a married woman* or *he's a British citizen*). It must be emphasized that this duality of function constitutes a general tendency, and there is no hard and fast rule to separate the two types. The order of classes of Quality in modifier sequences in the nominal group gives support to the distinction, as is fully discussed in Chapter 10. The potential for tempering also provides further lexicogrammatical evidence; epithetic Qualities have this potential, whereas Classifying Qualities do not. The combined evidence suggests that the boundary falls between **colour Quality** and **substance Quality**.

An additional complication is that adjectives which are typically epithetic may be 'promoted' in an *ad hoc* way to assume a classifying function. The change of function from epithetic to classifying is reflected in the ordering of adjectives in nominal group modifier sequences. This is discussed more fully in Chapter 10.

Each of these features leads to a dependent system network (Figure 7.6). Examples of some types would be: [evaluative] *excellent*, [effect] *interesting*, [typical human quality] *happy*. As will be shown in Chapter 10, epithetic Quality senses precede classifying Quality senses in nominal group modifier sequences. For example, we would expect *an interesting American invention* rather than *an American interesting invention*. The two types exhibit other general tendencies as well. Classifying senses are typically not tempered and they do not occur as Adjuncts of Manner. Such constraints, as we shall see below, are taken care of by the system network in terms of (a) entry conditions to the TEMPERING network, and (b) the specification of [quality of thing] as an entry condition to Classifying Quality.

The system in Figure 7.6 represents the major features relating to epithetic Quality. The features are motivated primarily by categories of experience which, on the whole, have a formal reflex in the complex modifier sequence potential of the nominal group.

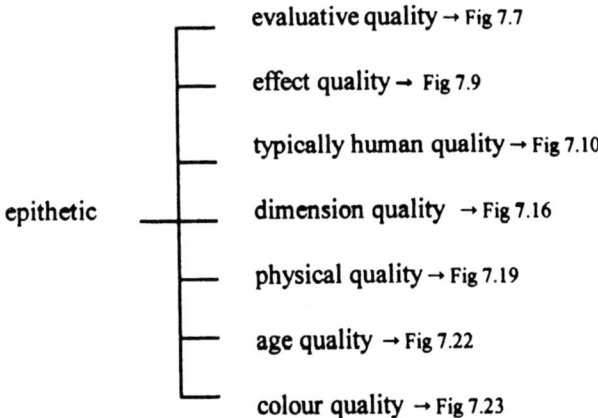

Figure 7.6. The initial system for epithetic Quality

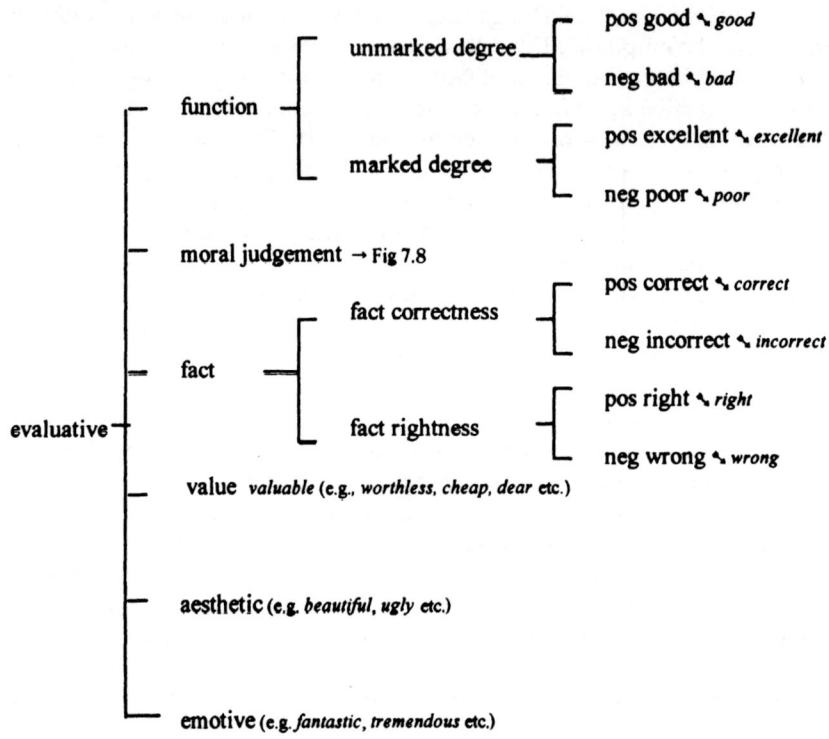

Figure 7.7. The system for evaluative Quality

7.3.4 Evaluative Quality

The six features in the system in Figure 7.7 relate to the potential for the expression of evaluation or judgement. Aesthetic and emotive evaluation are not further discussed.

Function Quality refers to speaker evaluation of the function or performance of Things, stereotypically artefacts (e.g. *a good engine*) and social roles (e.g. *an excellent teacher*). Natural Things are also modified in this way, but usually in terms of some function or purpose associated with them. Thus, for example, *poor coal* or *poor wheat* will relate to the coal's performance in producing heat through being burnt and the wheat's performance in producing a yield of grain respectively. Other senses of *good, bad*, etc. will appear elsewhere in the network.

In the subnetwork in Figure 7.8 we see the use of features to provide compound entry conditions to systems. For example, the feature [rightness] can only be selected if [quality as attribute] is also selected. This reflects the availability of *right* and *wrong* in this sense only in the Attribute function, as illustrated by (34) and (35).

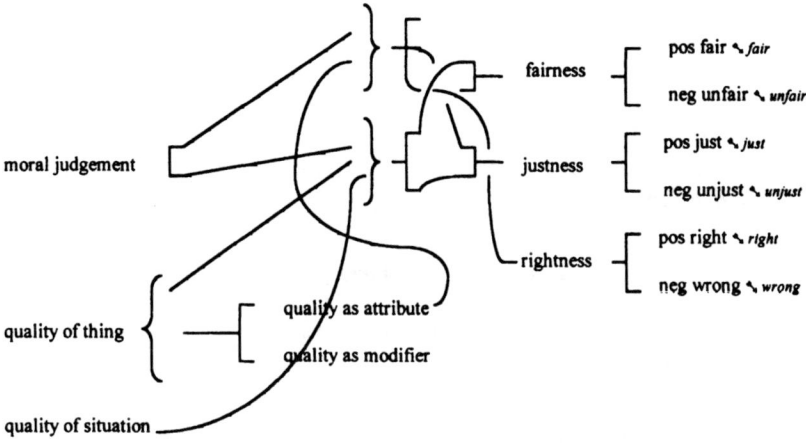

Figure 7.8. The subnetwork for moral judgement Quality

(34)   murder is wrong
(35)   *a wrong murder has been committed

This pair is typically used in expressions such as *it is right/wrong to protest about animal transportation*. The other options allow the adjective in either its Attribute or modifier function, and the adverbial equivalent, as a Manner Adjunct, if [quality of situation] is selected. The network in Figure 7.8 displays considerable complexity at this point. The reason for this complexity is that the co-selection of [moral judgement wise] and [quality as attribute] leads to a three-feature system. All other complex entry conditions exclude the feature [rightness wise], thus leading to a two-feature system.

The feature [fact quality] in Figure 7.7 refers to speaker evaluation of statements, facts and actions which are governed by rules, regulations or laws. Again, the nouns which are predicated in this way tend to be reified Processes associated with verbalization. The Qualities are transferred to humans as the utterers of mental and verbal Processes. Thus *John is right* in (36) implies that **what John has said about the necessity of leaving** is right.

(36)   John is right – We should leave

In a different sense, a person who is perceived as habitually behaving correctly is a *correct person* and this sense of the adjective is categorized as a **typically human Quality** along with others such as *careful, courteous, intelligent*, etc.

7.3.5 Effect Quality

Although the effect Qualities shown in Figure 7.9 are clearly attributes of a Thing, they are oriented towards the **reaction of** or **effect on** the perceiver. They are often 'de-verbal' in nature and can usually be re-expressed as a verbal

expression; e.g. something that is *amusing* is 'something that amuses people'.
Note that the feature [comfort] appears in this system, as it does in the system
for [typically human quality]. The sense of *comfortable* here relates to Things
such as chairs, beds, etc. which cause humans to be comfortable. This sense of
comfortable/uncomfortable is used in both the modifier and the Attribute function,
but is not available adverbially, as it is as a typically human Quality, e.g. *he was sit-
ting comfortably in his chair.*

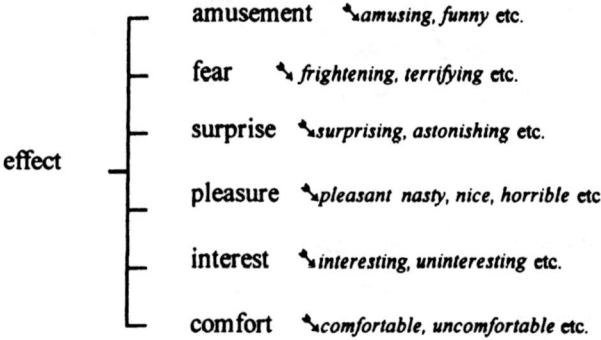

Figure 7.9. The system for effect Quality

7.3.6 Typically human Quality

It is unsurprising that, given the varied and complex social and psychological
existence of human beings, there exists an extensive lexical resource which
corresponds primarily to attributes of human beings. It is interesting to note
that typically human Quality, or 'human propensity' in Dixon's (1982) classification, exhibits considerable variation, from language to language, in terms
of whether the class is realized through adjectives, nouns or verbs (Dixon
1982: 61).

Of the categories posited in Figure 7.10, only [physical state] (Figure 7.11)
has any correspondence in the wider animal world. Many of the behavioural
and emotional Qualities that humans do attribute to other animals reflect a
high degree of anthropocentrism. Some, in fact, such as *kind, thoughtful, honest,*
etc., are predicated virtually exclusively of humans, outside of the imaginary
world of fable, fairy tale or contemporary animated cartoon films. The general
categories of [behaviour] and [emotion] are distinguished primarily on the
grounds that the latter is reactive, and is a consequence of the subject's capacity to be affected by some state of affairs; something makes someone *happy* or
angry. Behavioural attributes tend to be associated with the subject's personality
or character. Both types are, of course, perceived by others through outward
behaviour; we believe someone to be happy because of the smile on his or her
face, or the way they are talking. Permanent states of happiness or sadness can,
however, be taken as part of a person's overall personality. This is particularly

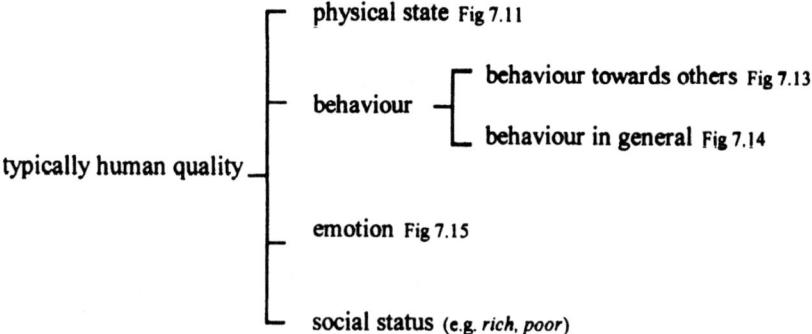

Figure 7.10. The system for typically human Quality

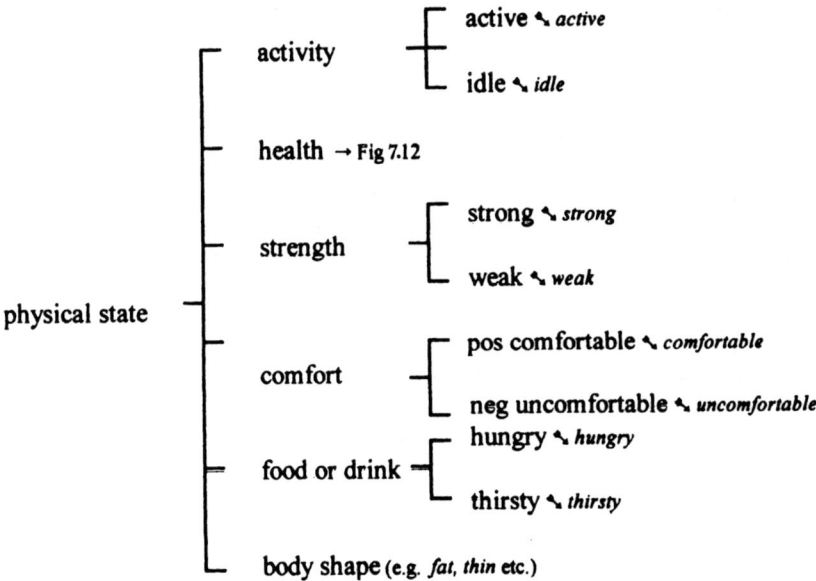

Figure 7.11. The subnetwork for physical state Quality

evident when these Qualities are represented as modifiers in relational clauses such as *he's a happy man.*[5]

The system for **health Quality**, given in Figure 7.12, distinguishes between **general health** and **specific health**. The former relates to the general, long-term condition of human beings, whereas the latter relates to health over a shorter period. There is no automatic association between *healthy* and *well* or *unhealthy*

133

and *unwell/ill* although there is a pragmatic implicature, as indicated by the different co-ordinating linkers in (37) and (38).

(37)   He's a healthy child, but he's ill at the moment
(38)   He's an unhealthy boy and he's ill again at the moment

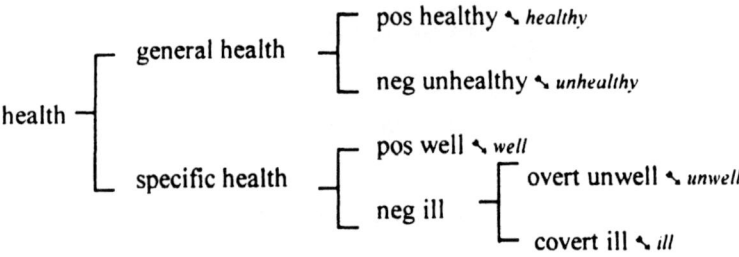

Figure 7.12. The subnetwork for health Quality

The senses available for [specific health] are always, or almost always, used only when the qlgp fills an Attribute, and they have no Manner Adjunct equivalent. This system network will need to specify [quality as attribute] as an entry condition to this feature. There is, however, a tendency for even the most typical 'Quality as Attribute' adjectives to be used as 'Quality as modifier', e.g. *I'm not a well man* or *there are three ill children in this house*. If one wishes to allow for this in the lexicogrammar, it can be represented probabilistically rather than being excluded in an absolute sense. Furthermore, when *ill* is itself tempered, as in *mentally ill* or *chronically ill*, it is acceptable in the modifier function. The realization rule on [pos well] will need to take account of the irregular comparative form.

It is debatable whether *strong* and *weak* should appear here as a 'typically human Quality', as shown in Figure 7.11. The entry for both words in COBUILD lists the 'people or animals' sense as the first sense and the 'objects' sense as the second. The senses will have to appear elsewhere in the network in any case, since the use of *strong*, for example, in *a strong wall* is not transferred in any way from a primary association with human strength. The two items will also appear as exponents of the behavioural senses, as in *a strong person will resist the desire to drink too much*.

The adjective *comfortable* as a modifier, in its direct 'ascriptive' sense (Ferris 1993: 19ff), relates typically to persons and their state of physical (and by extension mental) well-being. When the same item is used with a non-sentient Thing, predominantly items of furniture, it must be understood as a Quality which brings about that state in humans. Like *well* and *ill*, *comfortable* and *uncomfortable* are usually used as 'Quality as Attribute' when used with persons. With furniture, however, they may be used in both ways, e.g. *a comfortable chair*. The

Manner Adjunct sense, *comfortably*, on the other hand, is only available in relation to persons.

An example of this distinction would be the difference between *caring* (i.e. caring for people) and *careful* (careful in doing something). This is not to claim that Qualities such as *intelligent* are not important to social life, but rather that they do not necessarily involve another interactant. Qualities in the first category often take a scope which usually involves other persons, very much as if such scopes expressed Participant Roles in a Process. Their scope is typically introduced by the prepositions *to* or *towards* (e.g. *polite/kind to*). The systems for [behaviour towards others] are shown in Figure 7.13, those for [behaviour in general] in Figure 7.14.

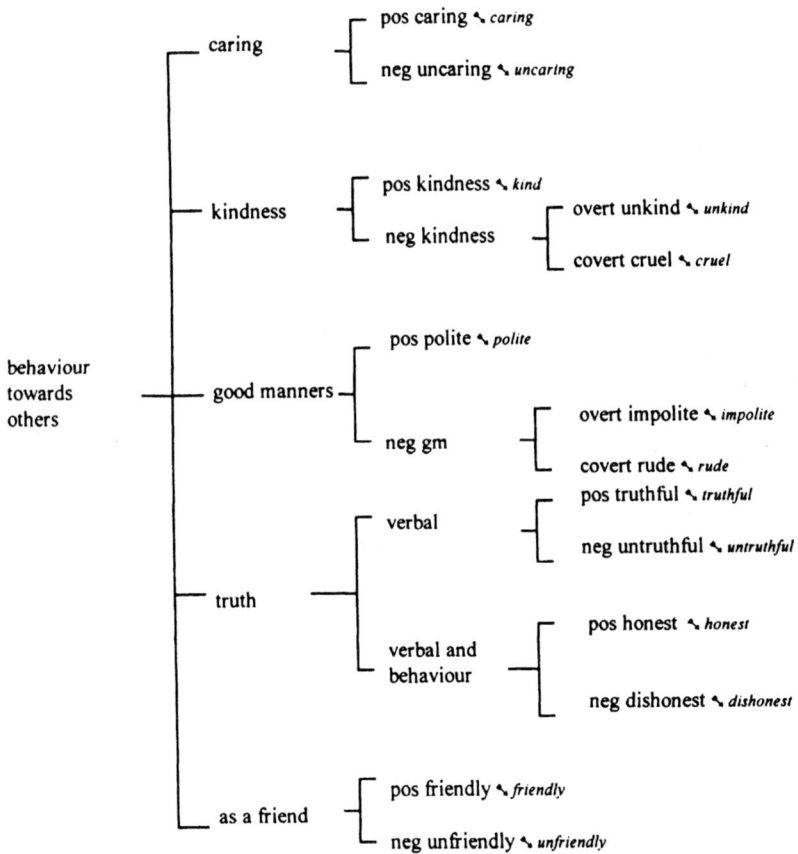

Figure 7.13. The subnetwork for behaviour towards others Quality

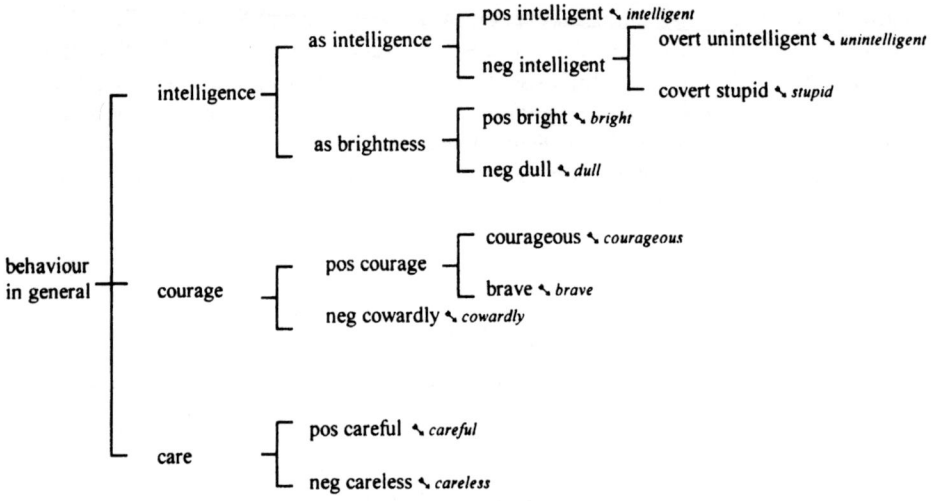

Figure 7.14. The subnetwork for behaviour in general Quality

The adjectives *bright* and *dull* have no corresponding adverb when used in this metaphorical sense as a human Quality. They must therefore include [quality of thing] in their entry condition.

Note that there is no overt negative form of *courageous* in regular use. Another candidate for an appropriate covert negative term is *timorous*.

Emotion Qualities, such as those represented in the subnetwork in Figure 7.15, are frequently associated with some form of scope (e.g. *happy to be alive, pleased that you could make it*, etc.). Since they are Qualities that relate to the emotions, speakers often include the source of emotion, expressed as another Situation. The potential for scope, in such cases, is restricted to the Attribute function of the adjective. Used as modifiers, such adjectives generally indicate a more permanent state of mind, rather than a provoked emotion, as example (39) suggests.

(39)   There were many angry young men in the fifties

There are two observations to make with regard to [pleasure] senses. First, despite their 'verbal' form, items such as *pleased* have clear adjectival status. This is verified by its potential for tempering, e.g. *very/extremely pleased*. Second, they have different and restricted use as modifiers, some collocating strongly with items expressing role senses, such as *customer*.

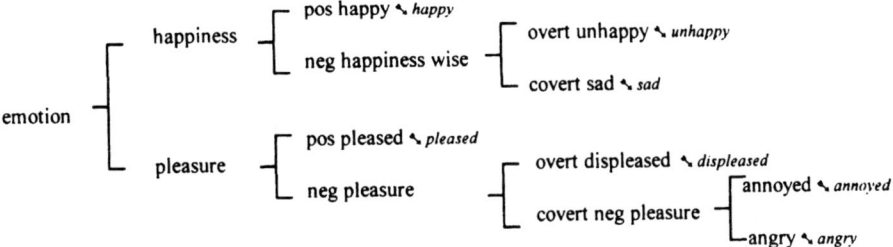

Figure 7.15. The subnetwork for emotion Quality

This network includes a reasonably full grammar of the scope of *angry*, which is discussed in detail in Chapter 9, and is therefore not represented or commented on here.

7.3.7 Dimension

The dimension Qualities constitute a system (Figure 7.16) on the basis of their individual position in modifier sequence, preceding other physical Qualities. In their basic sense, dimension Qualities have no Manner Adjunct realization as Qualities of Situation, e.g. **he jumped highly*, although some are found, in a different yet related sense, when a clause fills a modifier, as in *a highly valued skill, a widely acclaimed novel*, etc.). Others, such as *big, little, small*, have no adverbial form at all. They are organized on the basis of antonym pairs, consisting of what are termed here an **upper range** and a **lower range** (following Quirk *et al.* 1985: 471). It is clear, however, that the corresponding lexical items do not indicate absolute upper or lower range, but relative ends of a scale. The senses are in themselves inherently comparative, in that a Thing is *large*, for example, in terms of what is usual for the class of thing in question. This is illustrated by the COBUILD definition for *large*: 'something that is large is greater in size than usual or average'.

Moreover, the end-points in the scale may be modified by comparatives, and fuller lexical systems will include, in the case of size, other senses such as those realized by *huge, massive, enormous, minute*, etc.

7.3.7.1 Size, height, length and width Qualities

The multiple origins of modern English lexis often gives rise to near synonymous items such as *large/big* and *small/little*. There are thus contexts where *large* and *big* are practically in free variation as in (40) and (41) below.

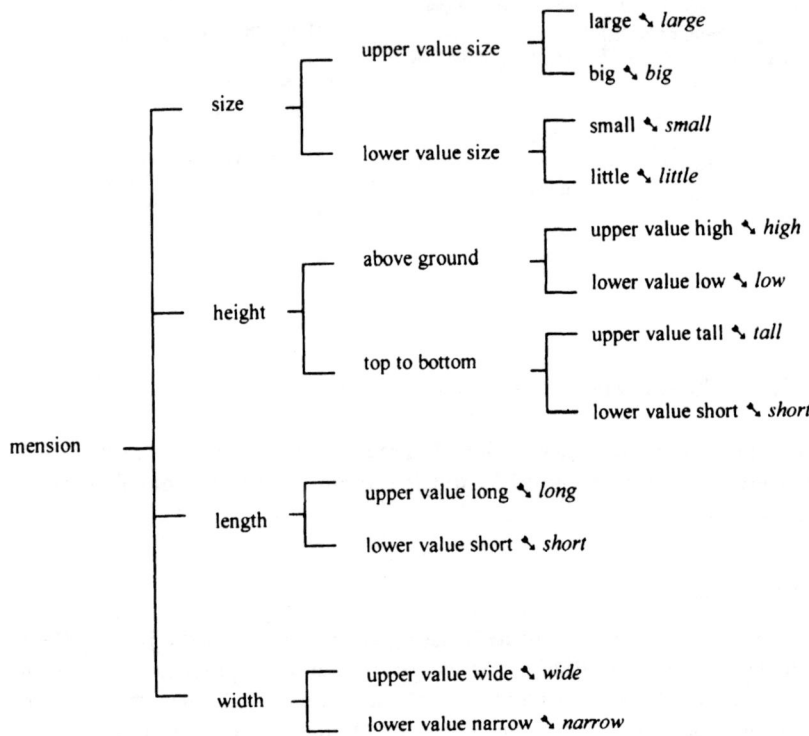

Figure 7.16. The subnetwork for dimension Quality

(40)   They live in a big/large house
(41)   She has large/big blue eyes

It is felt by many speakers that *large* is the acceptable item in more formal or careful speech. Beyond such considerations, the pair have distinct collocational behaviour, which removes free choice in many contexts. Such collocational restrictions, however, often hold for classes of Thing, especially those outside the field of concrete objects. One example of this is the collocation of *large* with abstract nouns of size or measurement as shown by (42) and (43).

(42)   a large/*big number of books
(43)   a large/*big amount of cash

138

There are also a considerable number of idiomatic expressions which involve one rather than the other, e.g. *as large as life, too big for his boots, The Big Bang* and *in large part.* The adjectives in such expressions, if they are realized by re-entry into the Quality network, will be preselected by the specification of 100 per cent probability on the relevant features.

The items *tall* and *high* also have some overlap in terms of synonymy, albeit to a much lesser extent than *large* and *big.* The adjective *tall* collocates with *person, building, tree, mast,* etc. which constitute a class of Things which have their base on the ground and extend upwards. Only with *person* (*man, woman,* etc.) is *tall* the exclusive collocate in this sense.

7.3.7.2 *Markedness in measure expressions and how–expressions*

Members of the antonym pairs *big/little, high/low, long/short,* etc. are also associated with markedness/unmarkedness in 'measure expressions', such as *how tall is it* and *it's three feet tall* (see Quirk *et al.* 1985: 470). The unmarked term, or the 'impartial' term for Cruse (1986: 244), is the upper range term – with the exception of *large* and *big* which are not used in measure expressions – and is used in expressions such as *three feet tall, two inches long,* etc., irrespective of whether the measured thing is of a greater or a lesser dimension than the norm (see Lyons 1977: 275–6). All dimension Qualities follow this markedness principle in interrogatives containing '*how*-questions' as in (44).

(44)   How big is it?

Speakers may also select the marked option for a '*how*-question'. Once something has been identified as *narrow,* for example, a *how*-question may be formulated using *how narrow,* as is shown in (45).

(45)
    A.   The driveway is rather narrow for your car
    B.   How narrow is it?

In a generative SFG, the choice of Quality in *how*–questions originates at clause level. Any unmarked information-seeking Situation concerning the degree of Quality, as in (46) below, involves Operator and Complement placement. Clauses expressing 'confirmation seeker', such as *it was how big?*, have declarative word order, yet still have a *how*–expression. The feature [quality as attribute] is the entry condition to a system [quality presented] and [quality sought], as shown in Figure 7.17.

The feature [quality sought] will lead to expressions such as *what colour is it?* or *what size nail is it?*, which themselves raise problems in building an explicit generative grammar. The choice of a *how*–expression depends on the feature [quality presented] – given that the Quality itself is specified in either information-giving or information-seeking Situations – and this feature leads to a system [degree of quality given] versus [degree of quality sought]. This last feature must be selected if [information seeker] in the MOOD system has been selected, since only a *how*–expression involving Quality can occupy the

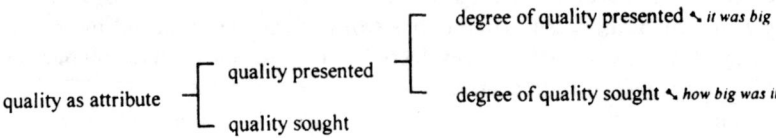

Figure 7.17. The subnetwork for [quality as attribute] in the network for Relational Processes

pre-Subject place in clause structure which is reserved for WH-elements. Thus, **very big is it?* is not possible as an information-seeking Situation. The feature [seeking degree of quality] is associated with a re-entry rule into the network for Quality which specifies the preselection of certain features. This ensures that [tempered quality] and [tempering sought] (Figure 7.2) are preselected and these lead to the exponence of the temperer element in the qlgp by the item *how*. The preselection of [tempered quality], as part of the conjunctive entry condition, also ensures that no how-expression can be generated for Qualities that cannot be tempered. Thus, strictly non-gradable qualities will not be available and the grammar will not generate interrogatives such as (46).

(46)   **how plastic is it?

For each system of Quality where the markedness principle applies (e.g. dimension, age, etc.), a further system with the two options of [unmarked] or [marked] must be available. When the feature [unmarked] is selected it must give rise to exponence by the unmarked term (e.g. *high, tall, old*, etc.). But the selection of the feature [marked] brings both options (e.g. *high* and *low, old* and *young*) into the system. This ensures the availability of the otherwise unmarked term as a marked option as well. We might characterize the unmarked situation as one in which the *how*–expression is neutral, or 'impartial' for Cruse (1986: 244), in terms of orientation towards the upper or lower ranges.[6] Thus if we ask how tall someone is we are not presupposing that the person is taller or shorter than the norm. When we ask how **short** someone is, there is generally a good reason for presupposing that they are shorter than the norm and that this is contextually significant. The good reason is usually based on a previous speaker mentioning that the person in question is shorter than average. Yet, the same principle applies equally to a presupposition that someone is taller than the norm. This is illustrated by the exchange in (47).

(47)
    A.   Howard is far too tall to be a scrum half
    B.   Well, how tall is he exactly?

Marked dimension Qualities are not typically associated with measurement in terms of appropriate units of measurement. The unmarked term is used irrespective of (even substantial) deviance from a norm towards the lower range. This is illustrated by (48).

(48)   John has suffered from a growth disorder and is only four feet tall

Marked terms do, however, co-occur with measurement in at least two ways. First, they are used to create a humorous effect as in (49).

(49)   Howard is ninety years young today

Second, they are used in comparative expressions to measure the deviance from an expected, desired, necessary dimension, as illustrated in (50) and (51).

(50)   James is two inches too short for eligibility for the police force
(51)   James is two inches shorter than the regulation height

The network fragment in Figure 7.18 illustrates the way in which it is proposed to handle the markedness convention, with **length Quality** as an example.

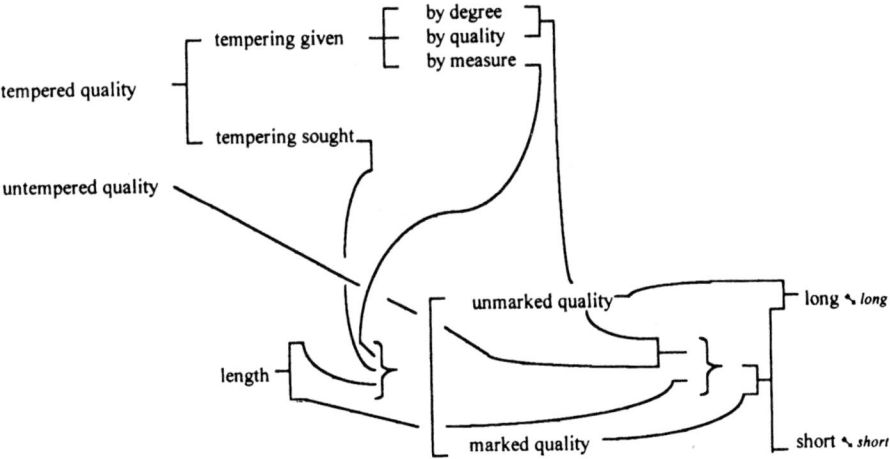

Figure 7.18. The system network for length Quality and markedness

7.3.8 Physical Quality

In many respects, physical Qualities are prototypical adjectival senses. They are central to our experience of objects which constitute the human world of experience. They concern the ways in which we perceive objects, predominantly

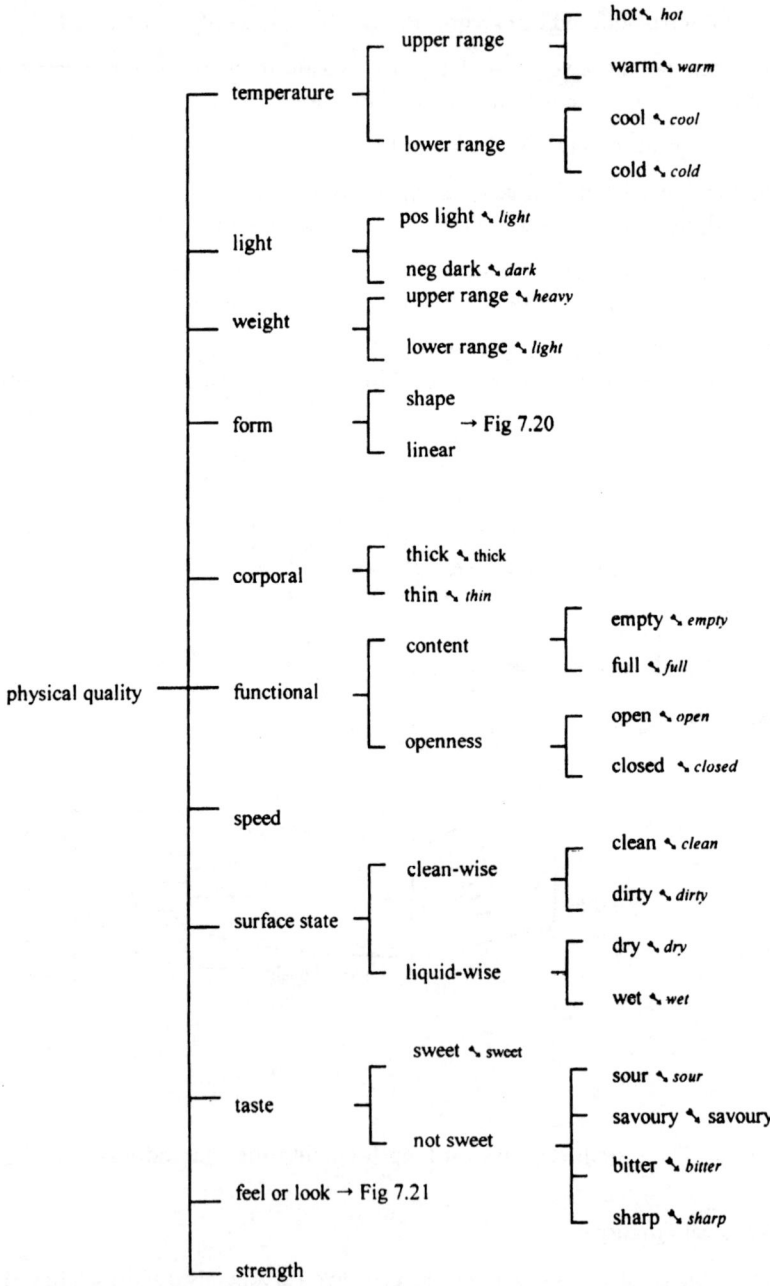

Figure 7.19. The subnetwork for physical Quality

through the visual processing of them, although all the human senses contribute to the perception of physical distinctions. In the human universe of artefacts and the exploitation of natural objects, and as in the network for Thing, physical Qualities interact with function. A typical example of this interaction can be seen in the COBUILD definition for *spoon*: 'a spoon is an object shaped like a small shallow bowl with a long handle, which is used for eating, mixing, stirring and serving food'. This is representative of one important aspect of cross-classification, which is discussed in Chapter 6. Although it is reasonable to suggest that we classify an artefact such as a spoon by function, it is also linked to a visual image in which shape and size are important in identifying it as one object rather than another and identifying the parts, e.g. *long handle*, which link it to its function.[7]

The major categories of physical Quality are represented in the system network in Figure 7.19. It will be noted that **dimension, colour** and **age** are represented as separated Quality subclasses on the grounds that they have an independent position in modifier sequences.

Several general characteristics of senses in the categories below are noteworthy. First, in their basic sense (as attributes of Things), relatively few have adverbial forms. There is, for example, no *roundly, squarely, bitterly* or *sourly*. Second, many of them have secondary senses, usually in the sphere of qualities of humans (e.g. *a cool/sweet/hard person*); transference to human behavioural Qualities brings with it the potential to be used adverbially (e.g. *he spoke sweetly to her*).

7.3.8.1 Temperature

The senses of temperature Quality, given in the subnetwork in Figure 7.19, differ from the 'environment senses' discussed above in that they refer to the temperature of objects. In many cases, the temperature of objects is a direct consequence of environmental conditions, typically the power of the sun. As sources of perceptible high or low temperatures (e.g. sun, fire, wind, ice) emanate heat or cold, certain forms of adverbial expression are found as in (52) and (53).

(52)   the fire glowed warmly in the hearth
(53)   the wind blew coldly over the plain

The adverbial form *hotly* in this sense is not found, however, although it is of course found in other senses of *hot* as in (54).

(54)   the goal was hotly disputed in the pub afterwards

The unavailability of *hotly* is ensured by introducing [quality of thing] into the system as an entry condition on [hot].

The question of unmarked terms is problematic with temperature. The correlation between Things and an unmarked temperature depends on the individual Thing. The same applies to the environmental use of temperature qualities. This often depends on 'real world knowledge' such that with a reasonable knowledge of seasonal variation and geographical position the following terms, in (55) and (56), would be used.

(55) How cold is it in Siberia in the winter?

(56) How hot is it in Egypt in August?

It can therefore be argued that there is no unmarked term, since with every use of a temperature Quality in a *how*-expression there is an expectation orienting towards one value in the range.

7.3.8.2 *Light Quality*

Like environmental Quality, light Quality relates to the presence or absence of natural or artificial light, and is frequently used as an Attribute with the dummy subject *it*, as illustrated in (57).

(57) It's light/dark in here

The adjectives, as modifiers, also collocate with enclosed spaces, e.g. *light/dark room, house, hall, church*, etc.; with periods of the day, e.g. *dark morning, dark afternoon*; and with surfaces exposed to or deprived of light, e.g. *a dark shadow*.

A closely related sense of *light* and *dark* is that used to distinguish groups of colour, and consequently objects, which are identified by the lightness or darkness of their colour, e.g. *a dark overcoat*. This semantic closeness raises the lexicographical problem of whether or not to recognize one or two senses with regard to such pairs. LDOCE offers a separate sense: 'tending towards black: *dark hair, dark green/dark clothes*'. The definition alone, however, does not provide sufficient explanation of the decision to separate them, whereas the different collocational sets do. There are no adverbial equivalents of *light* and *dark* in the above sense, hence the entry condition [quality of thing].

7.3.8.3 *Weight Quality*

The relationship of weight Quality to measure expressions and *how*-expressions has been discussed above. The two senses, *heavy* and *light*, are also exceptional in terms of adverbial use. Thus we find examples such as (58).

(58) she pressed lightly/heavily on the man's chest

It should be noted that [pos light], e.g. *a light room*, and [lower range light], e.g. *a light suitcase*, share the same realization rule number. In this way, all recognized separate senses of *light* which appear in different parts of the Quality network share the same realization rule. This has the form:

84.41 : pos light or lower range light or . . . : 'infl', a < "light".

In the current Cardiff Grammar, homonyms across word classes (e.g. *light* as verb, noun and adjective) are repeated for each individual word class. This allows the appropriate nominal, verbal or adjectival morphology to be expressed. There is in principle no reason why all senses from whichever word class should not have one exponence rule with morphological instructions expressed by conditions on the rule as illustrated below. However, given the exponence relation between an element of structure and an item, it would still be necessary to repeat the item for each condition, i.e. **M < "light", h < "light"** and **a < "light"**.

7.3.8.4 Form Quality

Form Qualities involve human perception of outlines of things and the form of lines. Shape, especially in geometrical terms, comprises a set of mutually exclusive terms, none of which enter into relations of complementarity. They are determined by our perception of the number of sides they have, if the lines are straight, and the degree of curvature in the case of circular, oval and round shapes. Lines on the other hand are either **straight** or **'not straight'**. There is no single complementary sense to *straight*. This is clearly because there is more than one way in which a line deviates from straightness. The subnetwork for form Quality is shown in Figure 7.20.

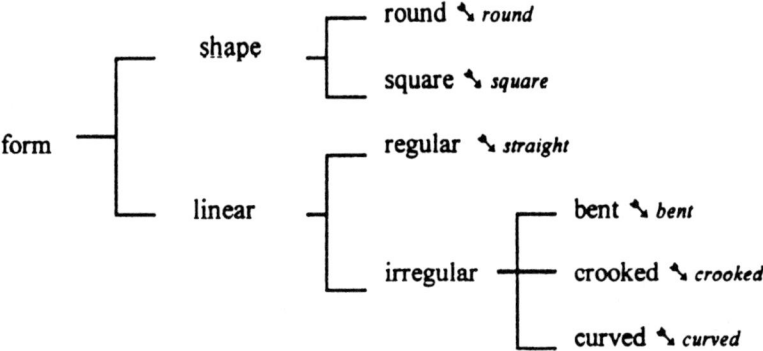

Figure 7.20. The subnetwork for form Quality

7.3.8.5 Feel or look Quality

It could be argued that our primary interaction with the surfaces of objects is through touch, but clearly we are able to see different surface qualities as well; hence the name of this function. In general this category relates to the evenness or unevenness of surfaces and to their rigidity, as in the case of *hard* and *soft*. In their primary sense these adjectives have no Manner Adjunct equivalent. One apparent exception to this, at first sight, is the use of *sharply*, as in COBUILD: 'He had on sharply pointed brown shoes'. However, this sense can be distinguished from the primary sense, to which LDOCE offers the definition: 'Not rounded, marked by hard lines and narrow angles'. If this is the case, then *sharp* in this sense relates to the shape 'as observed' rather than to the effect of feel, as in the primary sense. Sharply pointed shoes, unless made of metal, would be unlikely to be sharp as is a knife or a needle. The subnetwork for feel and look Quality is therefore as given in Figure 7.21.

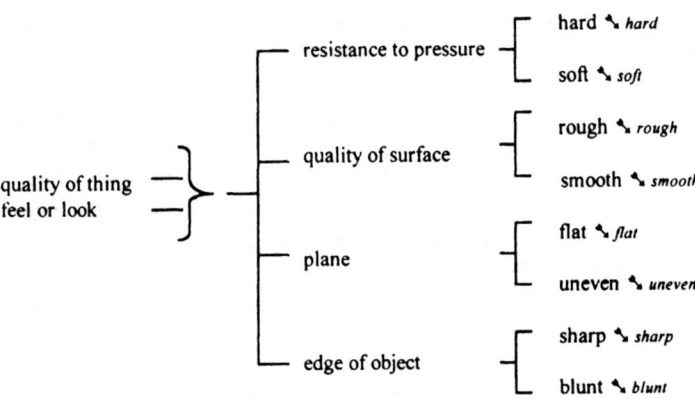

Figure 7.21. The subnetwork for feel or look Quality

7.3.8.6 Taste Quality

The sense of *sweet* is opposed to a number of senses in English, including *sharp* and *savoury*, which are shown in the subnetwork for taste Quality in Figure 7.19. This suggests that *sweet* is the primary taste perception. The various terms covered under [not sweet] have individual collocational relations with different food terms (e.g. *bitter almonds/chocolate/coffee*), and also collocate strongly with *taste*, both as a verb and a noun. When the association between a food type and a Quality of taste is strong, with cake(s) and *sweet* for example, the Quality is either redundant or, if expressed, co-occurs with adverbial intensifiers as in (59).

(59)   This chocolate cake is very sweet

7.3.8.7 Surface state Quality

Objects, and especially their surfaces with which we interact through contact, are subject to a number of states. Surfaces can be *wet* or *dry*, *clean* or *dirty*, or through the presence of some other element *sticky* or *slippery*.

7.3.8.8 Functional state Quality

A small group of Qualities stand apart from other categories posited here, and arguably from one another. The proposed feature, **functional state**, is set up to generalize across the meanings of the two pairs of words by highlighting their inherently functional nature. Thus containers are typically intended to be filled, and doors, windows, etc. to be opened and closed. With each, the particular functional state is determined with respect to some other Thing: the wall, building, etc. in the case of *open/closed*, and the contents in the case of *empty/full.*

One central state of **containers** concerns their degree of 'fullness' in respect of their contents. The two terms used to express these states are *empty* and *full*, which Cruse (1986: 225) includes in the class of 'antipodal opposites'. The terms express the absolute extremes in respect of a container and its contents. Unlike 'complementary opposites' there are degrees of content of a container which are expressed through appropriate temperers, usually fractional quantifiers or approximatives (e.g. *half full/empty, three-quarters full/*empty, almost/practically full/empty.*

It is an interesting point that, although the terms represent extremes on the scale, they still participate in comparatives, as in (60).

(60)   The rain tub is much fuller after all the rain

In this sense *fuller* implies 'more content' since the tub cannot be 'fuller than full'. Cruse treats this kind of comparative as a **pseudo-comparative** since it has the meaning 'of greater content' rather than 'full to a greater degree' (Cruse 1986: 207).

I would argue that *full* is itself an approximate extreme, and as such can be tempered in order to indicate something like absolute fullness. Thus we find:

(61)   Be careful not to spill your coffee. The cup is **very full**

Finally, we should note that *full* can also be accompanied by scope expressions, such as *full to the brim, full to bursting*, etc. There is therefore a lack of symmetry of behaviour between *full* and *empty*, the latter term less likely to be found with degree temperers or scope elements.[8]

The terms *open* and *closed/shut* are essentially complementary opposites. As in the case of doors, windows, drawers, gates, etc., there are differing states of openness, which are expressible through a small set of temperers, e.g. *half open, wide open*. The adjective *ajar* is also available, but can only function as an Attribute and collocates uniquely with *door*. Although containers have an opening and can therefore be either open or closed, in many cases there is no inherent duality of state as in the case of doors, windows, etc. Once a bottle of wine is open, it cannot return to its original state as an 'unopened' bottle of wine, even though the cork may be replaced. The deverbal adjectives *opened* and *unopened* express this relationship.

The Qualities *open* and *closed* are used predominantly in the Attribute function, and occur only rarely as modifiers. In many communicative situations, where doors or windows need to be described or identified, other Qualities or properties serve this purpose more effectively. As alternative states in a door's function, *open* and *closed* are similar to the terms *on* and *off* used with switches, taps, etc. Given that all doors can, in principle, easily be either open or closed at any point in time, the two states do not often provide an adequate basis for description or identification, unless the addressee can see the door in question at the time it is referred to.

The constraints on the range of temperers that *open* and *closed* accept must be expressed in the network by the inclusion of a separate TEMPERING SYS-TEM for these senses. It is interesting to note that *awake* and *asleep* share by and large the same set of temperers, which is explained by the fact that these latter states are typically signalled by the eyes being either open or closed.

7.3.9 Age Quality

Age Quality (Figure 7.22) occupies a separate modifier element in the structure of the nominal group (see Chapter 10). Three subtypes are recognized here, the first of which, **life or development wise**, relates to life forms. The second subtype relates to the time things have been made, created, built, etc. It is used with living Things in terms of their being possessed by or assuming some function or relationship with others, which is exemplified by *a new secretary, a new boyfriend*. The third subtype relates to the age of things in terms of their belonging either to a period in the distant past or to the period in which the speaker lives.

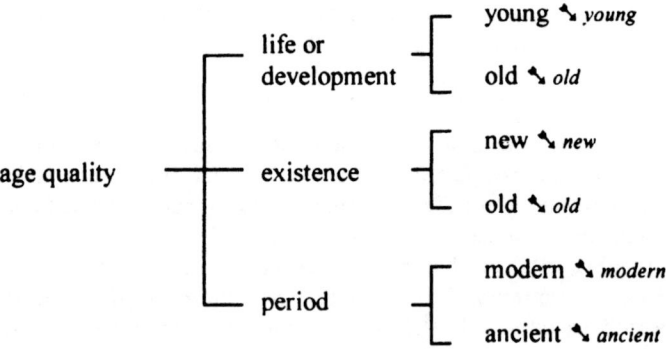

Figure 7.22. The subnetwork for age Quality

More specific age Quality is regularly expressed, in the modifier function, through Qualities relating to historical provenance, e.g. *nineteenth-century, Georgian, Roman*, etc. Age adjectives of all three subtypes form antonym pairs and all may be tempered. They have no equivalents as Quality of Situation.

7.3.10 Colour Quality

Colour terms have become prominent in theories of classification since Berlin and Kay's (1969) seminal contribution in the field of cognitive anthropology. An overview of the whole topic of colour classification is found in Lakoff (1987). The system in Figure 7.23 makes no attempt to present a detailed classification of colour. The overall network, however, does cover several linguistically significant characteristics of colour terms which the lexicogrammar must at least account for. First, colour Quality is set apart from other Quality types in terms of modifier sequence in the nominal group (see Chapter 10). Second, they have a specific set of temperers (e.g. *dark brown, pale blue, bright yellow*, etc. Third, the forms are both adjectival and nominal, so that this system is entered from the major system networks for Thing and Quality.

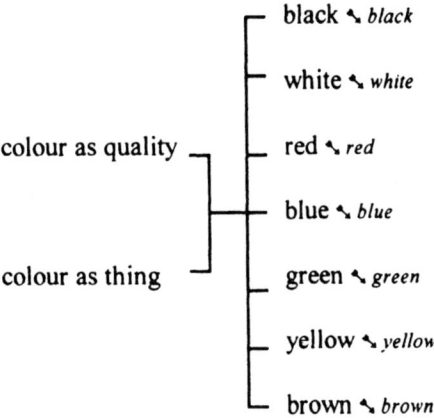

Figure 7.23. A basic system for colour Quality

7.4   THE CLASSIFICATION OF THINGS

7.4.1 Adjectives as subclassifiers

The term **classification** partially reflects Halliday's distinction between **classifier** and **epithet** (Halliday 1994: 184–6). For Halliday, the terms 'epithet' and 'classifier' are functions, and some adjectives may be used for either function (e.g. *a fast train*: (a) a train travelling fast (epithet) and (b) a category of express train (classifier). I adopt the term **classification**, and the network feature **classifying**, in contrast to **epithetic**, to distinguish those Qualities which are primarily used to classify and subclassify Things, and which correspond to a number of modifier classes in the nominal group. There is, I believe, good reason to suggest that this distinction is a more permanent one than might be suggested by Halliday's treatment of Qualities as functioning either as 'epithetic' or 'classifying'. The main justification for this is that certain classes of Quality **are** more or less significant in their potential to subclassify Things. Human beings can be classified according to whether they are happy or sad, intelligent or unintelligent, fat or thin, rich or poor, and yet their classification as being American or British or Chinese is socio-culturally more significant in the way we categorize experience. We thus talk about *happy French people* and *sad French people*, rather than *French sad people* and *American sad people*. Any modification of the role of Qualities in cultural subclassification represents an attempt to impose a different order of importance on our perceived classification. Epithetic Qualities may be 'promoted' to the function of classifier, as will be discussed in Chapter 10.

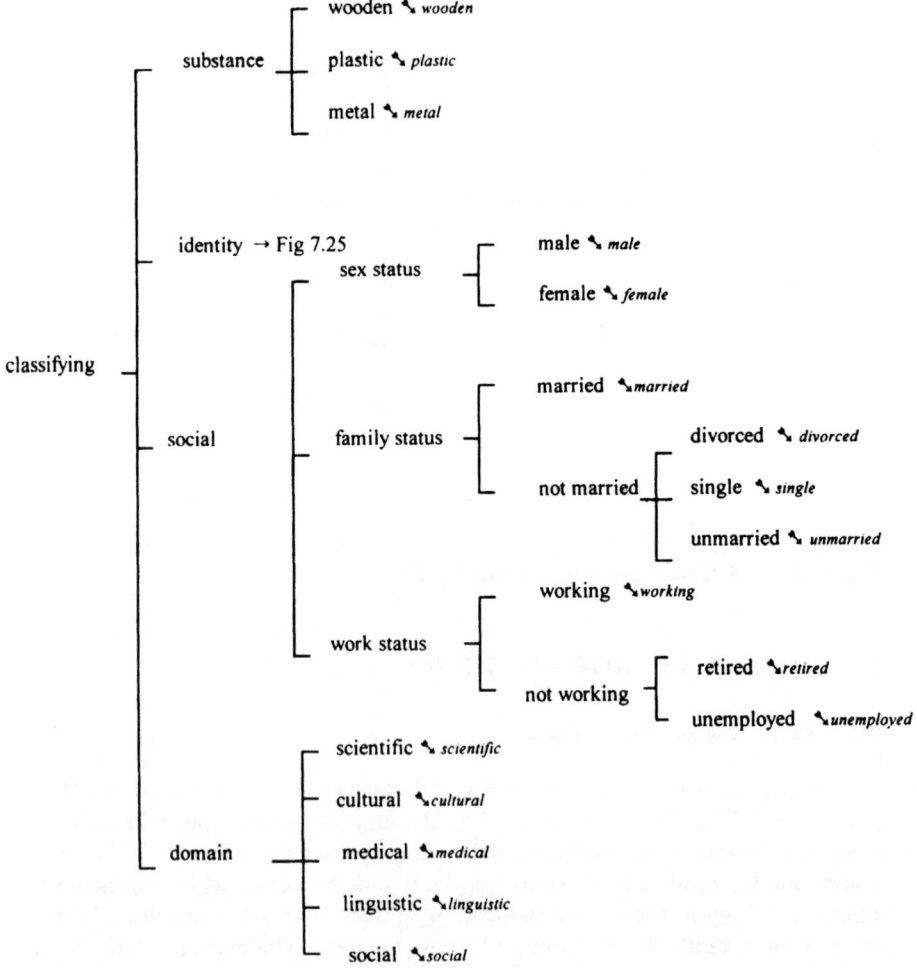

Figure 7.24. The subnetwork for classifying Quality

It is a general property of the classifying Qualities (Figure 7.24) that they do not accept degrees of comparison or intensity. Wherever such tempering is found, the adjective is understood as assuming a different, albeit related sense. Thus in (62) and (63) below, the sense of *English* concerns behaviour (i.e. behaving in a way typical of the English). This can even contradict the classifier sense of the adjective.

(62)   Gianluigi is more English than the English

(63)   Elke is very English in her mannerisms

It is also indicative of this behavioural function of typically classifying adjectives that they can occupy a separate and earlier modifier place in sequence. This is illustrated by (64) and (65).

(64)   An old English gentleman

(65)   A very English old gentleman

Classifying adjectives are found at the limits of prototypical 'adjectiveness'. Most items function equally as verbs or nouns. Prototypically, adjectives have four criterial characteristics, listed by Quirk *et al.* (1985) and discussed in Chapter 5. They occur (a) in attributive function, (b) in predicative function, (c) with intensifiers and (d) with comparatives. Classificatory modifiers, as we have noted, do not conform to (c) and (d). Criterion (a) is an essential characteristic, without which an item could not even be considered for adjectival status. It is, however, the criterion which gives no indication in respect of word class assignment since verbs and nouns occur as modifiers; one would not wish to classify *telephone* as an adjective on the basis of its occurrence in *telephone conversation*. Criterion (b) is more revealing, but is problematic with certain classes. The set of **materials** (e.g. *metal, plastic, cardboard*) barely, if at all, pass this criterion. Take for example the occurrence of *plastic* in (66) and (67).

(66)   This is a plastic spoon

(67)   ?This spoon is plastic

Furthermore, dictionaries are inconsistent in assigning materials to the class of nouns or adjectives. COBUILD and LDOCE give *metal, gold* and *silver* as both nouns and adjectives, but assign all other metals (in their basic sense), including *bronze*, solely to the noun class.

The criterion of predicative function shows more reliability with verb-like items. Past participial forms generally occur both predicatively and attributively, as (68) and (69) illustrate.

(68)   He is a retired electrician

(69)   He is retired

Note, however, the oddity of (70), caused by the incompatibility of the presence of a role term and *retired* which entails that the person no longer has that role.

(70)   The electrician is retired

The implicature present in (70) is that the electrician has retired from some other profession and is working as an electrician in his retirement.

Present participle forms generally fail the predicative function criterion for adjective assignment (i.e. as Attribute in the clause), since they are construed as verbal when following a copula, as can be seen from (71) and (72).

(71)   Working people have restricted freedom
(72)   Those people are not working

Notwithstanding this behaviour, *working* is generally assigned by dictionaries to both the noun and verb class.

Insufficient criteria, and the resulting inconsistency of lexicographers, affects word class assignment in peripheral cases. Lexical classification should not, however, be confused with function. All items used to modify nominal heads can be considered to have the function of modifier. As verbal and nominal modifiers gain significance and specialized meanings, they may be seen to cross the boundary in terms of lexical classification. Very little is gained by the ability to state categorically that an item is also an adjective. What is important to the grammar, and therefore to the speaker as a user of the resource, is that such meanings are made available. If verbal participles can be used as modifiers, then the grammar must make links between the relevant modifier element of structure and the process types. The same applies to nominal modification. In the Cardiff Grammar, **modification by Process** and **modification by Thing** will involve re-entry into the networks for Situation and Thing respectively. Once re-entry is effected, the whole range of verbal and nominal lexis can be exploited. Whereas with adjectives the modifier is filled by a quality group, in the case of verbs the modifier will be filled by a clause, in the case of nouns by a nominal group. Such units, of course, will have a greatly reduced meaning potential that essentially limits the generated structures to single lexical items.

7.4.2 Social Quality

The subnetwork for family status Quality in Figure 7.24 reflects the basic dichotomy, at least in Western society, between being married or not. It is perhaps significant that there are a number of possibilities for classifying how one is not married, whereas *married* tends to be subclassified through premodification, as in *happily married* or *unhappily married*. The term *unmarried* has a somewhat indeterminate status in either signifying 'not having a marriage contract' for whatever reason, or 'not yet or never having been married'. The system here opts for the latter, which therefore contrasts the sense from that of *single* and *divorced*. The term *single* may also reflect indeterminacy.

7.4.2.1 Work status Quality

The network for work status in Figure 7.24 raises the problem of adjectival status as discussed above. The terms for [not working] are clearly adjectives with a modifier and an Attribute function. Neither option for [working], however, is altogether acceptable in the Attribute function. In the case of (73) below, *is working* is taken to be the 'progressive' form of the verb, with *working* as the Main Verb element. In (74), the expression is at best ambiguous.

(73)   he is working
(74)   he is employed

A solution is needed for the treatment of such forms, however. If the grammar includes *working* as an adjective, it must be restricted to the modifier function, and therefore will have as part of its entry condition [quality as modifier]. If, alternatively, *working* is considered to be a modifier realized by a Process (and consequently a clause), then the sense will not be included in the network for Quality. The first alternative is adopted here, on the basis of expressions such as *working class, working hypothesis*, etc. This is further supported by the growing significance of work as no longer being the norm, where *a working docker/coal miner* is as marked a term as *an unemployed doctor*.

7.4.2.2 *Identity wise Quality*

Social identity is strongly related to geographical provenance and ethnic classification. The subnetworks in Figure 7.25 represent supra-national classification, although the full lexical resource would include sub-national identity as well, as reflected in adjectives such as *Liverpudlian, Glaswegian, Bristolian*, etc. It is assumed that identity is primarily an attribute of humans, given the status of nations as social artefacts. Other subclasses of Things, such as goods, products, produce, etc., may inherit this form of identity either directly or indirectly. Thus, *Italian fashion*, for example, is indeterminate between 'the fashion as adopted in Italy' or 'the fashion adopted by Italians'. Provenance, therefore, is not always a direct Quality of a Thing. Most current members of the *Italian community* in various parts of the British Isles, for example, do not come from Italy, but are descendants of people who did. The subnetworks in Figure 7.25 are clearly far from exhaustive and are not commented on in detail.

The term *foreign* is arguably deictic. A speaker either perceives others as coming from the same country as him/herself or coming from a different country, or alternatively (difficult though it may be for the English) perceives him/herself as coming from a different country from everyone around him/her, where he or she is foreign.

7.4.3 Domain Quality

An extensive range of Qualities derive from the nominal classification of areas of human knowledge, experience and activity. Thus, for example, relating to the domains of **science**, social activity such as **economics/economy**, **politics**, **music**, etc., and indeed **society** itself, are the Qualities *scientific(ally)*, *economic(ally)*, *political(ly)*, *musical(ly)* and *social*. The various relationships between the Qualities and their nouns include: 'relating to N', 'on the subject of N', 'from the domain

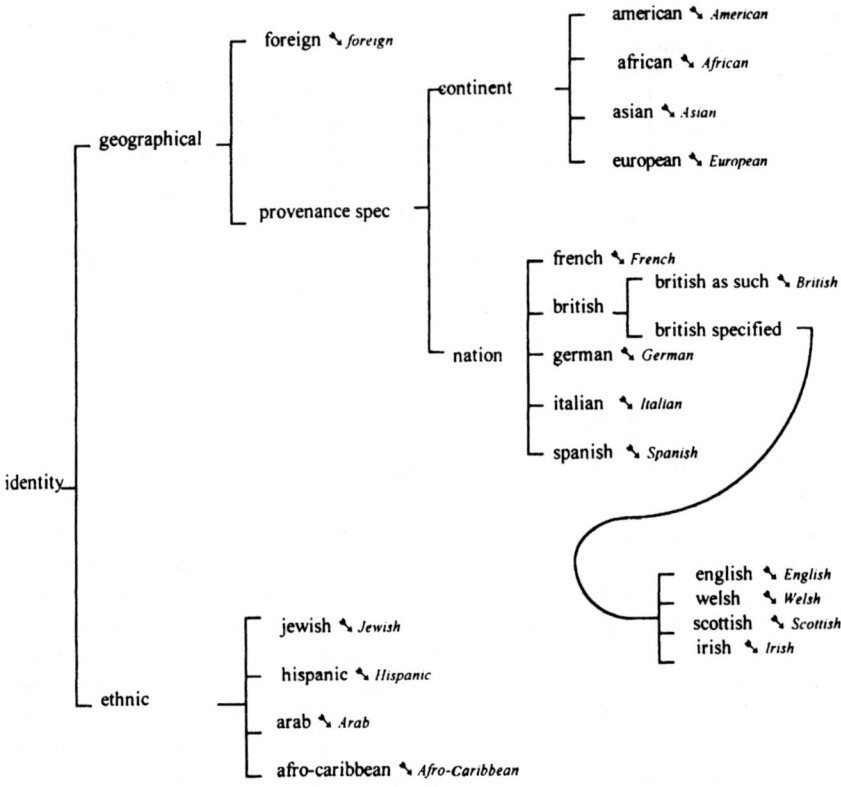

Figure 7.25. Initial systems for identity Quality

of N', etc. In general, such Qualities collocate with abstract and event nouns, such as *problem, question, phenomenon, failure, speech,* etc.

The indirect relationship of Quality (adjective) and Thing (noun), what Ferris (1993) terms 'associative', usually excludes the Attribute function of the qlgp, or at best imposes another interpretation on the qlgp. Take, for example, the behaviour of *economic* in examples (75) and (76).

(75)   They are studying the economic crisis in Britain
(76)   *The crisis in Britain was economic

Note, however, that this restriction on the Attribute function of such adjectives can be generally overcome by adding the prepositional group *in nature,* as in (77).

(77)   The crisis in Britain was economic in nature

The small system in Figure 7.24 is merely a placeholder for the whole range of Qualities of this kind.

7.4.4 Situation-oriented Quality

7.4.4.1 General overview

The term **Situation-oriented Quality** has been adopted to categorize Qualities that are primarily associated with Situations. Clear examples of this type of Quality are the range of adjectives and adverbs for expressing **usuality** and **probability** (e.g. *usual, rare, probable, likely*, etc.). As adjectives, they collocate strongly with event nouns (e.g. *the usual excitement, a rare occurrence, a likely event*, etc.). They also collocate with agentive nouns (e.g. *the probable winner, a rare finisher*, etc.) in expressions which can be re-expressed as *he will probably win, he rarely finishes*, etc. The association between other concrete nouns and Quality of event adjectives requires considerable processing and pragmatic implicature. For example, it is difficult to interpret (78) without contextual information of the type that someone is looking for a suitable tree to plant in their garden, i.e. *it's a tree that we might possibly plant there*. The systems for situation-oriented Qualities are given in Figure 7.26.

(78)   That's a possible tree

7.4.4.2 Usuality as Quality

The congruent expression of **usuality of occurrence** is through Adjuncts in clause structure. In the Cardiff Grammar, they are typically realized through the unit set up initially for Manner, and so they appear in the network for [quality of situation]. Examples of items which express usuality of occurrence are *often, seldom, generally, usually*.

Halliday (1994: 152) maintains that usuality of occurrence and frequency of occurrence are related categories, although not identical. In Halliday's words, 'usuality refers to position on a scale between positive and negative (always/never), whereas frequency is the extent of repetition'. For Quirk *et al.* (1985: 543), usuality – 'usual occurrence' to use their term – is considered a subclass of frequency, and is concerned with the expression of 'indefinite frequency'. In the present framework, frequency is reserved for expressions which state 'the number of times per unit', e.g. *five times a week, once a year*, etc., and is considered a sub-category of the overall phenomenon of usuality. It is, however, difficult to separate the two notions; both hold of Situations which repeat themselves over a given period. Even the 'loosest' of usuality expressions, such as *generally*, are based upon the number of times a Situation is repeated over some period.

Usuality is also closely related to **likelihood of occurrence**; usuality concerns the speaker's statement about the extent to which (between 'always' and

155

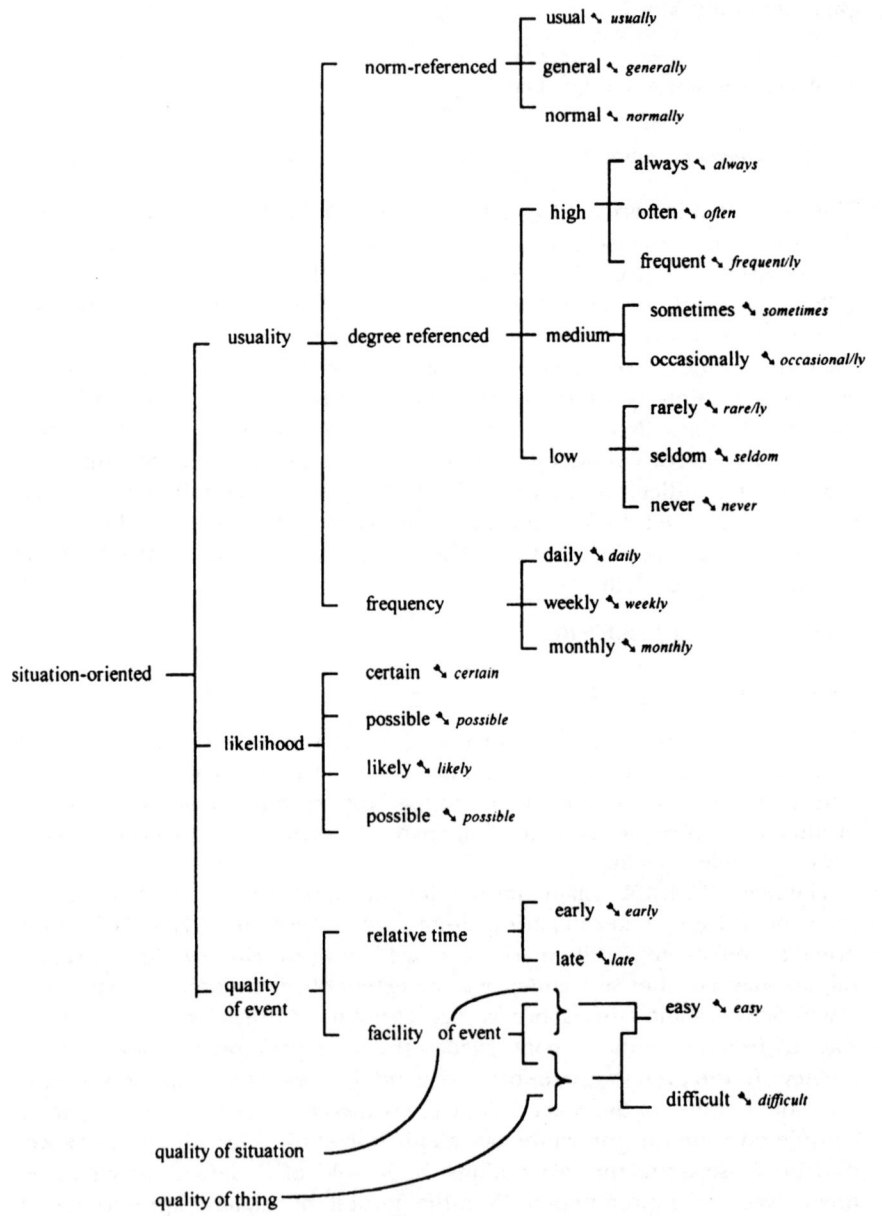

Figure 7.26. The subnetwork for situation-oriented Quality

'never') something is the case, whereas likelihood concerns the speaker's assessment of whether something is or is not the case. For Halliday (1994: 88) both usuality and probability are categories of 'modality'. The relatedness between the two categories is shown in examples (79a–c) and (80a–c).

(79a)   They seldom have a drink after the match
(79b)   They always have a drink after the match
(79c)   They generally have a drink after the match

(80a)   They certainly have a drink after the match
(80b)   They probably have a drink after the match
(80c)   They possibly have a drink after the match

One can of course assess the likelihood of the usuality of some Situation, as (81) illustrates.

(81)   They probably always have a drink after the match

Situations may be expressed in nominal form, and usuality expressed by adjectival structures (e.g. *occasional visits*). Furthermore, nominal expressions which indicate participation in Situations may also be modified in the same way (e.g. *an occasional visitor*), where *occasional* relates to the Process expressed in the nouns *visit* and *visitor*.

The considerable number of usuality Quality senses in English exhibit amongst them a range of syntactic and collocational behaviour typical of Quality senses as a whole. The only characteristic which they all share is their potential to function as Quality of Situation. A small set of the most common items expressing usuality cannot function as Quality of Thing. This set comprises *always, often, sometimes, seldom, ever* and *never*. Each of these, however, exhibits a different potential for TEMPERING. The item *sometimes* is never tempered, whereas others accept a small range, e.g. *almost/nearly always, quite often, very seldom, almost never*. Amongst these *often* has the potential for comparison and superlativization, e.g. *more often than before*, which is reflected in the forms *oftener* and *oftenest*, in certain varieties of English.

It is difficult to motivate the network organization of such senses on formal criteria, however, since other usuality items also exhibit idiosyncratic behaviour. The item *generally*, for example, has no potential for TEMPERING and does not have a usuality-related sense as Quality of Thing. In this last respect, it differs from *usually* and the adjective *usual*, both of which can express usuality, as shown in (82a–b) and (79a–c).

(82a)   They usually/generally have a drink after the match
(82b)   *Drinking is usual/*general after the match

In any full discussion of usuality/frequency on semantic grounds (e.g. Quirk *et al.* 1985: 541–9), the central criterion is the degree of usuality, on a scale from 'maximum' or 'absolute' usuality (*always*) to 'negative' usuality (*never*). The range of senses can be seen to reflect high, medium and low degrees of usuality. The items *always* and *never* may suggest absolute extremes on this scale, yet it should be noted that when they are tempered by *almost* they are no longer absolute.

In addition to reference to degree, usuality items reflect different orientations. One may express the regularity of the repeated Situation (*regular/ly*), express its continuity over a period of time (*continual/ly*, *continuous/ly*) or imply a high rate of frequency (*frequent/ly*).

The network in Figure 7.26 proposes three broad distinctions. The first and central category as discussed above involves usuality senses in terms of scalar degree. The second category groups together those senses which are 'norm-referenced', e.g. *generally*, *usually* and *normally*. These senses can only signal usuality/frequency in conjunction with another Situation. Note how (83) is meaningful in terms of usuality, whereas (84) is not, without some further indication of usuality/frequency.

(83)   They visit their parents quite often
(84)   They visit their parents generally

The third category allows for the specification of frequency, either in terms of 'periodicity', e.g. *weekly*, *daily*, *monthly*, etc., where 'once weekly, daily, monthly' is understood, or in terms of the explicit 'number of times per unit', e.g. *twice weekly*.[9] The network proposed here does not attempt to handle a large number of usuality senses. It does express, for the senses included, the potential and constraints concerning realization of Quality of Situation and Quality of Thing. As indicated above, it is clear that each of the senses must have their individual TEMPERING system.

7.4.4.3 Likelihood of occurrence

The four terms included in the system for [likelihood of occurrence] (Figure 7.26) represent points on a scale of values with which the speaker may indicate his/her assessment of the likelihood of occurrence of some Situation. This amounts to the speaker's confidence in the **validity** of the claim regarding the proposition. They constitute part of the resource for the general expression of 'epistemic modality' as distinguished from 'non-epistemic' or 'deontic' modality. Halliday expresses the distinction in terms of 'modalization' and 'modulation' (e.g. Halliday 1994: 89). In the Cardiff Grammar framework, modalization is treated as **validity assessment**. I have, however, retained the term **likelihood of occurrence** for the purpose of the expression of this phenomenon as Quality; the term 'validity' itself is not reflected in the lexical items available. The term 'probability' is used technically within the CG framework for the probabilities on features in systems, and 'possibility' has both an 'epistemic' and a 'non-epistemic' sense.

It is beyond the scope of the present discussion to pursue the exploration of modal meanings. Full accounts of the phenomenon are given, for example, in Palmer (1986) and Perkins (1983). What is relevant here is that 'validity assessment' or 'modalization' may be expressed through quality group structures involving adjectival and adverbial items. All that is attempted here is a specification of the lexicogrammatical behaviour of the Quality terms included.

All terms participate as adjectives in expressions of 'likelihood', most clearly, as in (85), in the Attribute function, a construction which Fawcett and Huang (1995) have referred to as an 'evaluative enhanced theme' construction.[10] They also occur in the modifier function as illustrated by (86) and in the Attribute function with event Things as in (87).

(85)   It is certain/probable/likely/possible that she will win
(86)   She is a certain/probable/likely/possible candidate
(87)   Victory is likely/certain/possible/probable

Two items, *certain* and *likely*, participate in what was known as the 'subject to subject raising' transformation in Chomsky's Extended Standard Theory (Horrocks 1987: 86–7), as shown in example (88). In the Cardiff Grammar, a different, functional approach is adopted, which brings out the similarity with expressions such as *Howard will win*, where 'likelihood' is expressed as a 'modal verb' at Operator in the clause. In this approach, *is likely* is treated as a 'complex' Operator/Auxiliary (O/X) construction in the clause, in which *is* is the Operator/Auxiliary, and *likely* is an Auxiliary Verb Extension (X^{ex}).

(88)   Howard is likely/certain/*possible/*probable to go

All the terms cited also occur in qlgps at Adjunct, as shown in (89), although *likely* is virtually obligatorily tempered by *most* in this role, at least in Standard English.

(89)   Howard is most likely/probably/certainly to be made captain

Given that the [likelihood of occurrence] Quality senses constitute part of the general resource for this area of meaning, their individual availability in the kinds of expressions illustrated above must be specified by preferences. Thus, if a speaker selects to express likelihood through a construction such as in (88), preferences must specify that only the features realized as *likely* and *certain* may be selected from the system given in Figure 7.26. The four senses appearing in this system are, of course, only representative of the much larger range available. A fuller system would include features such as [plausible], [sure], [unlikely], [definite], etc.

7.4.4.4 Quality of event

The two categories included in the system for Quality of event given in Figure 7.26 relate to the concepts of 'time' and 'ease' associated with Situations. As a consequence, the terms involved are primarily associated with event nouns, and secondarily, by extension, with participants in such events. Like the 'likelihood' adjectives, these adjectives also participate in evaluative enhanced theme constructions, as illustrated by (90) and (91).

(90)   It's late/early to be giving up
(91)   It's difficult/easy to learn how to drive

The Process to which *late* and *early* refer may be either left implicit or explicitly expressed as scope, as shown in (92). Indeed, there is such a strong association between these senses and the Process *arrive* that it is difficult to conceive of an interpretation of (92) other than in respect of 'arriving'. In its nominalized form, *arrival*, as an event Thing, the Process does not collocate with *late* or *early*, as shown by the anomalous nature of (93). When *arrival* has the sense of 'the person who arrives', however, it strongly collocates with either adjective, as in (94).

(92)   The plane was late (arriving)
(93)   *The plane's arrival was late
(94)   There have been a number of late/early arrivals

The terms [easy] and [difficult] co-occur typically with count nouns such as *examination, test, task, question,* etc., as in (95).

(95)   That was a very difficult question

In such cases, the Process is inherent in the noun and is unlikely to be expressed as scope, as in *a very difficult question to answer*. If there is no such inherent reference to the Process, the degree of recoverability of the Process will determine the optionality or obligatoriness of a scope, as in (96) and (97).

(96)   This book is easy (to read = optional)
(97)   This beer is easy (to drink = obligatory)

Lexical semantic insight into the nature of the relationship between such Qualities and Things is provided by Pustejovsky's 'Theory of qualia' in which he posits 'four basic roles' that constitute the qualia structure for a lexical item (Pustejovsky 1991). One of these four is the 'Telic Role', which concerns the 'purpose and function of the object'. Now if we apply this role to an 'object' such as 'question', for example, we can specify that questions are intended to be **answered**. Thus the Quality *difficult* or *easy* can be interpreted in terms of the possibility of answering the question. The difference between the optionality and obligatoriness associated with the realization of scope *book* and *beer* can be explained in terms of whether difficulty or ease are appropriate aspects of 'reading' or 'drinking' respectively. It is rather an esoteric issue of whether a beer is easy to drink, which does not depend so much on the fact that it is a liquid or not, but rather on whether it has the quality of 'smoothness' and 'taste' which appeals to the 'expert' drinker.

It is an odd fact that, despite its association with Processes, the term [difficult] has no adverbial form. If this sense is selected for [quality of situation] a prepositional group structure *with difficulty* must be chosen.[11]

7.4.5 Environmental Quality

Environmental Qualities are not primarily associated with Things or with Situations. They are thus found principally in the Attribute function with the dummy Subject *it.* It will be noted that environmental Processes have the same dummy

Subject, e.g. *it is raining*, in that they are not associated with any Participant Role. The occurrence of environmental Qualities in the modifier function is restricted to 'periods of time', e.g. *a rainy day, a sunny afternoon, a wet Sunday*, or with 'places', e.g. *a windy part of the country*. Places often indicate a 'micro-environment', e.g. *a hot/dark room, a hot/dark house*, where it is not the 'physical building' which is hot or dark, but the enclosed environment that it creates. Thus, *this is a hot/dark room* can be re-expressed as *it's hot/dark in this room*. Temperature and Light Qualities become 'properties' of objects, when they are affected by sources of heat and light. As Qualities of Things, temperature and light are treated as a class of physical Quality and the respective subsections. The adjective *wet* is included since it also participates in dummy Subject constructions. The inclusion of [temperature] ensures neatly that the temperature terms in the system discussed above under this heading are available to environmental Qualities. Environmental Qualities are not realized as Manner Adjuncts, and thus require [quality of thing] as an entry condition. The subnetwork for environment Quality is given in Figure 7.27.

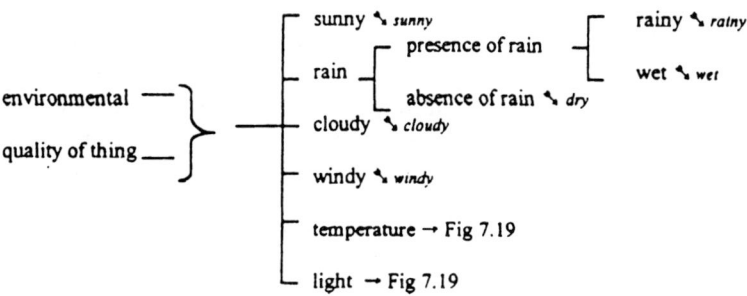

Figure 7.27. The subnetwork for environmental Quality

7.5   CONCLUSION

It will have become apparent to the reader, if it were not already so, that the task of modelling even a small part of the overall lexical resource is virtually limitless and unending. It may even be reasonably argued, as Sells reports Chomsky to have said in a course lecture, that 'it would be a mistake to come up with a grammar of English full of lots of rules and little riders that got all the facts right down to every detail' (Sells 1985: 27). Chomsky is primarily concerned with generalizations in order to make claims about universal principles behind human language. There are other objectives in developing linguistic theories, however, and they may well be served by lexicogrammatical descriptions of the kind presented here. From the viewpoint of developing systemic functional theory further, the delicacy of description attempted here provides a constant check on and stimulus to the theory itself, especially a theory in which 'syntax' and 'lexis' are not seen as independent components of an overall model. From a descriptive viewpoint, any such attempt is likely to advance our understanding of how English works. And finally, from the viewpoint of computational linguistics, if we are to develop machine systems which incorporate language, then such generative models with an extensive lexical resource are clearly necessary.

In the context of the total adjectival and adverbial resource of English, the network described above is clearly insufficient and inadequate. However, its shortcomings, I would argue, are a question of depth of description or, to use a key term in this general debate, of **delicacy of description**. Delicacy represents a development of the lexicogrammar in terms of coverage. The ultimate task of the lexicogrammarian might be to increase his or her grammar to a point which reflects the potential of some actual speaker of English. Indeed, that is all that could be achieved. To do otherwise would be to raise the issues of 'where language is'. Perhaps the issue is raised by my own statement of the task of the lexicogrammarian. No two individual speakers of any language have exactly the same linguistic resource. There is not a grammar of English, for example, which exists independently of individual minds, except for the generalizations which linguistic observers can capture. What, after all, is a dictionary or a descriptive grammar of English other than an account of the linguistic behaviour which a number of people share? And it is not surprising that we share a great deal, given that we acquire our own resource from interacting with others who already have a resource of their own. Human societies are based on the commonality of individual beliefs and the extent to which such beliefs are shared by the community at large. There is no reason to assume that beliefs about how language works (in the sense of a grammar or an individual's theory of language) should be any different. Language, like any aspect of human behaviour, is subject to control. The most powerful elements in a given society will always attempt to control any aspect of behaviour which potentially threatens their power. Language is no exception. Unwittingly, perhaps, the descriptive linguist is suggesting how a language is by drawing attention to those common elements which he or she uncovers. This is the dilemma of the corpus linguist in particular, who is making statements about a language on the basis of a large and varied cross-section of individual users. The findings of corpus linguistics represent what individuals have in common, but not what any one individual possesses. Any attempt to base a description of English on a corpus of one individual would simply result in a linguistic profile of that individual and nothing else. And yet, in terms of modelling linguistic behaviour, what alternative is there?

The goal of a project such as the COMMUNAL Project is to create an interactive system within a computer. It is a machine model of an interactive human being, to the extent that such a model is useful in replacing a human being for the purpose of certain tasks. Yet in so doing, the computational 'creator' creates another individual, providing it with a set of beliefs and 'working theories' about the universe in which it is to operate. The categories of experience which the machine endows are those assumed to be culturally relevant according to the 'creator'. To the extent to which such categories can be posited from various fields of research, they can be considered to be valid categories for the intended purpose. Yet they can only reflect in a generalized way the categories of an individual mind.

The point which I am labouring to make is that we cannot fully understand the categorial organization of an individual mind without an exclusive investigation of that mind. I do . not know how I or any other individual organizes Quality senses. At best I have some knowledge of how they might be organized by the way in which they are used in language. But again we have to generalize across many speakers of a linguistic community to establish such underlying organization and, in the process, factor out aspects of such organization which do not fully correspond to the general picture. We can assume, for example, that there is a relevant distinction between the categories represented by *angry* and *sad*, and we can also assume that there is a generally accepted categorial difference between the two. What we cannot verify is the extent to which each speaker conforms to the same apparent categorization.

This line of argument might seem to constitute an *apologia* for setting up whatever categorial organization one wishes, thereby protecting it from critical examination. To some extent, perhaps it is. Being unable either to interrogate the whole of the English-speaking world – or indeed any community of English speakers – or to bring to consciousness my own individual organization, I have built the system network for Quality on whatever evidence there is available. It is not the case that grammar, in the sense of 'most delicate grammar', will provide the answers, since our current knowledge does not, and probably never will, allow us to explicate all such semantic and conceptual organization.

The reader will therefore both find *lacunae* in the presentation and disagree with details of its organization. I am unaware, however, of any other presentation which claims definitiveness in this respect which itself is not open to the same criticism. It may well be that this approach simply avoids the criterion of falsifiability, although I would maintain that this criterion is not applicable to such categorization.

Despite its imperfections, due mainly to the impossibility of ever getting it all right (if indeed that is a humanly possible task), I would claim that the approach taken is capable of reflecting or modelling the lexicogrammar of Quality. Every individual lexicogrammar is a constantly evolving organism, in an ontological sense, from the onset of language to the grave. All the linguist can hope to achieve is to produce a model which is capable of reflecting this evolution, even if there is little chance of keeping pace with it.

NOTES

1 The expression *what kind of* would be generated as typic determiner (d^t) in a nominal group. The d^t is filled by a further nominal group which has a **head** expounded by *kind* and a **deictic determiner** expounded by *what*.

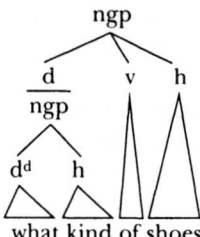

The expression *what was the party like* would be generated as a discontinuous **prepositional group** at Attribute, introduced by the element **p** (*like*) with the **cv** element placed in an early clause reserved for WH-elements.

2 This is currently one of the 'hot topics' in Natural Language Generation, e.g. Meteer (1992).

3 There are instances of these senses which do appear as modifiers, especially when they are tempered. An example of this would be *a half-asleep child*. Such exceptional cases can be included in the grammar by using probabilities.

4 It should be noted that some items which function as Binders (subordinating conjunctions) in the clause occur with a related meaning in linking two groups (coordination). Subordination is a relationship between clauses alone, and so all conjunctions used between groups can only be Linkers. This of course means that an item such as *although* is analysed differently in the clause and the quality group.

5 The distinction between 'happy' as a temporary Quality and as a permanent Quality is indicated in Spanish, for example, through the use of the two verbs 'to be' *estar* and *ser*, the first, in general, indicating temporary states of affairs, and the second permanent ones. Thus *está alegre* means that someone is cheerful at the moment, whereas *es alegre* signals a permanent personality trait. The distinction, however, is also made lexically, however; the adjective *feliz* corresponds with personality and is used with *ser*, whereas *contento* is a temporary state and is used with *estar*.

6 There is not one single set of unmarked terms which co-occur equally with measure expressions and how-expressions. The set which accepts measure expressions is restricted to the members *deep, high, tall, old, thick, long* and *short*. A notable absentee is *heavy* in the sense of 'weight' (in metric or non-metric units), which is a socially significant statistic alongside height and age. One might hypothesize that, in human terms at least, *heavy* carries negative connotations which excludes it from use in measure expressions and particularly noticeably from *how*–expressions. Outside the measurement of human weight, *heavy* is largely unmarked in how–expressions as shown in (f2).

    (f1)   I want to send this parcel to Canada, please
    (f2)   How heavy is it?

Even here, however, one might argue that *heavy* is still marked in terms of the equation *heavy* = *expensive to send*.

To capture a general principle of unmarkedness in *how*–expressions across a whole range of qualities, it is necessary to consider the quality which is positively associated with the thing it describes. Knives can be **sharp** or **blunt**, but by the nature of their function as artefacts they are more useful when they are sharp. The quality *blunt* is therefore negatively perceived for knives and to ask how blunt a given knife is presupposes that it is probably functionally deficient. The same hold for Quirk *et al.*'s example (1985: 471) given here as (f3).

(f3)   How accurate is your digital watch?

The function of a watch is to tell us the time and we assume that it does so accurately.

There is therefore a general correlation between (1) upper range qualities and qualities presupposed of things in a functional or behavioural sense, (2) the notions of positive and negative value, and (3) the notion of unmarkedness and markedness. If this is the case, the association of the values 'positive' and 'negative' with antonym pairs provides the grammar with a means of generalizing across all such cases. In terms of the grammar, the generalization may be expressed in the following way:

If the feature [tempering sought] is selected, then preselect the positively marked feature in the appropriate quality system.

The traditional systemic notation presents problems for representing markedness (see Martin 1987). Computational implementations, such as the COMMUNAL Project can suggest, provide better solutions. One such solution consists of a **same pass preference rule** associated with the feature [tempering sought]. Given that a computational system can be instructed to recognize an affix [pos] as in [pos old] or [pos accurate], the grammar is able to generalize across all such cases, without having to specify a complete list, e.g. **prefer [pos accurate, pos sharp, pos strong, pos ...]**. In technical systemic terms, preferences of this kind constitute a kind of invisible wiring, introducing a feature into the entry condition of a system which determines a single option or a set of options. In the traditional systemic notation, there is little alternative other than to wire in all cases or feature co-occurrence of this kind with a symbol such as (*). Clearly, however, each set of feature co-occurrences must be marked using distinct symbols, which shows that an alternative solution such as that proposed here is desirable.

7   Jackendoff (1990: 32–4) discusses the inclusion of a 3D model as part of the lexical entry for physical objects. In the case of the present model, 3D representations would be linked to the ontology component in the belief system.

8   The asymmetrical behaviour of *full* and *empty* might be partially explained by the fact that containers only accept a fixed volume of content, after which there is spillage. Thus, the utterance *be careful, the cup's very full* carries the implicature that if it is not handled carefully, the tea, coffee, etc. will spill out.

9   As often happens with other areas of meaning in the lexicogrammar, frequency senses raise the problem of **expressibility**. Frequency may be expressed by structures such as *three times daily* or alternatively by *three times a day*. Although I shall not pursue this issue further here, it is clear that such structures raise a real problem in terms of 'modifier–head' relationships.

10 This is the functional version of 'extraposition'; here the 'evaluative' Attribute *certain*, *possible*, etc. is an 'enhanced theme'.

11 The absence of the adverbs *difficultly*, *toughly* and *hardly* with a Manner Adjunct function constitutes a problem for rank-based grammars such as this. Having re-entered the network for Quality, one is committed to some realization involving the quality group. The network indicates, however, that in the case of [difficult] none is possible. Although the network prevents the erroneous application of the adverb realization rule, it does not permit the alternative, *with difficulty*, to be realized, since this involves the generation of a prepositional group. This illustrates the significant fact that we have to view the systemic grammar as a resource, including lexicogrammatical constraints, and not as a problem-solving device. In terms of natural language generation, it is necessary to incorporate some means of searching networks in order to ascertain whether realization is possible. In human processing terms, the lexicogrammar must be posited as 'linguistic knowledge'. Speakers will therefore 'know in advance' that adverbs such as *difficultly* do not exist.

8. Realization rules for the Quality network

8.1 INTRODUCTION

Having set out the system network for Quality in Chapter 7, we shall now explore the realization rules that are associated with features in the network. The general nature and typology of realization rules has already been discussed in Chapter 3.

The rules in a generative grammar are necessarily explicit and involve a considerable degree of detailed formalization. It is this aspect which sets such grammars apart from the tradition of descriptive grammars. In large-scale descriptive grammars, such as the *Comprehensive Grammar of the English Language* (Quirk *et al.* 1985), rules are expressed informally, often in terms of general principles. Examples of this type of rule are: 'The non-periphrastic superlative may be premodified by the intensifier *very*' and 'When *very* premodifies the superlative, a determiner is obligatory' (Quirk *et al.* 1985: 474). These observations are not intended as a criticism of such grammars. On the contrary, the work of descriptive grammarians is an indispensable source of information and linguistic insight. But, in attempting to formalize the body of linguistic behaviour which they describe, it is essential to provide the kind of rule framework which is found here. If we agree that language is at least in part rule-governed behaviour, then it is reasonable to postulate types of rule formalisms which account for the facts.

I would emphasize that the facts to be accounted for are **linguistic facts**. Gazdar *et al.* (1985: 5) argue convincingly against linguistic theorizing which claims psychological reality or which classifies linguistics as a branch of psychology, suggesting that:

> The most useful course of action (for linguistics) is... to attempt to fulfil some of the commitments made by generative grammar in respect of the provision of fully specified and precise theories of the nature of the languages that humans employ.

The same argument may be used in respect of the grammar described here. The two 'components' of the grammar, the system network and the realization rules, represent both the potential that speakers have and how that potential is realized. This is not a claim to any psychological validity for the nature of the organization of these components. Neither is such a claim implicit in the computational implementability of the Cardiff Grammar. Modelling language in this way, within or outside the domain of artificial intelligence, may well lead to insight about psychological processes, but that is an issue for the psychologist and psycholinguist to address, not the linguist. To emphasize the point made above, the system network and realization rules are designed to account for the facts, and such facts are primarily linguistic in nature.

167

As Fawcett has consistently argued (e.g. Fawcett 1988), no system network is complete without realization rules. Systemic functional grammar privileges paradigmatic relations through the central formalism of the system network; i.e. the choices in context which are available to speakers of a language. The realization of any set of meanings must, of course, exploit the syntagmatic potential of language structure. Any system network representation – or more precisely, any application of it – that cannot be fully translated into lexicogrammatical (and intonational) structure is therefore a device that is inadequate descriptively and, more importantly, generatively.

In an explicit generative account of language the notion of **constraint** is of central importance. Without constraints, a semiotic system would be unusable, since the means would not exist whereby users could be guaranteed some degree of constancy of the meanings to be exchanged. In specifying 'meaning potential' a systemic functional grammar in fact thereby also specifies the constraints, i.e. it states both what **can** be meant and what **cannot** be meant. Not all constraints, however, are absolute. At one extreme, if we give credence to the Chomskyan Universal Grammar (UG) hypothesis, all languages must conform to some general constraints if they are to be included in the set of natural languages. Within that framework, languages may vary in terms of different parametric settings for certain universal principles that account for linguistic formal organization. Furthermore, they may exhibit tendencies which cannot be explained by universal constraints and which are explained in terms of 'peripheral grammar' (Cook 1993: 201). An intermediate stage of constraint, in any given language, is that which governs possible forms from a synchronic perspective. Over time, these forms may undergo modification (albeit still within the parameters of some universal principle) or may be subject to change in terms of their relationship with meaning. At the opposite extreme, constraints are no more than tendencies which can only be expressed probabilistically.

A first impression of the realization rules used in systemic functional grammars such as the Cardiff Grammar, is often one of perplexity. Many realization rules appear to be the syntactic specification of the grammar of the language. And yet it is clear that, although these rules concern the syntagmatic relations of language structure, they do not on their own specify well-formedness. What they do express is a set of lexicogrammatical operations which generate structure and items. But the structures they sanction are dependent on the system network. Thus a given set of rule operations leading to some well-formed sentence is determined by the sets of possible co-occurrence of features selected from a traversal of the system network. A systemic functional grammar of English imposes constraints on the structural output through the collaboration of the system network's organization and the realization rules.

In Chapter 6 we discussed the constraints on system networks in terms of **system dependency**: the choice of any set of features in a given system is dependent on choices made in other systems. The realization rules are applied to possible co-occurring sets of features, each of which constitutes a **selection expression**. The realization rules attached to each selection expression must therefore specify a set of rule operations which account for one and only one formal configuration. It must (a) specify the relevant units, (b) insert the necessary elements of structure, (c) order them appropriately, and (d) expound them with appropriate items or fill them with further units which must subsequently undergo the same processes.

8.2 REALIZATION RULES IN THE NETWORK FOR QUALITY

8.2.1 Potential structure

The first statement in the realization rule component of each system network is the **potential structure**. The potential structure for the quality group is given below, together with a key to the symbols. (This structure was fully discussed in Chapter 5.)

unit (qlgp): & @ 1, ex @ 2, t^e @ 3, d^{qld} @ 4, t^d @ 6, t^a@ 7, d^{qlq} @ 8, a @ 10, t^d @ 12, f @ 16, sc1 @ 18, sc2 @ 20, f @ 22, e @ 24.

Key to symbols

&	= linker	**t^a**	= adjunctival temperer
ex	= extent	**a**	= apex
t^e	= emphasizing temperer	**sc1**	= first scope
d^{qld}	= quality deictic determiner	**sc2**	= second scope
d^{qlq}	= quality quantifying determiner	**f**	= degree temperer
t^d	= degree temperer	**e**	= ender

A **potential structure** is always specifiable, in the sense that it is possible to list the elements of structure which compose the unit, and state either the fixed place in structure that each one takes relative to others or the potential range of places which an element may occupy. In the structure of groups, such as the qlgp, most elements have a fixed place. Wherever this is the case, the initial potential structure specification will make the only reference to the placing of that element. Thus, if the element is present in a given expression of Quality, its place need not be specified by a realization rule on a feature. This means that any element is functionally significant only in terms of its place relative to other elements and to its presence or absence. Since it may occupy only one place, it cannot be functional in terms of its presence at that place rather than at any other. Elements that have more than one potential place typically carry additional functionality in terms of the opposition between potential place 1, potential place 2, potential place 3, etc. This is only true, however, when the same item or unit occurs at this element. The two temperers, for example, are not functionally different, since the second place allocated is only expounded by the item *enough*, and this item can only occur at this place. All other items expound the first temperer element. In the above potential structure specification the element f has two potential places in structure, to allow for the alternative ordering of scope and finisher as in (1) and (2) below.

(1) he is as happy with the outcome as you are
(2) he is as happy as you are with the outcome

As a consequence of the two possible orders, the place in structure of **f** cannot be automatically specified in the potential structure, and must be stated in a separate rule for each occurrence of the finisher.

8.2.2 Quality of Thing

Here is the first realization rule for Quality of Thing.

> 80.1 : quality of thing :
> **qlgp**

The purpose of this rule, attached to the feature [quality of thing], is to create a qlgp as the unit which fills either (a) a modifier element of structure in some nominal group, or (b) the Complement realizing the Participant Role of Attribute in relational Process clauses.

In the case of (b), the Attribute function of the qlgp, the filling relationship is straightforward. The qlgp at modifier, however, involves a potential complication, since, if scope and/or finisher elements are present, they are separated from the apex by the head of the nominal group, as in (3) (where elements of the qlgp have been italicized). The qlgp is therefore discontinuous.[1] The problem of discontinuity will be further discussed in 9.3.6.

> (3)   a *more successful* man *at business than his brother*

8.2.3 Quality of Situation

Now consider rule 80.2.

> 80.2 : quality of situation or quality of quality :
>   (a) **qlgp**,
>   (b) if not [irregular qs]
>   then **a <+ "+ly"**,
>   (c) if [quality of situation] and on mother pass
>   [manner as separate information unit]
>   then **e < ","**.

The selection of the feature [quality of situation] also creates a qlgp, but in this case it fills one of the Adjuncts in clause structure which can be filled by a qlgp. The rule for [quality of situation] is also responsible for the morphology which separates it from [quality of thing]. The general rule expressed in rule 80.2, **a <+ "ly"**, ensures that this morpheme is added to the base.[2] The morphophonological and graphological realizations are not handled by this rule; it simply produces a morphological string, e.g. *happy + ly*, and this, in turn, is processed by the 'graphological rules' component, to ensure the appropriate output. At the same time, the rule must ensure that the base form of any exponent to which *+ly* is not added to form an adverbial item is excluded from the generalization. Given that morphological affixation is determined through reference to the feature [quality of situation], exceptions are also stated through features in the negative condition on the rule.

It should be noted that this rule is not responsible for constraining base forms of adjectival Qualities such as *big, tall, blue, French*, etc., which do not have 'adverbial' equivalents with the suffix *-ly*. All such cases are covered by constraints in the system network for Quality. As was discussed amply in Chapter 7, if any Quality cannot be realized as a Manner Adjunct, it will not have the entry condition [quality of situation], and thus the feature will not be available in the relevant system.

Rule 80.2 also refers to the potential status of the qlgp as a separate **information unit** (see Tench (1991) for the basic model and Fawcett (1990) for the adaptation to the Cardiff Grammar). Manner Adjuncts, amongst other elements, may be realized as a separate piece of information from the rest of the clause in which it is located, by being given a separate information group (or 'tone group' in other frameworks). In the case of adverbial manner Adjuncts, this is more likely when the Adjunct is thematized as in (4) below.

(4)   //2- slowly //1 he walked into the room //

Subrule (b) of 80.2 makes reference to the feature [manner as separate information unit] which is an option in the Situation network, and therefore does not appear in the selection expression for the traversal of the network for Quality. For this reason, the condition specifies **if on mother pass**. This is an instruction to search the selection expression generated on the pass responsible for the unit (the clause in this case) in which the quality group fills an element of structure.

Note, finally, that rule 80.2 also applies to the feature [quality of quality]. This allows for embedded quality groups which fill the temperer element in the quality group.

8.2.4 Seeking Quality

80.4 : quality sought:
a < "how".

The option [quality sought] represents a brief incursion into the network for Quality. If Quality is 'sought' through the use of the 'interrogative adverb' *how*, rather than by expressions such as *what kind of*, then the only role of the Quality network is to offer this option and to realize it as in the rule above.

8.2.5 Exponence rules

In the Cardiff Grammar, the realization of elements of structure in items is referred to as **exponence**. Within the qlgp, items that **expound** the **apex (a)** are those which are traditionally classed, in word class terms, as either adjective or adverb. The item is an adjective if the quality group fills a modifier or an Attribute, and an adverb if the quality group fills a Manner Adjunct. This is essentially what a word class is, a set of items which share the same distributional properties. As this distribution is represented by the distribution of the apex as an element of the quality group, and of the quality group in terms of what it fills in other structures, the labels 'adjective' and 'manner adverb' are redundant in the Cardiff Grammar syntactic description. The simplest form of an exponence rule involving the apex is:

83.33 : low cheap : **a < "cheap"**.

Rule 83.33 on the feature [low cheap] states that the apex is expounded by the item *cheap*. Exponents of the apex are typically **morphologically free forms** in that they may appear in the output string in precisely this form. Under certain conditions, i.e. when [quality of situation] is co-selected, or when comparison or superlativization is expressed, the relevant morphological item (+ly, +er, +est) will be affixed. The conditions and operations involved in these cases are described in 8.2.8. The item that directly expounds the apex is, in one sense, the 'base' morpheme. Items that are affixed to the base are also considered partial exponents of the apex, and their status as **bound morphemes** is signalled by the presence of "+", as in **a <+"+ly"**.

8.2.6 The exponence of *good* and *bad*: a complex morphological case

The adjectives *good, bad* and the adverb *well* are clearly not covered by the general rules for the morphology of adverbs, comparative and superlative forms. The items *better, best, worse* and *worst* must therefore be realized through the individual rules on the respective features. Conditions on the rules make reference to features in the TEMPERING network, such as [greater degree c], [multi s], etc., which are features in the systems for comparatives and superlativization (to be described in Chapter 9). Most of the labels will be self-explanatory, in the context of the item realized, but note that [dual s] refers to cases of 'dual superlatives' such as *the better of the two candidates.*

83.11 : pos good :
    if [quality of situation] and not [greater degree c]
    then **a < "well"**
    else (if [greater degree c] or ([dual s] and [maximum degree])
    then **a < "better"**
    else (if [multi s] and [maximum degree]
    then **a < "best"**
    else **a < "good"**)).
83.12 : neg bad :
    if [quality of situation] and not [greater degree c]
    then (**a < "bad"** , **a <+"+ly"**)
    else ([if greater degree c] or ([dual s] and [maximum degree])
    then **a < "worse"**
    else (if [multi s] and [maximum degree]
    then **a < "worst"**
    else **a < "bad"**)).

The complexity of the two rules above is indicative of the difference between **informal rules**, as expressed in a descriptive grammar (e.g. Quirk *et al.* 1985 or COBUILD), and the formal, explicit rules which are required in generative grammars.

8.2.7 Polysemy, homonymy and exponence

As we saw earlier, in Chapter 7, there are numerous cases of polysemy and homonymy in all areas of English lexis, where a single form realizes more than one sense.

In the Cardiff Grammar, the realization operation specifying word form items is repeated only when they expound elements from different units. Thus, for example, the item *light* will appear as an exponent of (a) the Main verb in the clause, (b) the apex in the quality group, and (c) the head in the nominal group. Within the network for Quality, however, the two homonymous senses of *light* (*light* versus *heavy*, which is represented by the feature [positive light], and *light* versus *dark*, with the feature [low range light]), and any senses of either, will share the same exponent. This is done very simply by allocating the same realization rule to the various senses. Thus the exponence rule for the item *light* is:

84.41 : **positive light** or **low range light** : a < **"light"**.

8.2.8 Inflectional morphology

Adjectives typically form their comparatives and superlatives – in terms of how the temperer is realized – according to their syllabic structure. As a general tendency, all trisyllabic and longer adjectives use the 'periphrastic form' (tempered by *more/most*), whereas monosyllabic adjectives use inflectional morphology (*+er/+est*). One class of exceptions to this tendency, with regard to trisyllabic adjectives, is that in which the first syllable is the prefix *un-*, such as *unhappy*. These tend to follow the pattern of their bisyllabic bases, e.g. *happier* and *unhappier*. In the case of monosyllabic adjectives, most can use the periphrastic form, although as Quirk *et al.* (1985: 461–3) observe, this usage is more common in the predicative function and followed by a *than*–expression. On the other hand, a number of common adjectives (e.g. *small, wide, great, young,* etc.) are limited to inflectional comparative forms.

With bisyllabic adjectives, the question is even more complex. Those that most readily take inflection, as an alternative to the periphrastic construction, are adjectives ending in unstressed vowels (e.g. *early, easy, mellow, narrow, able,* etc.), so the criterion is again phonetic. Others, such as *worn* and *wounded*, have exclusively periphrastic comparatives, here on the basis of their participial origin.

Another important consideration is the status of any adjective as primarily 'gradable' or 'non-gradable'. In principle, if an adjective is non-gradable it cannot be tempered, and thus does not participate in comparative constructions. Secondary senses of non-gradable adjectives – typically those that are used with a classifying function, as discussed in Chapter 7 – often allow tempering, including comparison, as example (5) illustrates.

(5)   He is more French than the French themselves

As *French*, here, is epithetic rather than classifying, it is gradable, but its primary association with the classifying function appears to prohibit the use of the inflectional comparative.

The problem for lexicogrammatical generation is therefore how to control the application of the two forms of comparison. If the main criterion is length, in terms of syllable count, then the realization rules must make appeal to word phonology. As with some types of derivational morphology, it is difficult to know, in human processing terms, whether a general rule is in operation, or whether each case is learnt separately. Without some intuitive guidelines, speakers would be unable to make decisions when faced with using adjectives for the first time in comparative constructions. In the case of longer, less common and 'esoteric' adjectives, many speakers may never have been exposed to, or have no memory of exposure to, comparative forms. On the other hand, it is perhaps implausible that an exact 'syllable count rule' is in operation.

The solution adopted in the Cardiff Grammar, as with derivational morphology, is to handle all instances on an individual basis and to consider any general rule to be inductive.

Yet the problem does not end here. We have observed above that there are three categories of adjectives to be accounted for: (1) those that exclusively use the periphrastic comparative, (2) those that are exclusively inflectional, and (3) those that accept either construction. Constraining those under (1) and (2) is unproblematic, since there is effectively no speaker choice. They will simply conform, without exception, to a rule which determines which of the two comparative forms is required. Those under (3) are, however, problematic precisely because there is a degree of choice. The exact nature of the choice involved is not clear, although it would seem to be linked to stylistic or aesthetic concerns, rather than to differences in meanings.

One possible solution to this problem is, however, proposed in the framework of the Cardiff Grammar. As has been noted above, exponence can be affected by conditions on rules of the type **if [a] then a < "x", if [b] then a < "y"**. Thus, in the case of Quirk *et al.*'s (1985) observation that tempered comparatives occur more often with monosyllabic adjectives in *than* constructions at Attribute, the use of appropriate conditions such as 'if [quality as attribute] and [comparison explicit]' would lead to the use of periphrasis rather than inflection.

Alternatively, choice could be represented systemically, where applicable, in terms of two features, say [comparison by inflection] versus [comparison by periphrasis], each leading respectively to rules governing the two constructions. This approach would be sanctioned if the stylistic or aesthetic criteria were more fully understood, and, rather arguably, incorporated in the semantics of the lexicogrammar. In the absence of such criteria, the systemic alternative is not adopted. As a consequence, and for technical reasons, each adjectival item is specified uniquely for either the periphrastic or the inflectional construction.

The current solution to the 'temperer versus inflection' problem involves the application of subrules which are signalled in the exponence operation for individual senses. The status of each item, with reference to its comparative form, is stated as a simple opposition between 'inflection' and 'non-inflection', this being expressed by the subrule indicators 'infl' and 'non infl'. These are present in the body of each rule, as illustrated below:

83.33 : low cheap :	**'infl',**	a < "cheap".
83.76 : pos interest interesting :	**'non infl',**	a < "interesting".

The subrules for 'infl' and 'non infl' are described below.

8.2.9 The 'infl' subrules

Both adjectives and adverbs participate in comparative and superlative constructions. Manner adverbs, however, with the notable exception of *fast*, do not inflect after their adverbial suffix. They thus conform to the general pattern for Qualities which take *more* as a temperer. As a consequence, the feature [quality of situation] in the subrule below leads to the subrule 'non infl' and this neatly captures the generalization. If [quality of thing] has been selected, the 'infl adj subrule' applies.

> 'infl':
> (a) if [quality of thing] then **'infl adj subrule'**,
> (b) if [quality of situation] then **'non infl'**.

Before we come to this subrule, consider examples (6) and (7).

> (6) This apple is the bigger of the two
> (7) This apple is the biggest of them all

The 'infl adj subrule' below distinguishes between 'dual superlatives' and 'multiple superlatives', exemplified by (6) and (7) respectively. The exponence of the determiner by *the* is handled under the rule for **superlativization** and is discussed in Chapter 9. Dual superlatives share the *+er* inflection with comparatives, as part (a) of the subrule indicates.

> 'infl adj subrule' :
> (a) if [greater degree c] or ([dual s] and [maximum degree]) then
> **<+"+er",**
> (b) if [multi] and [maximum degree] then **a <+"+est".**

We turn now to the 'non infl' subrule. Unlike inflectional comparatives, the meanings of [greater degree s], [dual s] and [maximum degree] are not conflated with the adjectival apex. The exponence rules therefore specify that the temperer is to be expounded by the items *more* and *most*.

'non infl' :
(a) if [greater degree c]
then **t < "more"**,
(b) if [maximum degree
then (if [multi s] then **t < "most"**,
if [dual s] then **t < "more"**).

8.3   CONCLUDING REMARKS

The realization rules required for the system network for Quality do not constitute a special case. No realization operation is required here that is not already employed in other parts of the lexicogrammar. With the exception of the morphology for irregular items, most rules in this network are simple exponence operations.

However, the rules on features for meanings realized at scope and finisher, together with some meanings at temperer, are rather more complex. These are cases where the element in question is not directly expounded by an item, but is filled by another unit. They therefore involve re-entry into the network and the preselection of relevant features. The realization rules attached to features in the subnetworks for meanings realized at scope, finisher and temperer are discussed and described in the following chapter.

NOTES

1   As I have indicated elsewhere, in Section 9.3.6, discontinuity of this kind is a problem for 'rank-based', top-down natural language generation, yet in terms of the **mechanism**, rather than linguistic theory. The issue, in respect of qlgp discontinuity, is essentially as follows. The structure of the ngp is determined by traversal of the network for Thing, and the application of rules attached to features in this network. If the ngp includes a modifier, the structure of the qlgp which fills this element is built on a subsequent traversal of the network for Quality. And if options in meanings are then expressed at finisher and/or scope, they must be inserted at some place **after the head** of the nominal group, rather than at the place occupied by the modifier. This means either (a) anticipating the requirement of a place for the scope/finisher, during the generation of the ngp, or (b) returning to the ngp at a later stage to insert the scope/finisher element. Both solutions are problematic with the current computational mechanism of the Cardiff Grammar. If, as in (a), the scope/temperer is anticipated, then the meanings must be realized during the traversal of the network for Thing, despite the fact that they concern options in the network for Quality. If, on the other hand, the meaning at scope/finisher is realized during the traversal of the network for Quality, the scope/finisher element cannot be inserted into an ngp which has already been built. Since, as I have emphasized, these are problems of computational mechanism, I shall not pursue the matter further here.

2   The feature which acts as a negative condition on the application of adverb morphology is here expressed as [irregular qs]. This feature is a useful expedient which obviates the need to include all irregular adverbial forms as conditions to the rule. Any

feature in the network which corresponds to an irregular adverb form is an entry condition to a **gate** which has the sole feature [irregular_qs] as an outcome. Thus features such as [pos good], [neg bad], [fast], etc. which lead to the exponence of *good, bad, fast,* etc. specify [irregular qs] as a **dependent feature**.

9. Aspects of the lexicogrammar of Quality

9.1 INTRODUCTION

In this chapter we take up the discussion of the functions of tempering and scope, originally introduced in Chapter 5, and propose system network solutions to the various phenomena. The chapter falls into two main parts: (a) a discussion of **tempering** and (b) a proposal for an extension to the Cardiff Grammar in relation to **scope**, exemplified by the specific complementation potential of the Quality sense realized by the item *angry*, including a discussion of expressions such as *be worried about*.

9.2 THE MEANING POTENTIAL OF TEMPERING

9.2.1 The general nature of tempering

This section describes the system network for TEMPERING QUALITY, which expresses the potential for meanings realized at **temperer** in the quality group. (The three subclasses of temperer were described and discussed in Chapter 5.)

A number of factors must be taken into consideration in developing the lexicogrammar of tempering. First, not all adjectives have the same potential for tempering. There is a general correlation between the gradability of adjectives and the potential for premodification. Indeed, this is self-evident, given that tempering is largely concerned with expressing a 'degree of Quality'. Thus non-gradable adjectives, at least in their core sense, are not tempered by degree (cf. Allerton 1987: 21). In theory, however, non-gradable adjectives may be tempered by the adjunctival temperer as in *an **apparently foreign** presence*.

Secondly, tempering exploits a number of resources, which were listed in Section 5.6.3. In broad terms, these can be divided into: (a) expressions associated with degree, e.g. *very, too, quite, extremely, this, that, two inches*, etc., and (b) expressions which introduce the range of meanings associated with Quality itself, e.g *absurdly long, generously kind, apparently blameless*, etc. As these two general types may co-occur in the quality group, two separate elements of structure, the **degree temperer (t^d)**, and the **adjunctival temperer (t^a),** were set up (see Chapter 5). This distinction is not always a clear-cut one. A number of type (b) expressions have, over time, come to be used as type (a) with a consequential weakening, and eventual loss, of their core Quality sense. They therefore fall into the class of degree temperers. This is the case with temperers such as *frightfully good* and *terribly important*, which are no longer directly associated with original senses. It is often difficult to establish whether such cases have become completely associated with 'degree' or 'intensity', or whether they still retain something of their original sense. An example of such an expression is *unbeliev-ably*, as in *unbelievably stupid*. The extent of transfer can be measured by the extent to which a paraphrase such as (2) is entailed by an expression such as (1).

(1)   he is unbelievably stupid
(2)   his stupidity is unbelievable

A more reliable test of their status, as we saw in Chapter 5, is whether or not they co-occur with the more common degree temperers such as *very, too, rather*, and the comparatives and superlatives. This would seem to settle the question of *unbelievably* in (1), since although the paraphrase in (2) is compatible with (1), expressions such as *very unbelievably stupid, extremely unbelievably stupid*, are at best odd.

Thirdly, there is the question of the complex relationship of semantic classes of temperers to the semantic classes of adjectives. This is essentially a question of how the potential for Quality senses can be exploited for the purpose of tempering other Quality senses. Furthermore, numerous collocational patterns are also observable (Johansson 1993: 46).

9.2.2 Gradability and degree temperers

Allerton (1987: 18) observes that to postulate a basic distinction between grad-able and non-gradable adjectives is an over-simplification. He argues the need for three basic subtypes of degree intensifier, together with four cross-classified subtypes. The three subtypes he terms 'scalar', 'telic' and 'absolute'. Scalar degree intensifiers are 'those which indicate parts of a mental scale of assess-ment of degree', e.g. *extremely, very, pretty*, etc. Telic intensifiers are those that 'relate the actual degree of the adjectival quality to the degree required for a particular purpose', e.g. *easily, hardly, barely*, etc. Finally, absolute degree intensifiers 'emphasize that the degree of the adjectival quality is genuinely within the range required by the "superlative" type of adjective with which they occur' (e.g. *absolutely, utterly, totally*) (Allerton 1987: 20). Allerton also suggests a similar tripartite classification of adjectives: 'scalar' (e.g. *big, bright*), 'telic' (e.g. *sufficient, perceptible*) and 'absolute' (e.g. *huge, gorgeous*). He also recognized four further types, such as 'scalar-telic' (e.g. *noticeable, late*) and 'telic-absolute' (e.g. *dead, possible*), on the basis that they co-occur with more than one type of degree intensifier. With this classification of intensifiers and adjectives, Allerton is able to account for their co-occurrence patterns with classes of adjectives. Thus, he observes that 'while *beautiful* occurs with both *very* and *absolutely*, the purely scalar *pretty* occurs only with *very*, and the purely absolute *gorgeous* only with *absolutely*'.

The importance of Allerton's typology is not so much that it throws further light on the semantic classification of 'degree intensifiers', but that it provides further evidence of other semantic features by which Quality senses can be classified. Allerton does not present an overall classification of adjectives, as does Dixon (1982), or as is presented in the network for Quality described in

Chapter 7. The examples with which Allerton illustrates his categories of 'telic', 'scalar', 'absolutive', etc. cut across the categories in the network for Quality. His approach therefore offers us a means of **cross-classifying** Quality senses. As we saw in Section 6.6, cross-classification is an essential aspect of system network approaches to meaning. If his classification is valid for the whole range of Quality senses, with the exclusion of classifying Qualities, then it suggests a way forward to modelling their tempering potential. The primary classification of senses in the network for Quality does not, on its own, account for this potential. To take an example, the items *beautiful, pretty* and *ugly* are clearly closely related in terms of expressing 'aesthetic evaluative Qualities'. Yet, despite their semantic relatedness, they have a different tempering potential, as Allerton points out. It may well prove to be the case that the range of features in such systems – especially when they indicate a scale from the 'absolute positive value', e.g. *beautiful*, to the 'absolute negative value', e.g. *hideous* – correlate in a regular fashion with categories such as Allerton's. Further work through corpus investigation is required to establish the extent of such a correlation.

Other subclassifications of degree intensifiers have also been proposed. Quirk *et al.* (1985: 445) distinguish between amplifiers (e.g. *awfully, downright,* etc.) and downtoners (e.g. *almost, fairly*). Spitzbardt (1965), reported in Johansson (1993), analyses degree adverbs in terms of 19 semantic fields which fall into two main spheres: a 'predominantly objective-gradational sphere' (*largely, lightly, completely,* etc.), and a 'predominantly subjective-emotional sphere' (*attractively, exquisitely,* etc.). Again, I would suggest that all such classifications are ultimately related to the semantic properties of the Quality senses themselves. As with Allerton's classification, the above distinctions require further investigation if they are to provide significant categories by which to capture the relationship between Quality and tempering senses.

9.2.3 Other classes of temperers

In work based on the LOB Corpus, Johansson (1993: 40–6) recognizes a number of different semantic categories of temperer other than those indicating degree. He is careful to emphasize, however, that the task of classifying such expressions is far from straightforward and that this classification is not exhaustive. Johansson classifies temperers under the following headings:

- degree and extent: (discussed above)
- emphasis: e.g. *clearly different, positively embarrassing*
- manner: *agreeably spontaneous, arrogantly proud*
- time: *the ever delightful blacksmith, its once formal gardens*
- space: *internationally famous, locally resident*
- viewpoint and respect: *academically barren, politically relevant*
- evaluation of truth: *apparently blameless, seemingly authoritative*
- basic and typical Qualities: *a basically evil policy, typically British*
- value judgement: *acceptably small, frighteningly true*
- Quality and state: *calmly reasonable, gravely compassionate*

It is apparent from Johansson's classification that such semantic types cover the full range of Quality senses available for use as temperers. Yet this is the point that Johansson misses. The network for Quality itself, as I have pointed out, provides the basis for the potential for tempering. Most of the examples given in Johansson's classes above appear in the network for Quality, both as adjectives and as adverbs. As this is the case, and as such items derive their senses from their Quality sense, as represented in the network, or in whatever classification one sets up, it is surely preferable to understand the nature of this 'primary' categorization, rather than to establish a 'secondary' one for temperers alone. Clearly, degree temperers, as I have emphasized, are either items whose senses are almost exclusively associated with degree, e.g. *very, so, too*, etc., or are Quality-derived senses that now function as such, and are unrelated with the original Quality sense, e.g. *terribly, awfully*, etc. Other senses used in adjunctival tempering, however, can be seen to draw directly on the potential for Quality, which must already be in place, given that tempering senses are a function of Qualities and not the converse. As will be explained in 9.3.1, the potential for tempering that is available through the network for Quality initially involves re-entry into this network.

As I have suggested above, the complexity of 'temperer–apex' co-occurrence clearly indicates the impossibility of positing a system network for TEMPERING QUALITY which is simply entered simultaneously with the system network for QUALITY TYPE as shown in Figure 7.3. The potential for tempering associated with an individual Quality sense is determined both by its 'primary' semantic classification and by other less apparent factors, such as those suggested by Allerton's classification.

A major task in the development of the lexicogrammar of Quality tempering concerns, therefore, the **preselection** of appropriate classes of temperer according to some relevant semantic classification of individual Quality senses. This degree of delicacy has not yet been attempted in the current Cardiff Grammar, principally on the grounds that extensive work is required in both (a) understanding the semantic classification that determines the tempering potential and (b) developing the lexicogrammar accordingly for a considerable number of senses. Such relationships can, however, be modelled using the available architecture of the Cardiff Grammar, so that the implementation of a substantial network for Quality tempering is simply a matter of time. The particular range of temperers available for selection for any Quality sense or class of senses can be expressed through **preferences rules** on features in the system network for Quality. The effect of these rules is to guide and determine the selection of appropriate features in the network for TEMPERING QUALITY.

The current lexicogrammar of Quality and Tempering includes the following features in a small system network for TEMPERING:

(a) meanings realized as the most common degree temperers such as *very, so, too, rather*, etc.;

(b) meanings realized as comparative and superlative temperers (*more, most* and *as*);

(c) generally unconstrained re-entry into the network for Quality for selection of adjunctival temperers;

(d) meanings realized as finishers, e.g. *than he thought, as a plank of wood*).

9.3 DESCRIPTION OF THE SYSTEM NETWORK FOR TEMPERING QUALITY

9.3.1 Initial systems

The system network for TEMPERING QUALITY is entered from the network for Quality. It is only entered for those classes of Quality which can be tempered. The feature specification 'TEMPERING QUALITY' therefore appears as a dependent system, to be entered simultaneously with other systems, wherever the entry condition permits (see Chapter 7). Furthermore, given the complexity of temperer–apex relations referred to above, constraints need to be placed on options in the Tempering network on the basis of the varying potential for individual senses. As Figure 9.1 shows, temperable Qualities may either be tempered or remain untempered, or alternatively, tempering may be **sought** (expounded by the item *how*, as in *how arrogant is he?*).

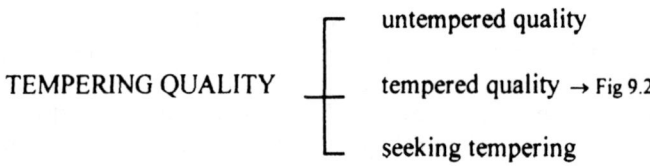

TEMPERING QUALITY
- untempered quality
- tempered quality → Fig 9.2
- seeking tempering

Figure 9.1. Initial systems in the network for TEMPERING QUALITY

Tempered Quality then selects from one of the three classes shown by the features in Figure 9.2. The feature [tempering by quality] involves re-entry into the Quality network. The items selected in this case are therefore considered to expound the apex of a further quality group which fills the temperer, even though it may be argued that in this context they cannot themselves receive any modification.[1]

As I emphasized in 9.2.3, tempering senses selected on the basis of re-entry into the Quality network do not require to be expressed as a separate system network, since the Quality network itself expresses the semantic potential which is available.

The selection of [by quality] in the system for TEMPERING QUALITY leads to the preselection of the feature [quality of quality] in the system for QUALITY ROLE, as discussed in Chapter 7. This ensures that only those Quality senses

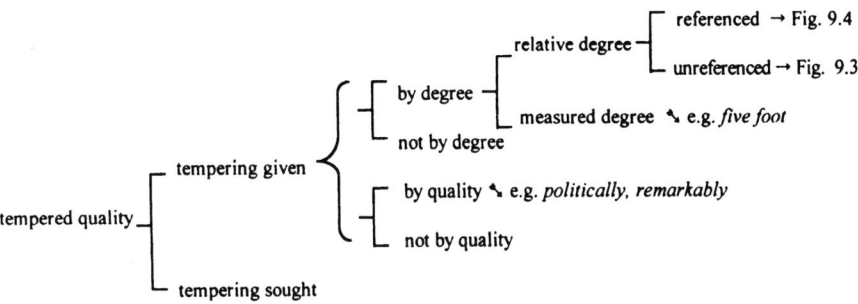

Figure 9.2. The system network for [tempered quality]

which have adverbial forms are selected, as is the case for Quality of Situation.

The feature [measured degree] introduces the potential for certain Qualities – notably dimension Qualities – to be tempered by expressions of measurement, such as ***three feet high*** or ***two miles wide.***

The remainder of the discussion of the network for TEMPERING QUALITY concerns the common degree temperers, and options in comparison and superlativization.

9.3.2 Degree

The subnetwork for tempering by degree is given in Figure 9.2. As the initial system shows, degree tempering presents a choice between [relative degree] and [measured degree]. The feature [relative degree] then leads to a system where the options are [unreferenced degree] (Figure 9.3) and [referenced degree] (Figure 9.4). The feature [referenced degree] involves tempering which makes some reference, either implicit or explicit, to some other phenomenon. Such tempering senses imply **comparison, superlativization, sufficiency** (with respect to some purpose) or **result**. Options in the system for [unreferenced degree] are the common degree temperers such as *very, too, fairly*, etc.

The high-frequency degree temperers constitute a set of meanings almost exclusively associated with their tempering role. Unlike temperers expressing Quality, and adverbs functioning as Adjuncts in clause structure, the set of degree temperers either have no basic Quality equivalent (e.g. *very, rather, quite, so*, etc.) or have assumed a different meaning from the basic equivalent (e.g. *fairly, awfully, terribly*, etc.), as discussed above. They differ in terms of a choice between high or medium degree of intensification, which, to some extent, reflects Allerton's distinction between 'scalar' and 'absolutive' (Allerton 1987: 19). The feature terms below (originally proposed by Robin Fawcett) constitute one attempt at capturing their individual sense, although it may be felt that they do not satisfactorily do so.

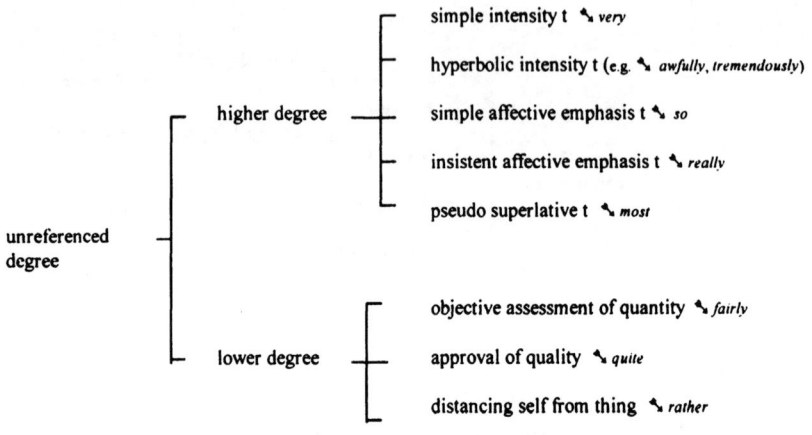

Figure 9.3. Systems for unreferenced degree

Following my proposal (presented in Section 5.6.4) for the treatment of one sense of *so* as an **emphasizing temperer**, realizing the feature [simple affective emphasis t], the item *so* is available either (a) alone with an apex or (b) in addition to other types of tempering sense. This is discussed further in 9.3.4.

9.3.3 Hyperbolic intensity

The feature [hyperbolic intensity] in the network above introduces the large and growing range of adverbial 'degree intensifiers' which, in this context, have become disassociated from their basic Quality sense. Examples are *tremendously, terribly, awfully, fantastically, incredibly*, etc. The main problem for their semantic classification as 'degree intensifiers' is that there often seems little difference in meaning between them beyond their association with individual speakers' idiolects. Unless any clear semantic distinction can be found on the basis of collocational behaviour, most of them are perhaps best handled as free variation choices, selected by reference to dialect, register and personal speech style.

Originally, in the Cardiff Grammar, such intensifiers were represented by features such as [pseudo amazing quantity] for *amazingly* and [pseudo terrifying quantity] for *terribly*. Such feature labelling is misleading, however, given the complete loss, in most cases, of association with the original adverbial sense, as can clearly be seen with *terribly* and *awfully*.

9.3.4 The emphasizing temperer

The emphasizing temperer was introduced in Section 5.6.4 in order to account for expressions such as *so very aware*. This additional emphasis is unavailable for temperers such as *too, fairly* and *quite*, or for comparative and superlative

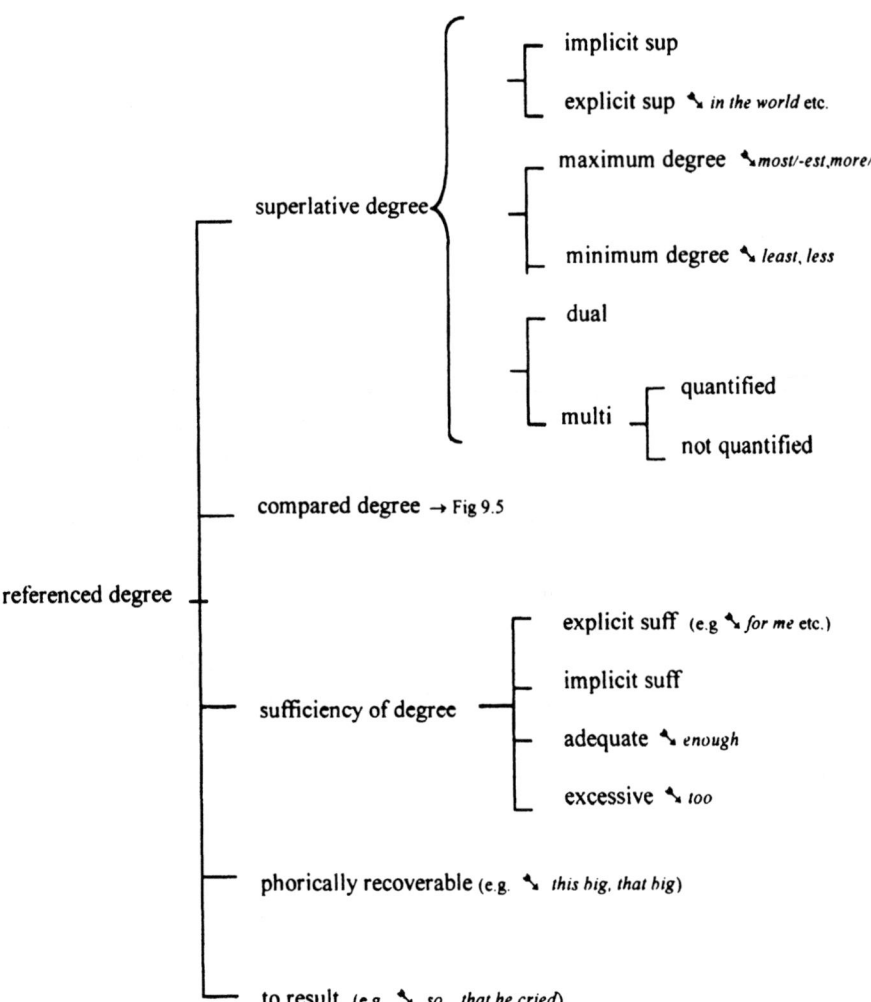

Figure 9.4. Systems for referenced degree

tempering. It must therefore be specified only as a further option with those classes of temperer which accept it. This system with its complex entry condition is given in Figure 9.5.

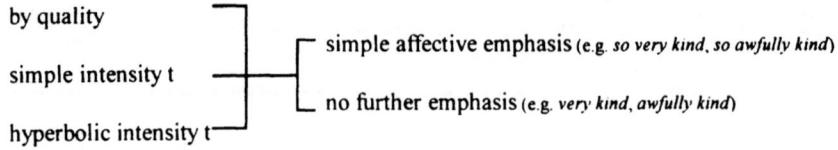

by quality

simple intensity t

hyperbolic intensity t

— simple affective emphasis (e.g. *so very kind, so awfully kind*)

— no further emphasis (e.g. *very kind, awfully kind*)

Figure 9.5: The system for temperers accepting further emphasis through *so*

9.3.5 Referenced degree

Besides indicating a degree of Quality by giving a scalar value, the degree may be indirectly indicated by reference to some other phenomenon. The temperer items *more, most, less, least, as, so, too* and *enough* have this function. Each of these is inherently associated with some other information which allows the relative degree to be interpreted. Yet they differ from other degree temperers in not directly assigning a scalar value. This is evident, especially in the case of dimension Qualities, from the examples below.

(3)   It's not very big, but it's bigger than the other
(4)   It's not very big, but it's too big to fit this hole
(5)   It's not very heavy, but it's heavy enough for the purpose

The exception to this is *so*, which, like its [simple affective emphasis] sense, does assign a degree of intensification. Thus the oddness of (6).

(6)   ?It's not very heavy, but it was so heavy that it broke the bag

The information with which these degree terms are referenced falls into three categories:

(a) reference to a standard: in the case of comparison and superlativization
(b) telic reference: in the case of temperers of sufficiency
(c) reference to result: in the case of *so*

In all cases except [to result], the standard or purpose may be implicit or explicit. If no result is provided with *so*, it can only be interpreted in its [simple affective emphasis sense]. The possibility of an **explicit** standard or purpose, and the **obligatoriness** of result, motivates the inclusion of a **finisher** element in the componence of the quality group, as was discussed in Chapter 5. In all such cases, therefore, the respective systems must provide for re-entry to the network in order to generate appropriate expressions, such as *big enough **for our house**, so big **that it wouldn't fit***, etc.

The lexicogrammar of finishers clearly demands re-entry to the system network to generate meanings realized through embedded clauses or prepositional groups, and this is a major area of research in its own right. The treatment of such phenomena in respect of the Cardiff Grammar is explored in Tucker (1992).

9.3.6 Temperers in the quality group at modifier in the nominal group

The discussion of tempering so far has been exemplified by quality group structures which express the Participant Role of Attribute in the transitivity of the clause. If we now turn our attention to the quality group filling a modifier in the nominal group, two further obstacles become apparent. The first of these concerns discontinuity between the apex and finisher as in (7), and between apex and scope as in (8). Elements which follow the apex in the quality group also follow the head of the nominal group. The problem of discontinuity was first raised in Section 8.2.2.

(7)   a *more difficult* book *than the other*
(8)   a *difficult* book to *read*

The second concerns the relative ordering of the apex and the quantifying determiner $a(n)$ when certain temperers are selected as shown in (10) compared to (9).

(9)   This is a difficult book
(10) ˙   This is too difficult a book

This is further compounded by the fact that the temperer *so*, in both its senses discussed above, may be replaced by the form *such*, which is separated from the apex by the determiner as in (12).[2]

(11)   She is so nice a person
(12)   She is such a nice person

Discontinuity of this kind does not present a problem for systemic syntactic description. Crossing branches in structural descriptions are fully acceptable in this approach.[3] Within a ranked-based approach to language generation, however, problems do arise. This is primarily due to the fact that structures are generated in a **top-down** direction. In the case of the phenomenon under attention here, the structure of the nominal group is built **before** the structure of the quality group embedded within it. As we have seen, the choice of a temperer such as *so* and *too* may lead to the presence of finisher and scope elements that occur **after** the head of the nominal group.

The solution adopted in the Cardiff Grammar, for cases of discontinuity, involves anticipating any options which may arise in subsequent re-entry of the network to fill an element of structure with another unit (such as the quality group at modifier) and which affect the structure of the unit in which they are embedded. Thus, the kind of meaning expressed by *too* must be anticipated in the system network for Thing in order to place part (at least) of the quality group before the determiner. The same applies to the placing of finisher and scope elements after the head of the nominal group. This is by no means an ideal solution, since it requires considerable duplication of systems for Quality in the network for Thing. An alternative approach – one which will need to be explored in the future development of the Cardiff Grammar – would be to postpone the final componence of the 'higher' structure until later options involving the 'lower' structure have been made.

However, it should again be emphasized that the current problem with discontinuity is a question of the mechanism required for computational generation rather than a problem for systemic description.

9.3.7 Tempering and comparison

The option to make explicit the **standard of comparison,** as shown by the system for COMPARISON EXPLICITNESS in the network in Figure 9.6, involves (a) re-entry into the network, (b) the further selection of features and (c) the building of embedded structures. This part of the lexicogrammar, which involves the expression of meanings at finisher, is described and discussed in detail in Tucker (1992). The discussion of comparatives is limited here to one general observation – that all three subtypes of comparison shown in Figure 9.6 accept a similar set of structures at finisher as illustrated in (13)–(18).

(13)   more important than the first one was
(14)   less important than the first one was
(15)   as important as the first one was
(16)   more handsome than him
(17)   less handsome than him
(18)   as handsome as him

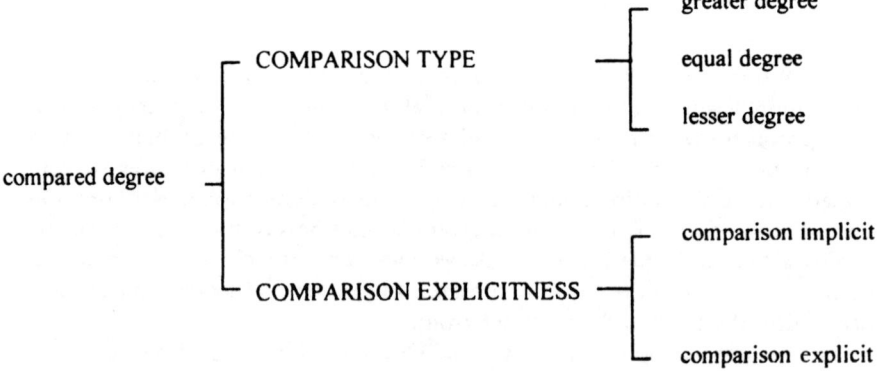

Figure 9.6. The system network for compared degree

This generalization is captured through a single network for COMPARISON EXPLICITNESS. The only essential difference between the types of explicit comparison is between *than* or *as* which introduce such constructions. The choice of one of the three types of comparison will, however, be affected by the same markedness principle as was discussed in Chapter 7, with reference to antonym pairs such as *old/young, tall/short*, etc. In comparing age, for example, the unmarked expressions *younger, older, not as young as . . .*, are preferred to the marked (and patently odd) expressions *less young, less old.*

9.3.8 Superlativization

The system for superlative degree allows for both 'dual superlatives' (e.g *the larger of the two*) and 'multi superlatives' (e.g. *the largest of all*). Superlatives, as I argued in Chapter 5, are considered to be structures realizing a class of determiner, (d^s), within the nominal group. As a consequence, the accompanying deictic determiner is considered to be an element of structure of the quality group and is generated at the same time as the Quality sense marked for superlativization, either inflectionally or periphrastically, with the overt temperer *more* or *most*. It was also argued that quantification preceding the Quality, as in *the three most important*, is also a function of the quality group. The system network for superlative degree therefore includes an option for quantification. Given that quantification is redundant in the case of dual superlative degree, the system depends on prior choice of [multi] (superlative degree), as is illustrated in the system network in Figure 9.4.

9.4   REALIZATION RULES FOR TEMPERING

9.4.1 Simple exponence and finishers

The realization rules for temperers typically involve a simple exponence operation of the type:

89.11 : simple intensity :
   t^d < "very".

For those tempering senses that select for explicit completion of reference at **finisher,** re-entry and preferences are specified by realization rule. Where a range of options is available, these are first expressed in the dependent system network and the respective realization rules stated as a consequence of the features selected. This is the case with comparatives and with *enough* and *too*. In the case of resultative *so*, the finisher is obligatory, and is realized as a clause of the proposition type, i.e. a *that*–clause as in: *so large that I had to wrap it separately.* Given the obligatoriness of both finisher and the clause structure which fills it, this may all be expressed in the same rule, together with the exponence operation for *so*.

89.4 : referenced to result:
   (a) t^e < "so",
   (b) **for f re-enter at referent,**
   (c) **for f prefer [situation, subordinate, proposition sit].**

9.4.2 Superlatives

The assignment of either morphological inflection (e.g. *larger/largest*) or of the separate temperer *more/most* for superlative degree is handled by the **inflection subrules** (described in Chapter 8). These subrules are attached to each sense in the Quality network through the terms 'infl' and 'non-infl'. They make reference in their conditions to the presence of [superlative degree] in the selection expression produced during the traversal of the network for TEMPERING QUALITY. Any morphologically irregular forms of super-latives (and comparatives), e.g. *good, better, best*, are stated in the individual exponence operations for such Quality senses. What remains to be stated in the realization rules in the network for TEMPERING QUALITY is: (1) the inser-tion of the determiner **d**^{qld}, and its exponence by *the*, and (2) re-entry and pre-selection of features for the quantifying determiner **d**^{qlq}, if this has been selected.

89.3 : superlative degree :
    (a) **dqld < "the"**.
89.32 : quantified superlative :
    (a) **for dqlq re-enter at [entity]**,
    (b) **for dqlq prefer [quantity]**.

9.5   SCOPE AND ADJECTIVE COMPLEMENTATION

9.5.1 The complementation of adjectives

In Chapter 5 we considered the structural complexity of adjective complement-ation, which is handled in the Cardiff Grammar through the inclusion of one or more of the scope elements (sc) in the structure of the quality group. Although the term **scope** may be considered inadequate as an umbrella term for the various types of complementation, it will be retained here.[4]

The notion of scope is related to adjective complementation in particular and complementation of heads of structure in general (cf. Quirk *et al.* 1985: 1220ff, Huddleston 1984: 305ff, Jackendoff 1977). Apart from the case of adject-ives such as *averse (to x), conscious (of x)*, where it is obligatory, scope constitutes an extension in meaning potential through providing the speaker with the means of giving additional information other than expression of the Quality itself. Thus, for example, a speaker may choose either simply to say that he or she is *happy* or to specify the source of the happiness. Moreover, because of the transitivity-like nature of apex-scope structures, in certain cases a number of dif-ferent options are available to the speaker. The range of options involve a num-ber of embedded structures filling the scope element. They are summarized by Quirk *et al.* (1985: 1120) as the following:

- Complementation by a prepositional phrase
- Complementation by a *that*–clause
- Complementation by a *wh*–clause

- Complementation by a *than*–clause
- Complementation by a *to*–infinitive clause
- Complementation by an *ing*–participle clause

As with the verb complementation, scope is a feature of individual adjectives or, at best, of classes of adjectives. In a functional approach to this phenomenon, one would expect the scope patterns of individual Qualities to reflect the meanings that they express. This is the case with items such as *angry*, which is discussed below. In the case of Qualities such as *answerable, close, similar,* the unit that fills the scope element is restricted to a prepositional construction which is headed by a uniquely specified preposition – *to* in the case of the above. There is therefore no semantic choice involved other than that between expressing or not expressing the meaning realized through a scope element.

The system network for Quality must therefore provide a further degree of delicacy, making explicit the range of meanings that may be expressed through scope, and specifying the realization rules necessary to generate the appropriate structures. The following section explores the modelling of scope with one Quality sense in particular, that realized by the adjective *angry*, selected because it provides an example of the range of possible scope patterns which express further meaning potential.

9.5.2 The scope of *angry*

A reasonably exhaustive range of scope types associated with *angry* is given in examples (19)–(25) below.

(19)   I am angry
(20)   I am angry about the government's education policy
(21)   I am angry about what they're doing to primary schools
(22)   I am angry about having to shake hands with the Minister
(23)   I am angry with/at the Minister
(24)   I am angry with/at the Minister for suggesting such a policy
(25)   I am angry that the Minister has not resigned

The range consists of scope by prepositional group with the prepositions *about, at* and *with*, and *that*–clause scope as in (25). The preposition *about* may be followed by a 'fused relative construction' (Huddleston 1984: 402), e.g. *about what they're doing to primary schools*, an *ing*–participle clause, e.g. *about having to shake hands with the Minister*, a nominal group, e.g. *about the government's education policy*.

9.5.3 The system network for the scope of *angry*

Let us now return to the relevant part of the system network for Quality described in Chapter 7, repeated here as Figure 9.7. The feature [angry] is located in the sub-network for Qualities of emotion. The first consequence of

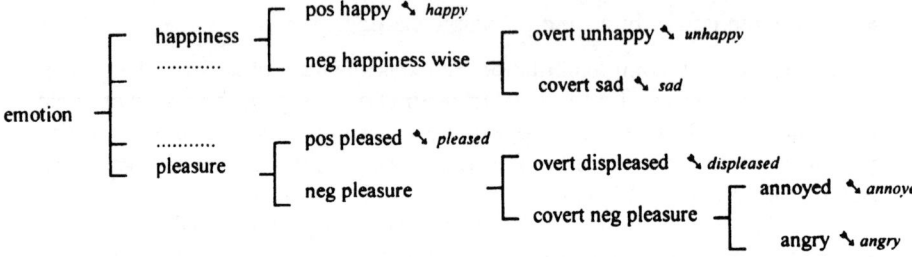

Figure 9.7. The sub-network for emotion wise Quality

the selection of this feature is the application of a realization rule which states that the item *angry* expounds the apex of the quality group. It further specifies the item as 'infl', thereby ensuring the generation of forms such as *angrier* and *angriest*, if the feature is co-selected with features relating to comparative or superlative meaning.

In one sense, the feature [angry] is a **terminal feature**. In this specification of the lexical resource, at least, there are no further distinctions reflected in the choice of lexical item. The feature [angry] is already in systemic opposition to [annoyed]. One would wish to claim, of course, that there are other fairly synonymous expressions, such as *pissed off*, but this introduces the interpersonal motivation for lexical choice and could be treated as a realization of [angry] determined by the co-selection of the feature [casual] or [intimate] in the TENOR system. In another important sense [angry] is not a terminal feature, since its selection must provide for the specification of the meanings that can be expressed at the scope element of structure. To emphasize one of the major claims of this work, scope is very much a part of the overall lexicogrammar of Quality.

The feature [angry] is therefore an entry condition to the system in which meanings relating to scope are expressed. Further features must be specified, however, in order to constrain entry to this system. Scope is restricted to the Attribute function of the adjectival quality group and is thus precluded as an option for the group at modifier in the nominal group, as example (26) illustrates.

(26)   *He is an angry man about the government's educational policy

Similarly, adjunctival expressions of Quality are not associated with this kind of scope. The features [quality as attribute] and [quality of thing] also constitute the entry condition along with [angry] to the system of SCOPE EXPLICITNESS.

The first general option in all such systems concerns the choice between expressing some meaning realized through a scope element or leaving it implicit. This raises the question of whether or not all senses expressed as adjectives at Attribute have scope options available to them. If such options are generally available, it can be argued that the system of SCOPE EXPLICITNESS is entered and selected from simultaneously with initial systems leading to Quality senses. Fawcett's examples of scope (Fawcett 1974–6/81), discussed in Chapter 5, suggest that many more adjectives associate with this type of meaning than is usually considered to be the case. The adjective *fat* in example (27) is not generally considered to take scope, yet Fawcett analyses *around the waist* as scope, therefore suggesting its similarity to more representative scope patterns.

(27)   He is too **fat around the waist** to wear his best trousers

If we accept Fawcett's inclusion of such expressions within the general category of scope, then clearly the option is available with a large number of the classes of adjectival Qualities recognized in Chapter 7. Moreover, this type of expression is not restricted to adjectives at Attribute, as (28) illustrates.

(28)   He is too fat a person around the waist to wear that kind of clothes

For present purposes we shall assume that scope is sense-specific, and consequently to be handled on the basis of individual senses, and as the network in Figure 9.8 shows, the system of SCOPE EXPLICITNESS is entered as a consequence of the selection of individual features. Similarly, the explicitness of the scope must be specified through the feature [scope explicit]. These are therefore the conditions under which further choices become available.

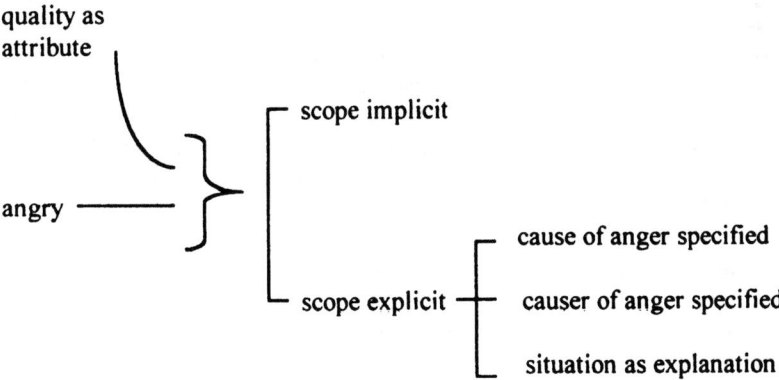

Figure 9.8. The system network for the scope of *angry*

The first system offers three choices leading to the generation of scopes of the kind: *about X, with/at X* and *that X*.

As the system for [scope explicit] and examples (20)–(25) suggest, there are three basic meaning options. Anger is caused by some event, which is often some form of act for which there is a (typically human) agent. We may thus express anger by reference either to the event itself or to the agent considered responsible for it. The first option, [cause of anger specified], involves a prepositional expression with *about*, the second, [causer of anger specified], a prepositional expression with *at* or *with*.

Alternatively, we may wish to present the event as an explanation for the anger, [situation as explanation], through a *that*-clause. Note that the cause may be expressed nominally, as a completive of the preposition element in a prepositional group. Typically, in this case, the nominal group contains an **event noun** associated with material or mental Process types. In other cases the presence of a concrete or abstract noun requires some pragmatic interpretation. The prepositional group *about the wall* in (29) will be understood to mean something like (30).

(29)   I'm angry about the wall outside my house
(30)   I'm angry about the council's building a wall outside my house

As we observed above, *about* may introduce a 'fused relative construction' (*what*-clause) or an *ing*-clause, with or without a Subject, as well as a nominal expression.[5] The choice of expressing the cause either as a Thing or as a Situation is therefore dependent upon the preposition. This may be modelled in one of two ways. First, the Thing or Situation option may be expressed systemically within the subnetwork for SCOPE EXPLICITNESS as a system dependent on [cause as scope], by the features [cause as thing] and [cause as situation]. Similar features will be necessary in the network for [**minimal relationship plus thing**], where prepositional meanings and their 'complements' are realized through the elements of structure **p(reposition)** and **cv (completive)**. The option selected would therefore involve a rule which indicated re-entry into the **minimal relationship plus thing** network and preselection of the corresponding feature there. This would ensure that the subsequent re-entry for the completive element would generate a nominal group or a clause respectively. The structural output for this generation is given in Figure 9.9.

Secondly, the choice of Thing or Situation could be left entirely dependent on the meaning realized by the preposition *about*, with no reference being made in the network for SCOPE EXPLICITNESS. In this case, the single terminal feature [cause as scope] would be associated solely with a re-entry statement into the network for [minimal relation plus thing]. There appears to be little significant difference between either alternative. The former is perhaps less economical, since, as was suggested, the option of completing the preposition with a nominal group must in any case be available for the meaning of the preposition *about*.

The second option entails specifying the causer of the action which provokes the anger as in (23) above. This is expressed again as a prepositional group headed by either *at* or *with* and with a completive filled by a nominal group (e.g. *with/at Mr Patten*). In (20) and (21) the causer may also be present, but as the Subject of the clause in which the cause is expressed. The prepositions *at* and *with* identify the causer unambiguously. The choice of the preposition *about* in

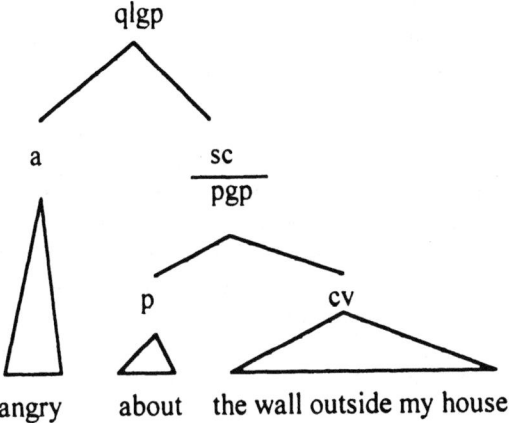

Figure 9.9. Analysis of *angry about the wall outside my house*

a Clause such as (31), on the other hand, does not entirely disambiguate the role of *John* in the situation at the root of the anger.

(31)   I'm angry about John

Without further information, *John* is open to interpretation as a victim in the unexpressed situation, or as the causer. In foregrounding the causer, a further option becomes available through a system which allows specification of the Situation for which the causer is responsible. This system is shown in Figure 9.10.

As in (24), the optional addition of the cause, in this case, takes the form of a prepositional group with the preposition *for* and the completive realized in an *ing*–clause. Note that this expression is only possible if the [causer of anger specified] option has been taken. Thus we do not find examples such as (32).

(32)   *I am angry for breaking the glass

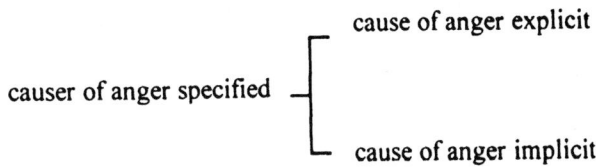

Figure 9.10. The system for adding cause to causer

195

The problem for the analysis of examples such as (24) is whether to treat the two prepositional groups as one expression filling the scope element, or to consider them as separately filling different scope elements. This problem is raised by Huddleston (1984: 307) and was discussed earlier, in Chapter 5. One solution would be to consider expressions such as *the minister for suggesting that standards are dropping* as a structure that can fill a completive in a prepositional group. This seems counter-intuitive, since the expression represents neither a possible nominal group structure nor a clause structure. The expression is therefore treated in the same way as a lexical verb with a 'double complement', with the causer and cause expressions filling a first scope element (sc1) and a second scope element (sc2) respectively. The realization rule on [cause explicit] must therefore include (a) a statement of re-entry into the network for Minimal Relationship Plus Thing to generate a prepositional group, (b) the preselection of the appropriate features to ensure the realization of *for*, and (c) the realization of the completive element as a non-finite clause. As the completive is filled by an embedded non-finite clause, further re-entry must be stated in the Minimal Relationship Plus Thing network in order to allow the obligatory clause structure to be preselected in the network for Situation.[6]

9.5.4 Realization rules for scope

As noted above, the purpose of realization rules for scope is to specify re-entry into the network for Minimal Relationship Plus Thing and the preselection of the appropriate prepositional meaning. No further specification is necessary at this point. The features that determine the nature of the completive as a Thing or Situation are expressed within the network for Minimal Relationship Plus Thing. A sample rule for [cause of anger specified] is given below.

> cause of anger specified :
> **(a) for sc1 re enter at [entity],**
> **(b) for sc1 prefer [thing, minimal relationship plus thing, subject mrpt].**

Given the range of meanings and uses of prepositions, it is notoriously difficult to arrive at an acceptable feature label with which to represent them in the system network. Here the label [subject mrpt] has been adopted for *about* on the basis of its general meaning, which can be roughly paraphrased as 'on the subject of'.

A simplified system for prepositions is given in Figure 9.11 in order to illustrate the option of Thing or Situation on the feature [subject mrpt].

In this network, the feature [subject mrpt] bears a rule which expounds **p** with the item *about*. The features [subject as thing] and [subject as situation] bear rules which specify re-entry and preselection in order to fill the **cv**. These rules are exemplified below.

> subject mrpt:
> **p < "about".**

subject as thing :
    (a) for cv re enter at [entity],
    (b) for cv prefer [thing].

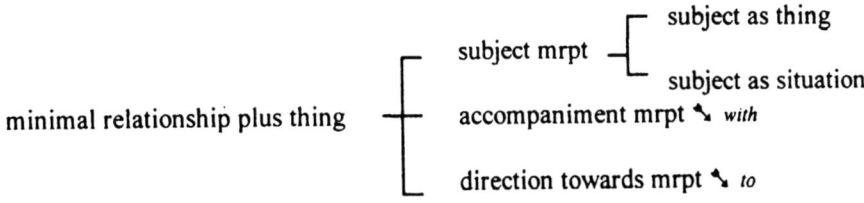

Figure 9.11. A highly simplified network for Minimal Relationship Plus Thing

9.5.5 Wh–questions and the scope of *angry*

A common feature in contemporary English is the 'fronting' of the wh–element associated with completive of prepositional group at scope, thereby inserting it into the structure of the clause. This is illustrated by (33) and (34) below.

(33)   What are you so angry about?
(34)   I'm angry about that broken window

Unless we were to adopt an analysis that treats *be angry about* as a single complex lexical item, we would be forced to model discontinuity in the prepositional group that realizes the scope element in the quality group. The potential structure of the prepositional group must allow for a single **p** element without a following **cv**, when the **cv** is a wh–element. However deeply embedded the prepositional group is, the wh–element **cv** will be inserted at the beginning of the highest clause, as is illustrated by (35).

(35)   What did Caroline think that John said Howard was worried about?

Where the completive is 'sought', discontinuous prepositional groups of this kind constitute the norm in contemporary English, despite prescriptive attempts to disparage this practice. Indeed, it would be difficult to accept (36) below as an alternative to (33), except in the usage of a speaker deliberately attempting to conform to the prescriptive rule according to which 'one should never end a sentence with a preposition'.

(36)   ?About what are you so angry?

The solution proposed in the Cardiff Grammar for the 'completiveless' group is to posit a structure **pgp*cv**.[7] The asterisk indicates that the completive is absent from its typical place, but appears elsewhere. The **cv** is in fact directly inserted into the structure of the higher clause at the place assigned for this purpose, as is shown in Figure 9.12.

Whilst the structural description in Figure 9.12 is largely unproblematic, the

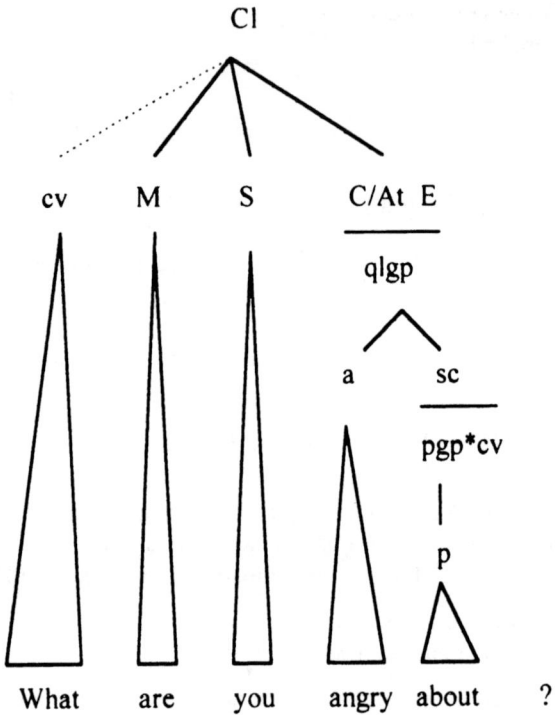

Figure 9.12. An analysis of discontinuity in the prepositional group at scope

generation of such a structure in terms of the necessary system network and realization rules is not. Firstly, the **cv** is not an element of structure of the clause, even though it must be inserted directly into the clause. Secondly, the **cv** does not fill the Attribute of the clause; this is an Attributive relational clause which has a quality group filling the Attribute, and this completive comes lower in the structure of that quality group. The wh–completive does, however, affect the structure of the clause in requiring the **Operator** (here *are*) to be inserted in its pre-Subject position. Semantically, the clause realizes the MOOD option of 'new content seeker', where the new content sought is the completive of the preposition *about*. The MOOD feature [new content seeker] must therefore be selected on the first traversal of the network for Situation, in order to guarantee the appropriate **Operator placement**. Unlike simple content-seeking clauses such as (37), the interrogative pronoun *what* is not an exponent of an element of structure in the clause.

(37)   What do you want?

It cannot, therefore, be realized by preselection in the network for Thing.

9.6   CONCLUSIONS

This chapter has highlighted the variety of meanings which are associated with the temperer, scope and finisher elements of structure in the quality group, and which modify or extend the meanings of the Qualities found at the apex. Each choice of a Quality sense brings into play further options of the kind discussed and illustrated here. The full lexicogrammar of Quality is therefore constituted by the interaction between all the subnetworks described above, together with the Quality network described in Chapter 7.

Both **interaction** and **dependency** are crucial. While it is possible, in theory, to describe the separate components as parallel or simultaneous networks, in reality, choices in meaning from one subnetwork are often constrained by choices made in another. In essence, it is the individual Quality sense, or some subclass of senses, which determines further choices in terms of tempering and scope. We are reminded yet again of Sinclair's notion of the unique lexicogrammar of an individual word. The full extent of the dependency relations which this notion presupposes cannot, of course, be modelled on the basis of our current knowledge of individual lexical behaviour. Yet in a lexicogrammar rich in meaning potential and equipped with formal means for constraining choice and expressing relative preferences, there should be no insuperable obstacle to gradually refining the description.

NOTES

1   An alternative solution to this problem, if we reject the analysis of an embedded quality group, is to treat all quality senses used as a temperer as direct exponents of the element **t**. This would require a condition on the realization rule of the type:

> factual :   **if [quality of quality]**
> **then t < "factual" else a < "factual".**

2   It could be argued that *such* expounds an element in the nominal group rather than in the quality group, given that it has this function in expressions like: *such a person should be admitted.* This solution, if it is accepted, does not, however, solve the discontinuity in the case of *so nice a person.*

3   In transformational grammar approaches, structural descriptions cannot contain crossing branches. For a discussion of crossing branches see Radford 1988: 120–2. Radford proposes a formulation of this constraint in the following way:

> NO CROSSING BRANCHES CONSTRAINT
>> If one node X precedes another node Y, then X and all descendants of X must precede Y and all descendants of Y (A is a *descendant* of B if A is dominated by B) (Radford 1988: 121)

4   One might be tempted to label such an element **complement (c)**, but this is already used, albeit with an uppercase letter, for Complements in clause structure.

5   I take the position here that forms such as *about* are prepositions, even though they can be completed by a clause structure. As Huddleston (1984: 340) observes, the question

of whether such forms are prepositions or conjunctions is problematic and a satisfactory solution to their classification has not been arrived at in grammatical theory.

The fact that the Cardiff Grammar does not make use of word class or part-of-speech labels does not obviate the problem. In the terms of this description, prepositions, as word classes, are items which expound the **p** element of structure, which is a functional specification, and subordinating conjunctions expound the **B** (Binder) element of structure in the clause. The analysis of *about having to shake hands*, therefore, can be analysed in two ways. In the first, *about* is treated as a **B**, introducing a non-finite clause, and consequently there is no further embedding, since *about* is a component of the clause. In the second, *about* expounds the element **p** in the prepositional group, and *having to shake hands* is a non-finite clause filling the **cv** (completive) element in the group. In the Cardiff Grammar, this means providing for further **re-entry** into the network for Situation, in order to generate the non-finite clause structure.

In the present work the second position is adopted. The two clause-like structures after *about*, namely *ing*–clauses and 'fused-relative clauses', are themselves completives which are considered, along with Huddleston (1984: 340), to be peripheral clause structures with clear affinity with nominal expressions (e.g. *I am angry about my having to shake hands*). Other items such as *until* would still need both analyses in the proposed framework, since, unlike *about*, they introduce finite clauses, as well as nominal structures (e.g. *I won't leave until he arrives* and *I won't leave until the morning*). Even non-finite *ing*-clauses with *until* differ from those with *about*, as is seen from the oddity or unacceptability of **I won't leave until his arriving*.

6   The complementation of *angry* is a good illustration of the centrality of **re-entry** and **preselection** in the Cardiff Grammar. The original selection of [angry] in the network for Quality, together with the selection of features relating to its scope, imposed considerable constraints on the structure of units through which the scope is expressed. As we have seen, there is restricted, or obligatory, selection, not only for the preposition but also for the structure of clauses which may fill the completive. Such constraints can only be imposed by re-entering subsequent networks and preselecting the features which lead to the structures in question. Clause structure is determined by the network for Situation, but without preselection; the full range of meanings (and therefore the full range of clause structures) would be available. An unconstrained system network would then produce ill-formed embedded clauses such as:

(f1) I am angry at John for John has been careless

Constraints arising from a systemic choice can therefore be seen to percolate down through the structure being built, via preselections in the various networks (and so embedded units) which are necessary to account for the structure.

7   This solution, originally suggested by Clive Souter of the University of Leeds, is comparable to the 'slash feature convention' of Generalized Phrase Structure Grammar (Gazdar *et al.* 1985: 12).

10. The syntactic environment of the quality group: nominal group modification

10.1 INTRODUCTION

We move away from the internal structure of the quality group to consider the role of the group in its **filling** relationship with elements of structure of other units in the lexicogrammar. Given the emphasis on adjectival lexis throughout this book, the discussion here will be restricted to the 'adjectival' quality group. In Chapter 4 we listed both central and peripheral roles of the Quality Group in this respect. They are repeated below.

(a) Pre-head modifiers in nominal structures (*a big parcel*)
(b) Complements of a copula in clause structure (*he is kind*)
(c) Complements expressing the result of the process denoted by the verb (*he shot him dead, he pulled the tooth loose*)
(d) Postpositive modifiers of certain types of nominal expression (*something nice*)
(e) Complements of prepositions (*in short, for good,* etc.)
(f) Premodifiers of certain adjectives (*pale blue, red hot*)
(g) Adjuncts in clauses (*I'm receiving you loud and clear*)
(h) Contingent adjective clauses (*Strange, I never suspected him*)
(i) Supplementive adjective clauses (*Soaking wet, he walked into the room*)

As was made clear in Chapter 7, the organization of the system network for Quality must reflect any variations in both meaning and structural potential as a consequence of the role it plays in different structures. Notable examples of this are the differences in the potential of the quality group to serve as modifier or Attribute. Furthermore, as the Quality network also represents the potential for Manner Adjunct expressions, similar constraints must be expressed for the potential of Quality senses to be used either adjectivally or adverbially. The range of structures which are filled by an adverbial Quality group will be mentioned only briefly here. In general, this class of Quality group will fill a Manner Adjunct in clause structure. Quality groups which are used to modify adjectives in temperer–apex structures were discussed in Chapter 9.

Of the nine filling functions listed above only types (a), (b), (c), (d) and (f) have so far received attention within the Cardiff Grammar. Moreover, with the exception of (a), filling the modifier element in nominal group structure, little need be said about the lexicogrammar of the units which the quality group fills. The major part of this chapter will be concerned with the Quality group at modifier, given the important relationship between modifier sequences and the organization of Quality senses.

10.2 FILLING REVISITED

The structural relationship of **filling** was introduced in Chapter 3. It is, essentially, the relationship between an element of structure of one (class of) unit and the structure that is used to realize the specific meanings selected for that element. It allows, importantly, the lexicogrammatical description to distinguish between the function of a (class of) unit, in terms of its own componence and its external function, determined by its environment. Thus, once the quality group has been described in terms of its own structure and the meanings it realizes (as was done in Chapter 5), it is then possible to specify the role of this structure elsewhere in the lexicogrammar. This may be stated for the adjectival quality group as below. It may also be expressed syntactically, as shown in Figure 10.1. The quality group may fill:

(a) the modifier element (m) in the structure of the nominal group
(b) the Complement element of structure (C) in Attributive Relational Process clauses
(c) the Main Verb Extension (Mex) in certain types of Process.

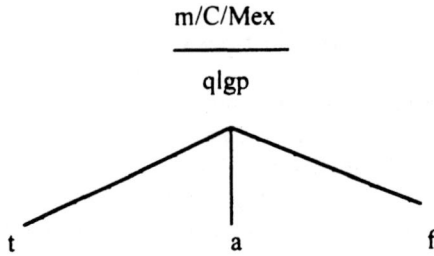

Figure 10.1. The filling relationships for the adjectival quality group

10.3 THE QUALITY GROUP AT COMPLEMENT IN RELATIONAL CLAUSES

One option in the system network for Attributive relational Processes is the feature [attribute as quality]. This is in opposition to [attribute as thing] where the Complement is filled by a nominal group. These two types are illustrated in (1) and (2).

(1)   Howard is happy
(2)   Howard is a happy man

The feature [attribute as quality] is accompanied by a realization rule which specifies re-entry into the Quality network, and the preselection of at least the features [quality of thing] and [attribute as quality]. As was explained in Chapter 7, these features are always preselected from other parts of the network, and it is through their function as entry conditions to features in the network for Quality that the potential for occurrence in this syntactic environment is stated. In interrogative clauses, such as (3), where the degree of Quality is sought, pre-selection is again necessary to ensure that tempering is selected, and that the temperer is expounded uniquely by *how*.

(3)   how happy are you now?

It is when it fills the Attribute in a relational clause that the quality group may exhibit its full structural potential, and therefore the full meaning potential expressed in the system network for Quality. The only constraint on this potential is the exclusion of the range of Quality senses which only have a modifier function. Such senses are exemplified by adjectives such as *utter*, *sheer* and *total*, all of which collocate strongly with certain subclasses of Thing senses, e.g. *disaster*, *flop*, etc. A number of Quality senses of the **domain** class in their basic sense are also unlikely to occur as Attributes, which is seen in the oddness of (4).[1]

(4)   ?this disaster is economic

Furthermore, in its Attribute function the quality group is never discontinuous, as it may be in the modifier function, as shown in (5).

(5)   a more important man than I imagined

Options involving a scope are constrained when the quality group is in the modifier function, as illustrated by (6) and (7).

(6)   the man was extremely unhappy with the result
(7)   *he was an extremely unhappy man with the result

Finally, unlike Quality senses at modifier, there is no ordering principle associated with more than one Quality senses at Attribute. This does not mean that a series of Quality senses may not follow the order typically found in modifier sequences, but that, if they do, they are always co-ordinated, as illustrated in the comparison between (8) and (9).

(8)   It was a large red wooden box
(9)   The box was large, red and wooden

10.4 THE QUALITY GROUP AS 'RESULTATIVE COMPLEMENT'

Adjectives commonly occur in English as a Complements of a Main Verb, where they indicate the resultant state or quality brought about by the Process itself. Amongst the numerous examples are: *tear x open*, *shoot x dead*, *drive x mad*, *scrape clean*. A number of solutions have been proposed for their analysis (e.g. Halliday 1967, Fawcett 1987, Ferris 1993). The question will not be pursued here beyond indicating the current Cardiff Grammar analysis. In brief, following Fawcett (1987), the relational clause analysis is extended to all such Processes, on the grounds that the same Participant Roles are involved in each case. Thus both *He made her happy* and *He painted the shed green* have an **Agent** (*he*), an **Affected-Carrier** (*her/the shed*) and an **Attribute** (*happy*).

On the other hand, cases such as *push open, shoot dead,* etc. exhibit two main characteristics that *make... happy, paint... green,* etc. do not. First, they are associated with two places in the structure of such clauses, either directly following the Main verb or following the **Affected** Participant role, as in (10) and (11) respectively.

(10)   he tore open the envelope
(11)   he tore the envelope open

Second, such expressions are typically associated with apex-only quality groups, especially when the Attribute directly follows the verb.[2] This, however, depends essentially on the nature of the Quality sense, and on the distinction between the 'causative' and 'resultative' types of construction. With the former type, the full range of tempering and scope options appears to be possible, as in (12).

(12)   She made him so very happy to be alive

These two characteristics suggest that the *tear... open* and *shoot... dead* cases should be analysed as a Main Verb + Main Verb Extension.

10.5   THE QUALITY GROUP AT MODIFIER IN THE NOMINAL GROUP

10.5.1 The centrality of the modifier function in modelling Quality senses

The most complex and problematic filling relationship that the quality group enters into is with modifier elements of structure in the nominal group. Despite the fact that this phenomenon primarily concerns the structure of the nominal group, which is not central to the purpose of this book, it is given detailed consideration here for a number of reasons. First, the modifier function of the quality group is itself a primary function, alongside the Attribute function. Second, the modifier–head relationship in the nominal group reveals a great deal about how Quality senses are related to Thing senses. Third, the typical ordering of premodifiers in sequence reflects certain functional and semantic aspects of the classification of Quality senses. Finally, the potential of other word classes in such modifier sequences throws some light on the similarities and differences between adjectives and other word classes.

In this section we examine the range of modifiers and propose a number of **modifier functions,** which are realized in the structure of the nominal group in a sequence that is relatively fixed. The different types of modifier recognized here are those which are found necessary to classify, identify and describe the various semantic classes of **Thing** which are realized as the lexical head of the nominal group. Various aspects of such sequences are discussed, including the principles governing the stereotypical ordering of modifiers, the distinction between **sequence** and **co-ordination** in respect of such meanings, and the nature of nominal and verbal modification. At the end of the section, the lexicogrammar of nominal modification within the Cardiff Grammar is described.

10.5.2 Overview of modification

As we have observed, the **modifier** function of the quality group is a primary function of the group. This function is indicated in the system network for Quality by the feature [quality as modifier]. Its place and function as an initial system in this network were described and discussed in Chapter 7. It is well known that in English a number of adjectives may be found in sequence, and that this sequence is typically not broken grammatically by the use of co-ordinating conjunctions.

The presence of some form of preferred sequential ordering of adjectival classes is an argument for considering that this phenomenon falls within the domain of lexicogrammar. It can of course be argued that sequences such as that in (13) are syntactically well formed, and that therefore the oddness of the ordering is of a purely semantic nature.

(13)   a green large cabbage

Furthermore, (13) may be perfectly acceptable in a world where size constitutes an important means of subclassifying cabbages.

Given the syntactic and semantic similarity of the expressions in the sequence, one solution to the problem of modelling this phenomenon might be to consider it an instance of co-ordination. This approach immediately runs into problems on several counts. In the first case, the absence of co-ordinating markers, such as conjunctions, or commas in the written language, suggests that it is not co-ordination. We would want to exclude strings such as (14).

(14)   *a large and green cabbage

Secondly, co-ordination does occur, but apparently when the adjectives involved belong to the same semantic class. And in such cases it is obligatory. Thus, in example (15), the membership of a particular semantic class of Quality which is shared by *intelligent* and *sensitive* requires that some overt marking of co-ordination be present.

(15)   an intelligent and sensitive person

Finally, there is general agreement that co-ordination typically occurs between two identical syntactic categories or units.[3] Given the presence of not only adjectival but also verbal and nominal elements in pre-head sequences, adherence to the 'same category' principle would rule out a model that related them by co-ordination.

Thus, although the phenomenon of sequential relations is semantically determined, it exploits the syntagmatic axis for linguistic realization. Even if we were to simply posit a syntagmatically recursive element of structure – call it **m**(odifier) – which might be expressed in terms of nominal group structure as $d < m_i < m_j < m_n < h$, we would not have solved the question of stereotypical ordering or indeed that of the possible number of modifiers permitted. These questions, the first especially, would have to be addressed in some conceptual or semantic component. The clear danger of this approach is that the explanatory power of the grammar is severely weakened. The ordering of surface strings must be a prime concern of any theory of language.

So far, the problem has been expressed in terms of modifier sequence involving adjectives. It is further complicated in at least two important ways. The first is the fact that nominal and verbal elements are also exploited to express modifiers of nouns. Thus for example we have strings such as the one in example (16).

(16)   a poorly delivered election address

Secondly, the adjectives, nouns and verbs present in such strings are themselves 'modifiable', giving rise to embedded structures such as (17).

(17)   a very important customer assistance service

It is clear that the items *important* and *assistance* in the example above are in fact heads of some other unit which intervenes between the element of structure in the nominal group and the lexical items themselves.

To summarize, an explicit grammar of English must provide for at least the following aspects of this phenomenon:

(a) the number and types of modifier (i.e. elements in the nominal group which express modifiers of the head noun)
(b) the preferential or stereotypical nature of this ordering
(c) the meanings of and reasons for alternative ordering
(d) the exploitation of members of the lexical classes of adjectives (in a quality group), noun (in a nominal group) and verb (in a clause) for the purpose of expressing such modifiers
(e) the place of embedded structures of which adjectives, nouns or verbs are the heads
(f) the difference between co-ordinated structures and straight sequence

10.5.3 Descriptive accounts of the phenomenon

A purely syntactic approach to the phenomenon which does not have recourse to semantics or semantic functions can have little to say. One notable attempt from the early transformational generative tradition is Vendler's (1968) account. This is based on the nature of the transformations which he maintains are inherent in the relationship between adjective and head nouns. Vendler claims that these transformational relationships correlate to a high degree with the derivational morphology of the adjectives. If we take this approach one step further, we can say that those transformational relationships may be motivated by the functional relationship between modifier and head word.

In descriptive accounts, ordering is generally considered to be semantically determined (as in Dixon's 1982 and 1991 accounts of semantic classes of adjectives). Halliday (1994) suggests progression along scales: from more subjective to less subjective, from qualitative to classificatory, from less permanent to more permanent modifiers. Other explanations are of a similar nature, but usually concentrate on the central adjectival classes (age, colour, shape, substance, etc.) and deal separately with other types of modifier (cf. Aarts and Aarts 1982, Sinclair 1972, Muir 1972, Quirk *et al.* 1985, Hetzron 1978).

Another explanation explored by Frawley (1992), drawing on work by Kamp (1975) and Siegel (1980), involves the notions of 'intensional' and 'extensional' modification. In Frawley's words (1992: 497–8): 'A modifier is intensional if, in its modification of a domain, it makes essential reference to the characteristics that comprise the denotation of the domain', whereas an extensional modifier 'makes reference to the domain as a whole, whatever its constituent properties'. Thus, for Frawley the modifiers *old* and *dark* (poorly lit) differ in respect of *house* in that *old* is interpreted according to the general domain of age as a whole, and is extensional, whereas a *dark* house 'is such by virtue of its constituent features, like lighting, windows, and so on'. The conclusion that Frawley arrives at is that intensional modifiers precede extensional modifiers. Intensional modifiers denote properties further away from those denoted by extensional modifiers. This approach has some explanatory power, and it appears to work well for Frawley's examples. But it fails to account for certain typical ordering. Why, for example, does *old* typically precede *red* as in an *old red car*, when, according to Frawley's classification, both are extensional? Neither age nor colour is a property of cars by virtue of the constituent features of cars.

There is, quite naturally, general agreement on stereotypical ordering of adjectives among most scholars, even if a number of different explanations are given, and this present account will not differ significantly in this respect. What is new here, however, is an attempt to bring together, in terms of ordering, all lexical and phrasal manifestations of modification, including modification through **nominal** and **verbal** expressions.

10.5.4 The structure for ordered modifier sequences

In structural and functional terms, adjective sequences are a phenomenon pertaining to the nominal group. The nominal group on the rank scale of units parallels and realizes 'Thing' on the semantic rank scale. Elements of structure of the nominal group serve to realize the kinds of meanings which are associated with the expression of Things. Amongst such functions are those of definiteness and indefiniteness of referents, their quantification, degree of lexical specificity or recoverability, and other forms of modification that help in both the identification of referent Things for the addressee and the speaker's subjective orientation to them. The kinds of choices available therefore reflect Halliday's tripartite metafunctional hypothesis in which language structure represents at one-time a mapping of meanings of an ideational, interpersonal and textual nature (e.g. Halliday 1994).

The three major functions beyond lexical expression and recoverability are **definiteness/indefiniteness**, **quantification** and **modification**. Here we are concerned exclusively with the third function, although there are important parallels between the way these systems operate. The overriding principle seems to be that of **selection**. In denotational terms, the nominal lexis of a language represents the culturally significant classes of Things to which we refer in interaction. A speaker's referent may be anything between a class of Thing and a unique, definite instance of some subclass. The grammar of determiners, both quantifying and deictic determiners, allows the speaker to select out from increasingly small sets. One major function of the grammar of modifiers is to provide additional means of subclassification beyond that which is lexically available. This subclassification may be simply a straight subclassification of the class of Thing denoted by the noun, or may interact with definiteness and quantification as a means of identification or as an *ad hoc* expressive device through which the speaker communicates his or her allocation of a referent to an interpersonally motivated class.

The function of modification itself (either pre-modification through **modifiers** or post-modification through **qualifiers**) does not encroach upon definiteness or quantification, although **qualifiers** function cataphorically to help the process of recoverability signalled by the deictic determiner *the*, as in *the girl with the red hair*. What modification does is narrow the denotational scope of the class of Thing at the head of the group. On this basis, the element(s) of structure recognized to realize this function can be considered to be different from the determinative elements which serve the other functions. A referring expression may simply be a reference to a subclass, however narrowly subclassified it is, as is shown in (18).

(18)   modern lightweight vacuum cleaners with extendable leads

The functional syntax of the nominal group, as described here, therefore recognizes four basic types of element of structure: **d**(eterminer), **m**(odifier), **h**(ead) and **q**(ualifier). The function of the last of these is similar in nature to the modifier, but is distinguished in terms of its post-head place in structure and by the structures which are found there, i.e. embedded (relative) clauses and prepositional groups. This 'starter model' can be represented as in Figure 10.2, without specification of the exact number of subtypes of the elements which bear the superscript n.

Now, as was suggested above, an account of modifiers which simply specifies their potential multiplicity does not resolve the problem of ordered sequence, given that such ordering is semantically determined. The same is true of determiners. A failure to specify the relevant subtypes and the syntagmatic relationship between them would lead to the generation of clearly ungrammatical strings such as (19).

(19)   *my of three racquets

If the lexicogrammar itself is to retain responsibility for the ordering of elements, it is clear that there must be some further subclassification of the general class of both determiners and modifiers. In (19), for example, we need to specify that the system is: **quantifying determiner** (e.g. *three*) + **selector** (*of*) +

ngp

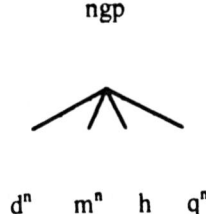

d^n m^n h q^n

Figure 10.2. A 'starter model' for the nominal group

deictic determiner (e.g. *my*). There are other types of element which serve as a precedent here, namely the types of Adjuncts in the clause and, within the nominal group, the subclasses of determiner: deictic determiner (d^d), quantifying determiner (d^q), superlative determiner (d^s), etc.

If a number of functionally determined subtypes of modifier can be recognized, we have the basis for ordering them, given the mechanism which exists for such purpose in the model as a whole. This, however, raises two problems: (1) establishing the number of subclasses that need to be recognized in order to account for all possible ordered sequences, and (2) accounting for some degree of freedom once the order of modifiers is fixed. The first of these questions is addressed in the following section.

10.5.5 Establishing the types of modifier function

What is claimed here is that any approach to the establishing of modifier subtypes must begin with an investigation of prototypical 'properties' of the various classes of Thing that are represented lexically in a language. This is a difficult enterprise without removing any rigid boundaries between lexical and conceptual semantics, if such things exist at all in their own right. Pustejovsky (1991) suggests that in order to explain the ability of speakers to interpret utterances successfully, a lexical semantic theory of associations is necessary. For this he postulates a 'theory of qualia' which consists of a number of semantic properties of lexical entries. Thus, for the successful interpretation of a sentence such as (20), it is necessary to know that books are produced by the activity of writing or used as artefacts for the activity of reading.

(20)   I've finished the book

A parallel can be drawn here with successful interpretation of the expression in (21).

(21)   a stupid idea

It is necessary to know that ideas are abstract entities, and that stupidity is a property associated primarily with animate beings – essentially humans – who exhibit cognitive behaviour. It is through our classification of ideas as mental artefacts or products that we can 're-attach' the property of being *stupid* to the creator of the idea. Part of our conceptual and lexical knowledge of Things is threrefore a set of more or less culturally useful properties for the purpose of identificational and subjective subclassification of the referents of linguistic utterances.

It can of course be argued that such concerns belong exclusively to the domain of conceptual organization, and that our choice of modifier to describe or identify a referent is determined by some kind of higher knowledge. Altern-atively, we could invoke the process of pragmatic interpretation. In this way, in the case of example (21) the interpreter would search for the most likely or most relevant association between *idea* and *stupid*, again the human creator. Sperber and Wilson's (1986) Relevance Theory, from a pragmatic viewpoint, Fass's (1986) Collative Semantics, from a natural language understanding view-point, and Pustejovsky's (1991) Theory of Qualia, from the lexical semantics paradigm, all offer approaches to the kind of interpretative process involved in (22). However, none of these approaches accounts for the sequential ordering of modifiers. Even with a set of typical modifiers, as in (22), there is a preferred ordering shared by the linguistic community which, only if modified on an *ad hoc* basis, might need some such interpretive explanation.

(22)   a large brown wooden box

In other words, our knowledge of the nature of Things and the properties that associate more or less prototypically with them is encoded in the language, both at the level of lexical semantics and at the level of structural organization.

As was pointed out above, modifiers are used for subclassification and iden-tification, and for the expression of some subjective, attitudinal orientation towards a referent. We might add to this list the function of providing informa-tion which will have retrospective or prospective usefulness in discourse. By making the statement in (23) the speaker is neither identifying *Howard* nor sub-jectively assessing him, but providing information which may prove to be useful as a basis for presuppositions in the development of the ongoing discourse.

(23)   Howard is an intelligent man

A functional theory of language attempts to relate structure to function, or at least to provide a structural environment into which the functions can be mapped and interpreted. Linear sequence is the only physically real means by which language can achieve this. Thus, we interpret what follows or precedes as functionally significant. General accounts of modifier sequence describe the phenomenon in terms of a 'more or less' scale: more or less objective, subjec-tive, permanent, identifying, etc. Such observations themselves reveal the role of sequence and the importance of early against late placing of modifiers. Yet again, apart from exceptionally marked sequences, where the speaker is exploit-ing sequence to set up *ad hoc* classification, a stereotypical order is laid down by the language itself which ultimately relates to our knowledge of Things and their properties.

Such an extensive discussion of sequences of modifiers might suggest that actual occurrences of such sequences are common. The fact is that they are not. The analyst is therefore thrown back on the scant evidence available in texts, which rarely amounts to more than two modifiers in sequence, or upon informants' judgements of whether sample orderings containing more than two or three modifiers 'feel right'. This constitutes an empirical disadvantage, but does not invalidate the claim that there is such a phenomenon. Each ordered pair of modifiers is itself evidence of a more extensive ordering principle; it is clear that members of such pairs are drawn from a number of classes of modifier. Furthermore, invented strings do find general acceptance among informants. The reason for the scant evidence is in the nature of the modifier function itself. If speakers do use modifiers for motives of identification, subclassification, personal orientation, etc., then it is clear that generally such goals can be successfully achieved with a minimal number. This would tend to conform with conversational principles of the type proposed by Grice (1975).

What is proposed here is that there is a wide range of modifier functions related to classes of Thing, and that each function is stereotypically ordered in respect of any other. At the expense of economy of description – indeed, emphasizing the semantic extravagance of language – as exhaustive as possible a set of functions will be proposed, which then serves as the general template for the ordering of any two or more. It would be foolish to lay claim to a definitive set at this juncture. Such a model must always be open to revision, capable of incorporating counter-examples as and when they are found. It is maintained, however, that the descriptive principles are sound, and that counter-examples will involve minor modifications rather than a complete revision of the principle.

This approach involves establishing which classes of modifier can be associated with what classes of Thing. Wherever possible, generalizations across different classes of Thing will be proposed. Major classes of Thing already fall out in the organization of the lexical resource. They tend to be those typically associated with superordinate categories in the semantic relation of hyponymy. Candidates are thus classes represented as systemic features such as [artefact], [human], [natural object], [abstract thing] and [event thing]. Of these, [human], in conceptual taxonomic terms, constitutes an exception, although it is clear that, linguistically, it is marked off from other life forms with 'humanness' reflected in the grammar of a language itself. We shall begin by considering the modification of artefacts.

10.5.6 The modification of artefacts

In a strongly anthropocentric world, artefacts have considerable prominence. Moreover, as cultures develop and progress, the number and specific purpose of artefacts grow. This places a strain on the lexical resource of a language, which in order to keep pace with developments must either be open to lexical innovation or provide a means of representing increasingly delicate subclassification. Artefacts are therefore a good point of departure for any discussion of modifiers. Not only are they prominent in the lexical resource, but they also exhibit considerable heterogeneity. It is perhaps for this reason that linguists' examples of modifier sequence revolve around them. Not surprisingly, they incorporate the properties of the more general class of physical objects, as well as the functional properties which single them out as a major class. We might therefore expect to find a greater number of modifier functions associated with artefacts. The following list is an attempt at characterizing such a range:

(a) what its function is
(b) what it is made of
(c) how it works
(d) what key process has been applied to it
(e) where it is found
(f) who owns or has created it
(g) for whom it is intended
(h) where it comes from (time or place)
(i) what colour it is
(j) what physical characteristics it has
(k) what age it is
(l) what dimensions it has
(m) what affective classification the speaker makes
(n) how it has been affected in some way
(o) how many there are
(p) how it relates to other Things of the same class

Whilst many of these functions are self-evident, several need explanation. The last two, (o) and (p), which would appear first in any given sequence of modifiers, have similarities with determiners. Cardinals numbers have both a quantifying determinative function and a quantificationally redundant role when preceded by deictic determiners such as (*my, the, those,* etc.). In an expression such as (24), *two* is recoverable in terms of quantification; it is not its function to say how many, but simply to reiterate a quantification which has been expressed in some previous utterance. I suggest that this is anaphorically relevant. This use can be contrasted with (25), where the cardinal number is selecting by quantification from the set of the speaker's friends. On the basis of this functional distinction, it is reasonable to set up a modifier subtype for numbers.

(24)   my (d^d) two (m) friends (h)
(25)   two (d^q) of (v) my (d^d) friends (h)

The relational function, (p), includes items such as *other* and *different*. They provide some aid to the identification of a referent Thing through direct association with some given referent. Thus, for example, in (26) some exemplar of the class *book* must be available to the interactants in order for another exemplar to be identified through not having the same properties.

(26)   give me a different book

The function expressed in (n) permits the expression of some 'affected state' of a Thing. It is realized by participial forms which relate the Thing to material

Process in the system of TRANSITIVITY. The Participant Role of Affected to which the Thing corresponds is often signalled by the presence of a Manner Adjunct with the participial Main verb form, as in (27).

(27)   a poorly maintained old bicycle

Function (d), the function of 'intendee', specifies for whom the class of Thing is intended. This involves the non-deictic use of genitives such as (28).

(28)   a (d^q) men's (m) tailor (h)

This is clearly distinct from deictics like (29) where the tailor is identified by being the one that the men use.

(29)   the men's (d^d) tailor (h)

This first function – the function of the Thing – is that most involved in cultural subclassification and re-lexicalization. There comes a point in the 'life' of certain artefacts at which they undergo some form of structural or design modification in order to serve a more specialized function. The lexis of 'cutting instruments' serves to illustrate this. Although knives and scissors are good prototypical examples of basic-level categories,[4] through the need for them to serve specialized purposes, they have developed into specialized instruments which often make them unsuitable for the generic function associated with them. A *fish knife*, for example, is of little use for most purposes for which we might require a knife as a cutting instrument. Similarly, any attempt to cut a piece of paper neatly in half with *crimping scissors* would prove unsuccessful. The change in function calls for a process of subclassification through lexical specification. This can be achieved in English through a form of modification of the Thing at head. As the examples above confirm, this can involve a verbal element indicating the function in terms of a specification of the Process in which it is a Participant, or a nominal element indicating the function, by using a Thing which represents the Affected entity. The cultural consolidation of this specialization process is often accompanied by complete lexicalization – that is, the modifying element becomes part of a compound lexical item. In many cases it is difficult to separate structures with the sequence 'modifying element + head' from those which have a compound lexical head. Word stress does not help here; *diving equipment*, which can be considered **m^{sc} (subclassification modifier) + h**, has the same stress pattern as *diving bell* or *diving suit*, which are considered by dictionaries such as LDOCE to be compound lexical items. (See Katamba (1994) for a recent account of 'compounding'.) This difficulty is reflected in contemporary lexicography, where we find variation across dictionaries in terms of whether the compound is specified as a separate entry or subsumed under the general lemma.

Thus, if we are to postulate this subclassifying function as a modifier with a separate head, we shall need to look for criteria for treating it in this way, rather than treating it as compound lexical item which is not syntactically decomposable.

By establishing these primary modifier functions we are able to propose both a number of modifier subtypes and their order in sequence. A first attempt at this is shown below, where the linguistic ordering is represented from bottom to top, terminating in the head of the nominal group.

Artefact: *torch*
subclass: *welding*
intendee:
owner or creator:
place:
material: *titanium*
mechanism: *electric/nuclear/gas*
internal property: *self-lighting*
state: *galvanized*
provenance (time or place): *Polish*
colour: *black*
physical state: *slim*
age: *new*
dimension: *big*
*quality: *useful*
*affective categorization: *fantastic*
*affected state: *poorly treated*
relative categorization: *other*

Interpreting such a nominal group may well stretch the reader's imagination and interpretative resources. Moreover, it is difficult to construct examples which contain all the proposed functions. Indeed, some functions appear to be mutually exclusive, and these are indicated by asterisks. The complementary distribution of such functions appears to be related to decisions which concern the degree of interpersonal meaning as expressed through modifiers. This is found among the earlier places in sequence, which may, in parallel with early places in the structure of the clause, have a 'thematic' flavour. Thus, once the degree of interpersonal meaning has been selected, it cannot be followed by another interpersonally motivated modifier which is in conflict with it. It is on the basis of the different nature of these predominantly interpersonally ascribed Qualities that separate functions are posited. One might argue that as the functions involved are mutually exclusive, they share the same place in structure. Yet, this would suggest that all realizations of this modifier belong to the same semantic class, and could therefore co-occur in a co-ordinated structure. If this were the case, they would not be semantically mutually exclusive.

10.5.7 The modification of other classes of Thing

What remains to be done is to set up a subclass of modifier for each of the major modifier functions and establish its place in sequence. So far, however, we have dealt only with the artefacts as a class of Thing. Before we move to a full set of modifiers we need to cross-check this already extensive list with modifier functions required for other subclasses of Thing. Although a detailed account of these will not be given here, it appears that few additions to the set established for artefacts are necessary. A general observation is that the other subclasses associate with fewer functions than do artefacts, and that most of those that are required are covered by the set which has already been proposed. Notable additions are those modifiers which refer primarily to events (or Situations), e.g **usuality** (*a frequent argument*), **likelihood** (*a possible meeting*) and **speed** (*a sudden outburst*), together with time specification, either relative (*an early arrival*) or specific (*an afternoon walk*). These represent the transfer of the meanings realized as Adjuncts in the clause to modifiers in the nominal group, as part of the process of nominalization. With regard to humans, **behavioural properties** must be added, corresponding to the feature [typically human quality] in the network for Quality and to Dixon's (1982) category of 'human propensity'.

Frames for **humans** (especially in their function as 'role') and **events** are given below.

Human being: *Colonel*
subclass: *army*
provenance: *Chinese*
state: *retired*
age: *old*
quality: *intelligent*
dimension: *little*
*affective categorization: *amazing*
*affected state: *poorly treated*
relative categorization: *other*

Event: *match*
subclass: *soccer*
time or occasion: *evening*
creator: *Bristol and District*
status: *official*
*quality of event: *quick*
*affective categorization: *awful*
*affected state: *poorly advertised*
*likelihood/usuality: *possible*
relative categorization: *other*

If a reliably accurate set of modifier functions can be established, together with a stereotypical order, we can proceed to the next stage of modelling the phenomenon. We shall therefore propose the following set of modifier functions as elements of structure of the nominal group, and their order in sequence:

m^{rel} (relative categorization) >
m^q (quantification) >

m^{ul} (usuality or likelihood) >
m^{afs} (affected state) >
m^{aff} (affective categorization) >
m^{dim} (dimension) >
m^{epi} (epithet) >
m^{age} (age) >
m^{phys} (physical quality) >
m^{col} (colour) >
m^{stat} (status) >
m^{prov} (provenance) >
m^{int} (intendee) >
m^{inpr} (internal property) >
m^{mech} (mechanism) >
m^{mat} (material) >
m^{cre} (creator) >
m^{time} (time) >
m^{place} (place) >
m^{sc} (subclassification) >
h (Thing)

10.5.8 Modifier function: epithet and classifier

The set of modifiers above has been established on the basis of the properties associated with Things and the syntagmatic order in which they are realized into the nominal group. Closer examination of typical realizations will clarify the relationship between the modifiers and the underlying semantic metafunctions which they serve. The major interpersonally oriented modifier function (Halliday's 'interpersonal Epithet') is m^{aff}, followed by the 'experiential' modifier functions (Halliday's 'experiential Epithets') m^{dim}, m^{epi}, m^{age}, m^{phys} and m^{col}. The remaining modifier functions correspond to Halliday's 'Classifier'. They are primarily concerned with subclassification of the Thing. From left to right, the sequence moves towards major subclassification culminating in m^{sc}.

10.5.9 The relationship between modifier and word classes

Three word classes are involved in the realization of modifiers: adjectives, nouns and verbs. It was observed in 10.5.2, however, that there is a more complex relationship between modifiers and the lexical items that realize them; the lexical items themselves can be 'modified', giving rise to embedded structures at modifier. Examples of the three kinds are given in (30), (31) and (32).

(30)   an (extremely interesting) film
(31)   a (good food) guide
(32)   a (efficiently managed) business

The lexical items must therefore be treated as **exponents of heads of units**, irrespective of the presence or absence of other elements of structure. As was suggested above, the relationship which links elements of one unit to a unit at the rank below, or to an embedded unit, is that of **filling**. In order to realize the appropriate items, it is necessary to fill a given modifier with one of the relevant units, that is **quality group, nominal group** or **clause**. A similarity may be noted here between the SFG approach to syntax presented here and X-bar theory in generative grammar, in which all non-head material is considered to be a maximal phrase category (i.e. an NP, ADP, ADVP, etc.).

The filling relationship, as was explained in Chapter 3, is handled through re-entry into the system network into those areas where choices are made for the expression of Situation, Thing and Quality, which are realized in the clause, nominal group and quality group respectively. There are naturally constraints on the structures of these units when they fill modifiers. Clauses, for example, are restricted to Main verb forms with **+ing** or **+en**, which may be accompanied by a preceding Adjunct or Complement, as, for example, in *a carefully preserved specimen* and *a telephone answering service*. Nominal group structure is similarly restricted, with few options available other than the lexical classification at head and the possibility of modification or quantification of the head, as in *a severe gale warning* or *a two-horse race*. As was suggested earlier, these constraints must be built into the system network itself by means of **preselection rules**, one of which is exemplified in Section 10.6. Furthermore, it is clear that the structures of such embedded groups are also restricted by the number of modifiers in the sequence. Tempering of the adjectival apex, for example, is typically reserved for the first of the modifiers, e.g. *a very pretty red dress*, although such a condition can be overridden by the phonological or punctuational fragmentation of the sequence as is exemplified in (33). The filling approach outlined above (see also a similar approach in Huddleston 1984: 257) allows us, therefore, to account for a structure such as (34) which is represented in Figure 10.3.

(33)   a very large, very solid mahogany table
(34)   a very interesting idea

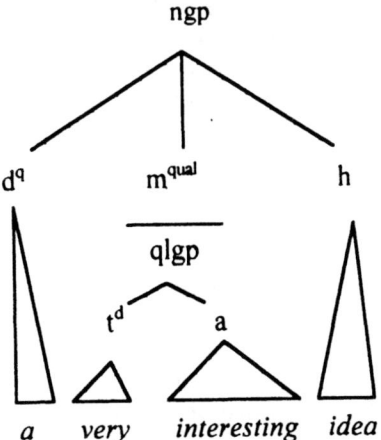

Figure 10.3. An analysis showing embedding through the filling principle

10.5.10 The lexical resource

The principal claim made in earlier sections is that modifiers are semantically or functionally determined on the basis of the kinds of 'Quality' that can be attributed to Things. The nature of 'attribution' also provides some insight into the semantic organization of Quality senses, and therefore the organization of the system network for Quality. Much of the organization of this network is indeed suggested by the modifier names themselves. Adjectives of age, colour, dimension, physical property (shape, weight, etc.) fall into identifiable semantic groups. Adjectives for stereotypically human Qualities fall mainly into the category of epithet. Lexical organization on these lines also shows some correlation with other characteristics of Qualities (such as gradability) and their resultant potential for tempering.

In moving from the modifier in the nominal group to the lexical resource represented in the quality group, it is possible to effect **preselection**, in the sense of opening up only that area of the resource which is available to express a specific modifier function. If m^{col} has been chosen, for example, we can preselect features in the network that lead exclusively to the subnetwork for [colour quality]. A similar procedure can operate for nominal and verbal expressions for modifiers, by preselection in the networks associated with 'Thing' and 'Situation' respectively.

10.5.11 Modification and co-ordination

As was made clear in 10.5.2, modifier sequence is complicated by the potential for the co-ordination of quality groups. Any two or more Quality senses from the same modifier function will be presented not as a sequence, but as co-ordinated units accompanied, as in other parts of the lexicogrammar, by co-ordinating devices. A typical example of co-ordination is given in (35).

(35)   a careful, intelligent and considerate employee

The lexicogrammar must therefore include a mechanism for this type of recursion, providing for the realization of a **linker (&)**, realized as an item (e.g. *and, but,* etc.), by punctuation (i.e. the presence of a comma), or phonologically, by information group (tone group) boundaries. It should be noted that co-ordination, unlike modifier sequence, is effected **at the level of the filling unit**. Thus, as in the example above, the m^{epi} is an element of structure which is filled by three co-ordinated qlgps, which can be represented as in Figure 10.4.

Co-ordination is planned, therefore, at the level of the nominal group, in the sense that a modifier function is selected (e.g. m^{epi}), but the network for Quality is entered only once. Within this network the various senses which correspond to [modification by quality] are generated one at a time, together with the selection of the feature [co-ordinated quality], which will ensure the presence of the appropriate co-ordination markers.

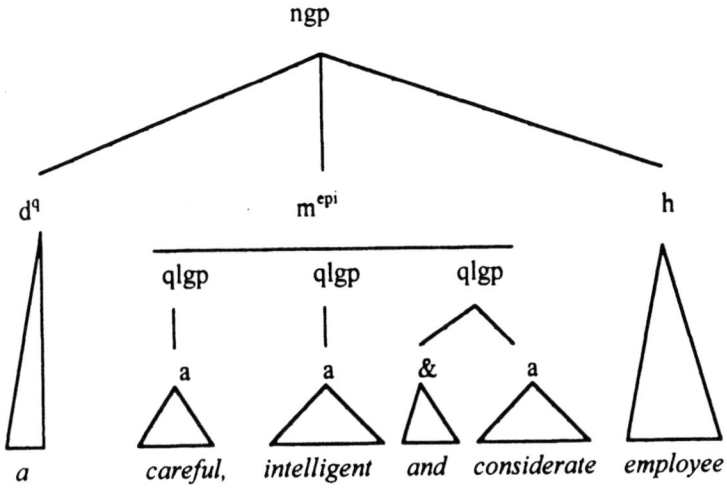

Figure 10.4. Group co-ordinating for modification

10.6   THE TREATMENT OF MODIFICATION IN THE CARDIFF GRAMMAR

10.6.1 The system network

This section describes major fragments of the system network for modification, together with the relevant realization rules. The initial entry condition to the system network in Figure 10.5 is [by attribute]. This feature is an option in an earlier system which allows for modification of Thing through modifiers and qualifiers. Qualifiers express modification through relative clauses and prepositional groups. The system must of course allow for all three types of modification to be present as in (36).

(36)   those tall trees with the red leaves that we saw in the park

This area of the grammar itself raises certain problems, such as the number of prepositional groups possible, but they will not be addressed here.

The central concern of this part of the network is to provide for the types of modifier, the number and sequence in structure and their relationship to other units of the grammar which realize them. We shall first examine the nature of the network and then describe the realization rules which are necessary to build the structure.

In order to allow for multiple modifier selection, the various attribute functions are presented as features in the system, as shown in Figure 10.5. It is from the system [attribute type] that these functions are initially selected. The

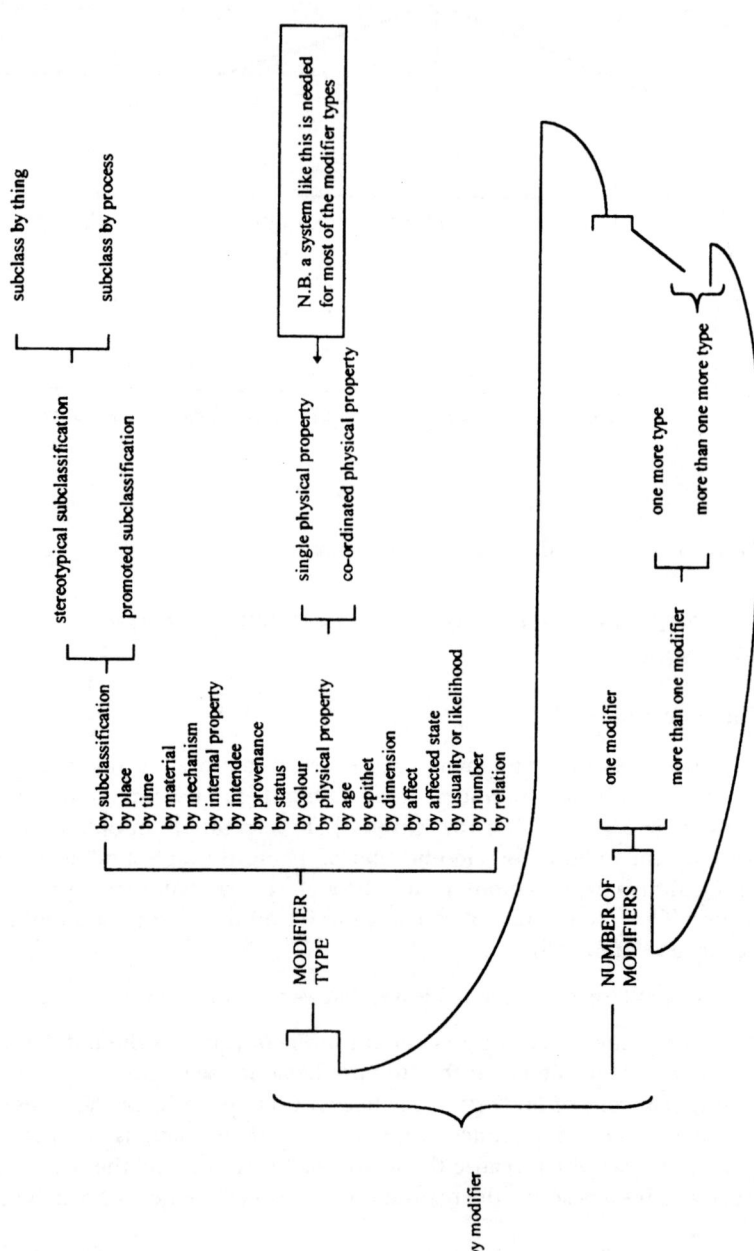

Figure 10.5. The system network for modifier function

number of attributes must also be specified by parallel entry into the system [number of attributes]. This system acts as recursive device to allows re-selection in the [attribute type] system.

Whenever the system is re-entered, however, any attribute function already selected must be excluded from the system; the same attribute type may be selected but, as has been argued earlier, this is a question of co-ordination of the group that fills the modifier, rather than two separate realizations of the same class of modifier. Each re-entry into the [quality type] system, therefore, must lead to a reduced set of available features. This is a non-trivial problem, although it can be solved within the Cardiff Grammar by the use of a **same pass rule (sp rule)**. Same pass rules have the effect of **resetting** the probabilities on features in a system as a consequence of the selection of a feature during the same pass through the network. This is a different, yet related, operation to that effected by **preference rules**, which cause probabilities on features to be reset on subsequent re-entry to the system network. Since it is possible to specify a 0 per cent probability for any feature, this will effectively remove the feature from the system.

Without the same pass rule, it would be necessary to express the revised system each time as a new system containing one less feature. The same pass rule is therefore a Type B rule, as described in Section 3.4.2, in the sense that it operates on the system network rather than operating on structure.

10.6.2 Co-ordination

The co-ordination of two or more Qualities, although effected at the level of the realizing structure, must be specified at the current level. Thus, for every modifier function where co-ordination is permissible, it must be expressed as a dependent system on that modifier type. For example, [by colour] leads to a further system [single colour] or [co-ordinated colour]. The latter of these features will involve a realization rule which preselects co-ordination of the unit upon re-entry into the relevant network.

10.6.3 Modifiers filled by a nominal group or clause

As we have observed, both nominal groups and clauses play a part in the realization of certain attribute types at modifier. Wherever this option is available, it must be expressed as a feature in the system network. A typical example of this is [by subclassification]. In this case, a dependent system specifies the choice of [subclassification by thing] or [subclassification by process]. This is necessary in order to re-enter the appropriate network (for Situation or for Thing) and generate the nominal group or the clause which fills the modifier.

10.6.4 Variation in modifier sequence: promoted subclassification

The potential for alternative ordering of attributes was pointed out in Section 10.5.4. If attributes are expressed as fixed modifier places in structure, this flexibility will not be accounted for. The phenomenon of alternative ordering is dealt with here by what I refer to as **promotion**; that is, some attribute may, perhaps in an *ad hoc* way, be 'promoted' to principal subclassifying status. Essentially, it involves a process of reclassifying Things. An example of this is the pair (37) and (38), where *sweet* in (38) has been promoted to the level of primary subclassification which overrides their stereotypical subclassification.

(37)   sweet green peppers
(38)   green sweet peppers

The selection of [promoted subclassification] therefore allows re-entry into the system, with the subsequent choice of any of the attribute types available for this role. Once this choice has been made, the option on subsequent re-entry is no longer available.

10.6.5 Realization rules

Certain features in Figure 10.5 are associated with realization rules. The range of operations covered by these rules, which are necessary for the generation of modifier strings, the lexical choices and structure, were described in Chapter 3 and are outlined again below. In general terms, it is necessary to:

(a) remove options from the attribute system on the same pass (same pass rules)
(b) insert any modifier into the structure of the nominal group (insertion rules)
(c) re-enter the network in order to fill modifiers with the appropriate units (re-entry rules)
(d) prefer features upon the re-entry described above in order to constrain lexical and structural choice

For the sake of brevity, the full set of realization rules necessary for the system network in Figure 10.5 is not given. Instead, we shall take examples of each of the types outlined above. Let us first consider **same pass rules**, e.g. rule sp20.1 on the feature [by subclassification] in Figure 10.5.[5]

sp20.1: by classification:
for same pass disprefer [by subclassification].

This rule has the effect of removing the feature [by subclassification] from the system when it is re-entered for a second choice of attribute. The system is re-entered if [more than one attribute] is selected from the system whose entry condition is [number of attributes]. The rule instruction **disprefer** assigns a 0 per cent probability to the feature in question which effectively ensures that it is no longer available for selection.[6] As a consequence of the choice of this feature, a new set of mutually exclusive features becomes available. Each attribute type feature bears a similar rule. Thus, on every subsequent re-entry, the system is reduced by one feature, ensuring that no selection of the same feature may be made twice.

Second, **insertion rules**. These are given in the potential structure for the nominal group and need not be specified again in individual cases. The potential structure assigns number places to each of the modifiers, e.g. **mcol @ 19, mstat @ 20, mprov @ 21**, etc.

Finally, **re-entry and preference rules**, e.g. rule 20.111 on [by thing].

> 20.111: by thing
> **(a) for msc re enter at entity,**
> **(b) for msc prefer [thing, stereotypical thing, outsider, cultural classification potential, cultural classification, not selected from by particularization, not selected from by superlativization].**

This rule first specifies in (a) that the system network must be re-entered in order to fill a modifier element of structure. Nothing more need be stated in this rule since all the relevant subnetworks for Thing, Quality, Situation, etc. are dependent on the unique entry condition [entity]. It is therefore in contrast with an **exponence rule** which would have expounded an element directly as an item, rather than building more structure.

Preference rules, such as that in (b), are responsible for most of the constraints that must be imposed on the structures that may fill a modifier. Yet they do so by constraining the choice of features in the network to be re-entered, as was clarified above. As in the case of rule 20.111, preference rules may activate, or make available, features which are not available in other contexts; subordinate or non-finite clauses, for example, are not available on the first pass through the network for Situation – the first clause generated must always be a main clause. The feature [thing as modifier] (and other systems or conditions on rules which depend on it) must, in fact, be·selected in the context of noun modification of head. This feature in turn controls and constrains options in the network, permitting only the limited range of meanings that can co-occur with nominal heads at modifier. Having selected [thing as modifier] there can be no particularization or quantification, only lexical realization of the head together with some further modification. Availability of the full range of options in the network for Thing would give rise to phrases such as:

(39)   *a (d^q) the sandwich (m^{sc}) box (h)

Options in modification will of course make available further modification by a nominal group leading to sequences like (40), which are common in some registers of contemporary English.

(40)   a finance committee meeting report scare

The extent to which preferences constrain the various networks for Situation, Thing, Quality, etc. cannot be specified in detail here, since this would entail a full account of these networks and the options they contain.

Preferences rules are also responsible for constraint in lexical choice. For example, if [by colour] is selected, then for the re-entry into the network to fill the m^{age} a series of features may be preferred which will guide the traversal directly into the area of the network which handles colour.

The question of ordering of the modifier elements is achieved through allocating each element a place in the structure of the nominal group. This is the insertion rule. This deceptively simple approach has the advantage of ensuring the correct placement of any modifier irrespective of which others may be present, and dispenses with rules which state the linear precedence of each modifier to every other. The promotion principle described in 10.6.4 re-assigns the 'promoted' modifier to the place reserved for subclassification, thereby placing it after any other co-occurring modifier.

10.7 CONCLUSION

Through examining the filling relationship between quality group and the elements of structure of other units, we have related adjectives to their wider syntactic and functional environments. We now have a picture of both the internal structure and functions of the quality group and its relationship to the functions and structure of the units whose internal meanings it is called on to express.

Further work is needed to incorporate the less common environments of the quality group listed in the introduction to this chapter. The treatment of modifiers is, however, a significant contribution to this thorny problem. When these proposals for modification were first presented at the International Systemic Functional Congress, at the University of Victoria (1993), one eminent member of the audience remarked with an air of belligerent scepticism that the presenter appeared to be claiming to have solved a problem which had beset scholars for many years. This is far from being the case. There is little doubt that, under close scrutiny, the above proposals will fall short of a definitive solution to the problem. Considerable fine tuning is undoubtedly required, and observers will inevitably find counter-examples. It is reasonable to suggest, however, that what has already been set in place is a plausible approach to the phenomenon within a systemic functional framework, and a way forward to a fully computer-implementable model of it.

As has often been emphasized throughout this book, the fruits of corpus investigation will constantly throw new light on such phenomena and force lexicogrammarians to revise their accounts. The model which has been presented here is robust and flexible enough to incorporate such revisions without irretrievably undermining the foundations on which it is built.

NOTES

1 It is of course necessary to distinguish here between adjectives which do not appear in their role as Attribute and those which cannot be Attributes because of the semantic relationship between the two word classes. In essence, as Ferris (1993) points out, where there is an indirect 'associative' relationship between noun and adjective,

rather than a direct 'ascriptive' one, the use of an adjective as an Attribute leads to anomaly, e.g. *foreign policy* versus *this policy is foreign.*

2   It will be observed that many of the adjectives found in resultative expressions are classed as **complementary opposites** in lexical semantics. As such, they are typically untempered, since they are not susceptible to being tempered by degree. The temperers which can accompany complementary opposites (e.g. *wide open, half open*) may also be present in resultative complements, as in *he pushed the door wide open.* They are less likely to occur, however, when the adjective directly follows the verb, e.g. **he pushed wide open the door.*

3   In Government-Binding approaches to syntax, co-ordination is deemed to be possible between two or more members of the same category at the same bar level (e.g. N + N, N" + N") (see Cowper 1992: 19ff). In the SFG approach used here, **units** (e.g. clause, nominal group, etc.) are co-ordinated, rather than **elements of structure** (e.g. Subject, head, modifier, etc.).

4   For a good survey of prototypes and basic-level categories see Lakoff (1987).

5   The **same pass rule** is a recent addition to the rule types employed by the Cardiff Grammar. This is a **Type B** rule in the typology presented in Chapter 3: it concerns an operation on the system network rather than direct realization in form. The effect of a same pass rule, e.g. **on same pass prefer [features *x*, *y*, *z*]**, is to reconfigure some part of the system network currently being traversed, in the sense of changing the probabilities on systems. As is by now clear, probabilities on features may be expressed as 100%–0%, which has the effect of making one feature in the system obligatory, or as a set of numbers on each feature in the system which totals 100%, e.g. (feature *x* 40%, feature *y* 40%, feature *z* 20%). Same pass rules therefore express the systemic potential which comes into play immediately as a consequence of some feature selection. As with normal preference rules, same pass rules do not necessarily make a later system dependent on the feature which invokes the rule. What they express is 'if the later system is entered during the traversal then its probabilities are reset differently from their original setting. It therefore constitutes a kind of markedness convention (see Martin 1987) which says, 'if feature *a* has been chosen then the system now being entered is to be reconfigured as . . .' It may of course be the case that the system in question is not entered, in which case the resetting is irrelevant. This relationship of co-occurrence, where one system is not obligatorily dependent on feature selection in another, cannot be expressed in traditional systemic representations, hence the need for the same pass rule type. This innovation to SFG was developed jointly by Robin Fawcett and myself, in conjunction with Yuen Lin.

6   The operator **disprefer**, unlike its opposite, **prefer**, has not yet been defined in the GENESYS system which runs the grammar in the computational implementation. I have been assured by Yuen Lin that its addition to the system should not present any problems.

11. CONCLUSIONS

11.1 THE PROBLEMS OF PRODUCING DESCRIPTIVE MODELS OF A LANGUAGE

It is a truism that a language defies exhaustive description. Noam Chomsky ruffled many feathers by stating that linguistic theory is 'primarily concerned with an ideal speaker–listener, in a completely homogeneous speech community' (Chomsky 1965: 3). And yet the linguistic models that we build are, to all intents and purposes, precisely those of 'ideal speaker–listeners'. Contemporary sociolinguistics has highlighted the multiplicity of dimensions along which language can vary, and the difficulty of providing a useful definition of such elusive notions as a 'language'. If, as it would seem, a language such as English is simply a label for a large number of related varieties which differ one from another along geographical, social and temporal dimensions, then the task of 'modelling' English is an impossible one.

It is undeniably the case that each individual speaker has his or her unique knowledge of language and engages in unique language behaviour. No two speakers of a language have the same grammatical or lexical resource. So it is natural that the lexicogrammarian focuses on what speakers of a language are assumed to share. This amounts to idealization, i.e. to describing Chomsky's 'ideal speaker–listener', for in opting for the 'shared' we are suggesting that the essential linguistic knowledge and language use of each speaker is one and the same. How, otherwise, could we explain in linguistic terms how people with different linguistic knowledge understand one another? If one speaker's lexicogrammar contains a number of rules that are not shared by another speaker, then he or she will produce utterances which are uninterpretable in terms of the other's lexicogrammar. In day-to-day interaction, this happens all the time. We understand utterances such as *I ain't done nothing*, even though our individual 'productive' lexicogrammar may not cover this variety of clause. And if we claim to understand such utterances, then should they not be part of our lexicogrammar?

Linguistic theory is concerned with the nature of languages, and the nature of language in general. The Chomskyan preoccupation with Universal Grammar is an investigation of the general properties of human language which, naturally, must generalize across language varieties such as *I ain't done nothing* and *I haven't done anything* (and *je n'ai rien fait*, equally). The linguist who builds a model of a particular language must, by the same token, generalize across varieties of that language, or decide to exclude all but one of them.

Systemic functional grammar is no less 'universalist' than Chomskyan generative grammar. It makes claims about how languages are organized in terms of the realization of options in meaning, in terms of universal functionality. If it were not universalist in nature, its theoretical validity would need to be seriously re-assessed.

The difficulties begin when one applies the theory to an individual language. This is because one is no longer exclusively involved in universals, but in language-specific properties and instantiations – and, moreover, in generalized and idealized instantiations or even in individual instantiations. At this point, linguists may decide to turn to large corpora to inform them of 'what really happens'. Ultimately, there are only two kinds of corpus: one recording the linguistic realizations of an individual speaker, the other recording usage across a number of members of the speech community. The first type underdetermines – and cannot be entirely representative of – the output of the linguistic collectivity, whilst the second type allows us to generalize across collective use and, at the same time, to isolate individual uses. The corpus linguist attempts to draw some statistically determined line between what is shared usage and what is individual. And that is reflected, naturally, in descriptions (either lexicographical or grammatical) that are based on corpora. Thus, the corpus-driven dictionary will foreground consensus usage and exclude the idiosyncratic.

I am now ready to make my point. What really counts about a model of language is the extent to which it explains some aspect of linguistic organization, accounting for both the general **and** the specific. As such, the Cardiff Grammar is both an implementation of general principles **and** a demonstration of the way in which those principles can handle the range of linguistic phenomena that emerge in the course of investigating language. The 'lexicogrammar of adjectives' which I have proposed is therefore just as important for the aspects of linguistic theory that it embodies as for the exhaustiveness of its coverage.

11.2 ACHIEVEMENTS, INADEQUACIES AND LOOSE ENDS

I began developing the lexicogrammar of Quality in the Cardiff Grammar with what seemed to be no more than a handful of adjectives extracted from the LDOCE defining vocabulary. Although the number, in terms of items, has not increased exponentially over the past years, the lexicogrammar has begun to reflect the extensiveness and complexity of description which is needed to incorporate them in the overall model. It will not come as a surprise to any linguist that the universe of adjectives and their organization is as much a bottomless pit as any other aspect of language. As I have delved into the multiple aspects of Quality, I have often been reminded of a remark (perhaps apocryphal) attributed to various American politicians: 'I know how to spell *banana*, but I don't know when to stop.' What I have learnt in my attempt to investigate and describe this phenomenon is that, paradoxically, there is no point where one can stop – and yet there is a point where one must stop.

If I am asked to summarize the value of the proposals set out in this book, I would wish to claim that they have laid solid foundations to an area of lexicogrammar which can now continue to grow without serious risk of collapse. In particular, I have shown how lexis can be incorporated into lexicogrammar, and how lexis is as central as grammar in the lexicogrammar. Furthermore, I would wish to claim, as I have elsewhere (Tucker 1996), that my approach is one that can reconcile the positions of the grammarian and the lexicographer, as described by Halliday 1991:

> Sinclair is by nature a lexicographer, whose aim is to construct the grammar out of the dictionary. I am by nature a grammarian, and my aim (the grammarian's dream, as I put it in 1961) is to build the dictionary out of the grammar.

These are complementary positions, not alternatives. Once the 'dictionary' is indistinguishable from the 'grammar', one cannot but attend simultaneously to both. Words engender grammar, and grammar words.

I now turn to certain aspects of my proposals which I feel to be less than fully adequate in terms of the detail of description, yet far more satisfactory in terms of theoretical approaches to certain phenomena. Three aspects of the lexico-grammar come to mind.

First, there is the question of modifier sequence, as discussed in Chapter 10. While I would claim that my general proposal for the treatment of multiple modification in this way is sound, the account that I have produced is open to revision and modification. The number of modifiers is probably about right, but it will inevitably transpire from detailed language investigation in this area that the types recognized are not fully adequate to cover all the data. In Chapter 10 I introduced the notion of 'promoted classification' to provide for some flex-ibility in the sequencing of modifiers. This notion goes some way to explaining why such sequences are not rigidly fixed, but it may well not account for other orderings that observers might wish to argue are possible. Furthermore, the number and types of modifier recognized may be found to be inconsistent with future data. Again, there is room for improvement. It may well be the case that the lexicogrammatical description has been taken as far as it can go in terms of 'delicacy', and some would argue that it has already gone too far. This question is perhaps best resolved through an adequate lexical semantic theory of the modification of Things, based upon extensive corpus research. Yet, as long as it is the delicacy of the description which is found to be inadequate, and not the principles behind the description, the essential structure of the proposal remains intact.

Second, there is the question of the status of certain elements of structure of the quality group proposed here – the **extent (ex)** and the **emphasizing temperer (t^e)**, which were introduced in Chapter 5. I have already indicated that there is a tension between what is happening in one part of the grammar and what is happening elsewhere. The case in point here is the notion of **quantification,** typically associated with Things, and its 'transfer' to Qualities, for the expression of **degree.** This transfer may be considered a process of 'grammatical metaphor' and, as Halliday (1994) observes, it is a common phenomenon. The notion of grammatical metaphor raises the problem of two alternative descriptions of the same phenomenon, and the dilemma for the lexicogrammarian – at least as far as language production is concerned – is which alternative to opt for. It is my view that, in such cases, the immediate paradigmatic relations should influence the decision. It is for that reason that I have analysed expressions such as *I haven't got the faintest idea* as mental Process expressions, related to *I don't know*, rather than as relational Process expressions, on the grounds that *have* is a relational Process. This means offering a different account of the structure than that given for relational Processes. In a similar way, I would argue that solutions suggested in this book to the problem of analysing expressions such as *far more* in *far more important* and *so very* in *so very silly* should be considered as possible alternatives to the use of the quantity group. This debate – largely a Cardiff Grammar internal one – will inevitably continue, as part of the process of refining the descriptive mechanism.

Third, the conflation of the adjectival group with the adverbial group may continue to cause some perplexity. While **by and large** adjectives and adverbs share both a common set of Quality senses and a common group structure, there are also differences that remain, even when set beside the main difference between them in terms of their respective function in the grammar as a whole and their respective syntactic distribution. At this stage in my thinking, I am rather more convinced of the 'separation' argument than I was before. Yet I would advocate a separation only in terms of the syntax, retaining a common Quality network for both the 'adjectival' and the 'adverbial' group. Although I have not yet articulated this proposal, or fully examined the consequences, there appears to me to be no insuperable problem within the current Cardiff Grammar formalism.

Finally – and perhaps most controversial of the proposals – is the organization of the system network for Quality itself. The case for the proposed organization of Quality senses in this way has been argued in Chapters 6 and 7. Nevertheless, many parts of the network appear not to have any direct lexicogrammatical corroboration and so are open to criticism, if only on the grounds that the categories may not be psychologically motivated. This possible criticism presumes that there is a more universal psychologically verifiable conceptual organization for such meanings. If this is the case, then (a) it is still unexplored, (b) it has yet to be published or (c) I have been less than thorough in my research. If the first of these alternatives proves to be the case, then what I have presented is an account of such organization which stands as a reasonable hypothesis, and so as a point of departure for possible psycholinguistic investigation.

11.3 FUTURE DIRECTIONS

It is clear from the remarks in both sections above that a descriptive model of the type can never reach completion or be fully adequate. A number of factors influence the directions in which we may proceed from here. The first of these is the obvious need for constant revision and firming up of the current proposals. This is necessary even without extending the coverage of the lexicogrammar. The second is that the proposals are just one part of a computational lexicogrammar of English, and – in the eyes of the Cardiff Grammar research team and especially in the eyes of the sponsors – part of a 'deliverable' natural language interactive system. In this sense, not only must those parts of the lexicogrammar be firmed up, but they must also be extended to include other aspects of the linguistic coverage that were originally specified for the 'final product'. This involves extending the lexicogrammar to include well over 500 Quality senses. The network described here covers about 200.

The third factor, which I consider the most influential, concerns the future development of both linguistic theory and lexicogrammatical description. With regard to linguistic theory in general – and systemic functional theory in particular – there is a need for constant development. Any theory that rests on the laurels of its original formulation, however impressive this might be, is destined for obscurity. I can think of no area of scholarly scientific endeavour where this is not the case. Theories must evolve in order to achieve the goals for which they were set up, unless such goals are trivial or insignificant. Regardless of the personal or intellectual contempt in which Chomsky's ideas have been held by some, transformational generative grammar has evolved extensively since the ideas were first presented in the mid-1950s. With these observations in mind, the Cardiff Grammar serves, and will continue to serve, as a test bed for the development of systemic functional theory itself. The current Cardiff Grammar itself is the outcome of theoretical evolution, as can be observed by comparing Fawcett's (1980) account with recent accounts such as Fawcett *et al.* (1993).

With regard to language description, there are both positive and negative aspects. On the positive side, the development of the Cardiff Grammar has led, as I hope I have shown in the course of this book, to the better description of particular linguistic phenomena. Much of the output of the developmental research is presented, and will continue to be presented, as a contribution to the description of English and other languages (so far, Chinese and Japanese, and to a lesser extent Arabic). On the negative side, the Cardiff Grammar's description of English, i.e. a generative grammar format with system networks and realization rules, is not the most transparent or explicit way to present language description to a wider public. Description is needed for a multitude of purposes, notably for language learning and teaching and for scholars working in other areas of language-related enquiry. It is important to ensure that the important aspects of one's description are not unnecessarily obfuscated by the technical machinery that the grammar uses. I do not wish to suggest that the Cardiff Grammar is altogether unuseful in this respect. The functionally-oriented descriptions of structure which have been presented here for the lexicogrammar of adjectives, like those available for the whole of the lexicogrammar, may serve as an important tool for the purposes of applied textual analysis, as the forerunner of the Cardiff Grammar has done, for example in the description of children's syntax (Fawcett and Perkins 1981).

11.4 CONCLUDING REMARKS

The main purpose of this book has been to propose a description of one area of the lexicogrammar of English which is more overtly 'lexical' than 'grammatical', and to further explore the plausibility and practicability of Halliday's notion of 'lexis as most delicate grammar'. In one sense, we might do well to reformulate Halliday's notion as simply 'most delicate lexicogrammar', since lexis and grammar are so clearly interwoven, as we have seen at many points in this book. Moreover, in claiming that lexis is most delicate **grammar**, one might be seen to be suggesting that lexical distinctions are simply more delicate grammatical distinctions. Yet as we have seen – especially in the case of adjective scopes – some lexical distinctions lead to dependent distinctions realized through structures. Furthermore, there seems little evidence that the grammar of lexical items exhibits the kind of highly generalized distinctions that are recognized for syntax.

A reformulation of Halliday's notion is not my main concern, however. That has remained the modelling of language as meaning potential, and in terms of a unified system network of options which makes systematic connection with the structures and the items that serve to realize these options. It is this aim, which derives unquestionably from Michael Halliday's view of language, that the proposals presented here have sought to serve.

References

Aarts, F. and Aarts, J. (1982) *English Syntactic Structures: Functions and Categories in Sentence Analysis*. Oxford: Pergamon.

Aitchison, J. (1987) *Words in the Mind*. Oxford: Blackwell.

Allerton, D.J. (1987) English intensifiers and their idiosyncrasies. In R. Steele and T. Threadgold (eds) *Language Topics*. Amsterdam: John Benjamins, 15–32.

Bäcklund, U. (1973) *The Collocation of Adverbs of Degree in English*. Studia Anglistica Upsaliensis 13. Stockholm: Almqvist and Wiksell.

Bazell, C.E., Catford, J.C., Halliday, M.A.K. and Robins, R.H. (eds) (1966) *In Memory of J.R. Firth*. London: Longman.

Becker, J.D. (1975) The phrasal lexicon. In R. Schank and B. Nash-Webber (eds), *Theoretical Issues in Natural Language Processing*, ACL Annual Meeting, Cambridge, MA, June, 38–41.

Berlin, B. and Kay, P. (1969) *Basic Colour Terms: Their Universality and Evolution*. Berkeley: University of California Press.

Berry, M. (1975) *Introduction to Systemic Linguistics*, Vol.1: *Structures and Systems*. London: Batsford.

Berry, M. (1977) *Introduction to Systemic Linguistics*, Vol.2: *Levels and Links*. London: Batsford.

Bhat, D.N.S (1994) *The Adjectival Category: Criteria for Differentiation and Identification*. Amsterdam: John Benjamins.

Boguraev, B. and Briscoe, E.J. (1987) Large lexicons for natural language processing: exploiting the grammar coding system of LDOCE. *Computational Linguistics*, 13 (3–4).

Boguraev, B. and Briscoe, E.J. (eds) (1989) *Computational Lexicography for Natural Language Processing*. London: Longman, 208–18.

Browning, S. (1992) Collecting a corpus of unscripted speech using a Wizard of Oz technique. Memorandum No. 4675, Defence Research Agency, Malvern, Worcs.

Butler, C.S. (1985) *Systemic Linguistics: Theory and Applications*. London: Batsford.

Carter, R. (1987) *Vocabulary: Applied Linguistic Perspectives*. London: Allen and Unwin.

Carter, R. and Burton, D. (eds) (1982) *Literary Text and Language Study*. London: Edward Arnold.

Chomsky, N. (1957) *Syntactic Structures*. The Hague: Mouton.

Chomsky, N. (1965) *Aspects of the Theory of Syntax*. Cambridge, MA: MIT Press.

Chomsky, N. (1970) Remarks on nominalization. In R. Jacobs and E. Rosenbaum (eds), *Readings in English Transformational Grammar*. Waltham, MA: Ginn, 184–221.

Chomsky, N. (1981) *Lectures on Government and Binding*. Dordrecht: Foris.

Clark, E.V. (1993) *The Lexicon in Acquisition*. Cambridge: Cambridge University Press.

Clocksin, W. F. and Mellish, C.S. (1987) *Programming in Prolog*. Heidelberg: Springer.

Cook, V. (1993) *Linguistics and Second Language Acquisition*. London: Macmillan.

Cowper, E. (1992) *A Concise Introduction to Syntactic Theory: The Government-binding Approach*. Chicago: University of Chicago Press.

Cross, M. (1991) Choice in text: a systemic-functional approach to computer modelling of variant text production. Unpublished PhD dissertation, Macquarie University.

Cross, M. (1993) Collocation in computer modelling of lexis as most delicate grammar. In M. Ghadessy (ed.), *Register Analysis: Theory and Practice*. London: Pinter, 196–220.

Cruse, D. (1986) *Lexical Semantics*. Cambridge: Cambridge University Press.

Cumming, S. (1986) Design of a master lexicon. Research Report, ISI, University of Southern California.

Cumming, S. (1987) The lexicon in text generation. Lexicon Workshop, Linguistic Institute, Stanford University. First published as USC/ISI report, University of Southern California.

Dahlgren, K. (1988) *Naive Semantics for Natural Language Understanding*. Boston: Kluwer.

Davey, A. (1978) *Discourse Production: A Computer Model of Some Aspects of a Speaker*. Edinburgh: Edinburgh University Press.

Davies, M. and Ravelli, L. (eds) (1992) *Advances in Systemic Linguistics: Recent Theory and Practice*. London: Pinter.

Diller, K.C. (1978) *The Language Teaching Controversy*. Rowley, MA: Newbury House.

Dixon, R.M.W. (1982) *Where Have All the Adjectives Gone?: And Other Essays in Semantics and Syntax*. Berlin: Mouton.

Dixon, R.M.W. (1991) *A New Approach to English Grammar on Semantic Principles*. Oxford: Clarendon Press.

Downing, A. and Locke, P. (1992) *A University Course in English Grammar*. New York: Prentice Hall.

Eggins, S. (1994) *An Introduction to Systemic Functional Linguistics*. London: Pinter.

Fass, D. (1986) Collative semantics: an approach to coherence. Memorandum in Computer and Cognitive Science, MCCS–86–56, Computing Research Laboratory, New Mexico State University.

Fawcett, R.P. (1973/81) Generating a sentence in systemic functional grammar. In M.A.K. Halliday and J.R. Martin (eds), *Readings in Systemic Linguistics*. London: Batsford, 146–83. (First published 1973 as University College London mimeo.)

Fawcett, R.P. (1974–6/81) *Some Proposals for Systemic Syntax.* Cardiff: Polytechnic of Wales. (First published 1974–76 in *MALS Journal.*)

Fawcett, R.P. (1980) *Cognitive Linguistics and Social Interaction: Towards an Integrated Model of a Systemic Functional Grammar and the Other Components of an Interacting Mind.* Heidelberg: Julius Groos and Exeter University.

Fawcett, R.P. (1987) The semantics of clause and verb for relational processes in English. In M.A.K. Halliday and R.P. Fawcett (eds), *New Developments in Systemic Linguistics,* vol.1. London: Pinter, 130–83.

Fawcett, R.P. (1988) What makes a good system network good?: four pairs of concepts for such evaluations. In J.D. Benson and W.S. Greaves (eds), *Systemic Functional Approaches to Discourse.* Norwood, NJ: Ablex, 1–28.

Fawcett, R.P. (1990) The computer generation of speech with semantically and discoursally motivated intonation. In *Proceedings of Fifth International Workshop on National Language Generation,* Pittsburgh, 164–73a.

Fawcett, R.P. (1992) Language as program: a reassessment of the nature of descriptive linguistics. *Language Sciences,* 14(4), 623–57.

Fawcett, R.P. (1994) On moving on ontologies: mass, count and long thin things. In D. McDonald (ed.), *Proceedings of the Seventh International Workshop on Natural Language Generation,* Waltham, MA: ACL, Brandeis University, 71–80.

Fawcett, R.P. (forthcoming) *A Handbook for the Analysis of Sentences in English Text Using a Systemic Functional Grammar.* London: Cassell.

Fawcett, R.P and Huang, G. (1995) A functional approach to the 'it cleft' construction(s). Paper accepted for the Conference on Functional Approaches to Grammar, University of New Mexico, July.

Fawcett, R.P. and Perkins, M.R. (1981) Project report: language development in 6- to 12-year-old children. *First Language,* 2, 75–9.

Fawcett, R.P., Tucker, G.H. and Lin, Y. (1993) The role of realization in realization: how a systemic grammar works. In H. Horacek and M. Zock (eds), *From Planning to Realization in Natural Language Generation.* London: Pinter, 114–86.

Ferris, C. (1993) *The Meaning of Syntax: A Study in the Adjectives of English.* London: Longman.

Fillmore, C.J. (1977) Topics in lexical semantics. In R.W. Cole (ed.), *Current Issues in Linguistic Theory.* Bloomington: Indiana University Press.

Findler, N.V. (ed.) (1979) *Associative Networks: Representation and Use of Knowledge by Computers.* New York: Academic Press.

Firth, J.R. (1957) *Papers in Linguistics 1934–1951.* London: Oxford University Press.

Frawley, W. (1992) *Linguistic Semantics.* Hillsdale, NJ: Erlbaum.

Gazdar, G., Klein, E., Pullum, G.K. and Sag, I. (1985) *Generalized Phrase Structure Grammar.* Oxford: Blackwell.

Giles, H. (1973) Accent mobility: a model and some data. *Anthropological Linguistics,* 15, 87–105.

Giles, H. and Coupland, N. (1991) *Language: Contexts and Consequences.* Pacific Grove, CA: Brooks/Cole.

Grice, P. (1975) Logic and conversation. In P. Cole and J. Morgan (eds), *Syntax and Semantics 3: Speech Acts.* New York: Academic Press, 41–58.

Gross, M. (1993) Local grammars and their representation by finite automata. In M. Hoey (ed.), *Data, Description and Discourse*. London: HarperCollins, 26–38.

Halliday, M.A.K. (1961) Categories of the theory of grammar. *Word*, 17, 241–92. Reprinted in part in G. Kress (ed.) (1976), *Halliday: System and Function in Language*. Oxford: Oxford University Press.

Halliday, M.A.K. (1966a) Lexis as a linguistic level. In C.E. Bazell, J.C. Catford, M.A.K. Halliday and R.H. Robins (eds), *In Memory of J.R. Firth*. London: Longman.

Halliday, M.A.K. (1966b) Some notes on 'deep' grammar. *Journal of Linguistics*, 2(1), 57–67.

Halliday, M.A.K. (1967) Notes on transitivity and theme in English, Parts 1–3. *Journal of Linguistics*, 3, 37–81, 199–244.

Halliday, M.A.K. (1978) *Language as Social Semiotic: The Social Interpretation of Language and Meaning*. London: Arnold.

Halliday, M.A.K. (1991) Language as system and language as instance: the corpus as a theoretical construct. In J. Svartvik (ed.), *Proceedings of the Nobel Symposium 82, Stockholm 1991*. Berlin: Mouton de Gruyter.

Halliday, M.A.K. (1994) *An Introduction to Functional Grammar* (2nd edn). London: Arnold.

Halliday, M.A.K. and Fawcett, R.P. (eds) (1987) *New Developments in Systemic Linguistics*, Vol. 1: *Theory and Description*. London: Pinter.

Halliday, M.A.K. and Hasan, R. (1976) *Cohesion in English*. London: Longman.

Halliday, M.A.K. and Martin, J.R. (eds) (1981) *Readings in Systemic Linguistics*. London: Batsford.

Hasan, R. (1985). Lending and borrowing: from grammar to lexis. In J.E. Clarke (ed.), *Festschrift in Honour of Arthur Delbridge. Beiträge zur Phonetik und Linguistik* 48. Hamburg: Helmut Buske Verlag, 55–67.

Hasan, R. (1987) The grammarian's dream: lexis as most delicate grammar. In M.A.K. Halliday and R.P. Fawcett (eds), *New Developments in Systemic Linguistics*, vol. 1. London: Pinter.

Hetzron, R. (1978) On the relative order of adjectives. In H. Seiler (ed.), *Language Universals*. Tübingen: Gunter Narr, 165–84.

Hindmarsh, R. (1980) *Cambridge English Lexicon*. Cambridge: Cambridge University Press.

Hobbs, J., Croft, W., Davies, T., Edwards, D. and Laws, K. (1987) Commonsense metaphysics and lexical semantics. *Computational Linguistics*, 13 (3–4), 241–50.

Hoey, M. (ed.) (1993) *Data, Description and Discourse: Papers on the English Language in Honour of John McH. Sinclair*. London: HarperCollins.

Horacek, H. and Zock, M. (eds) (1993) *New Concepts in Natural Language Processing: Planning, Realization and Systems*. London: Pinter.

Horrocks, G. (1987) *Generative Grammar*. London: Longman.

Huddleston, R. (1984) *Introduction to the Grammar of English*. Cambridge: Cambridge University Press.

Hudson, R.A. (1971) *English Complex Sentences: An Introduction to Systemic Grammar*. Amsterdam: North-Holland.

Hudson, R.A. (1974/81) Systemic generative grammar. *Linguistics*, 139, 241–50. (Republished 1981 in M.A.K. Halliday and J.R. Martin (eds), *Readings in Systemic Linguistics*. London: Batsford, 190–217.)

Hudson, R.A. (1979) Pan-lexicalism. Paper presented at the spring meeting, Linguistics Association of Great Britain, Hull.

Hudson, R.A. (1980) *Sociolinguistics*. Cambridge: Cambridge University Press.

Hudson, R.A. (1984) *Word Grammar*. Oxford: Blackwell.

Ilson, R. (1985) *Dictionaries, Lexicography and Language Learning*. Oxford: Pergamon/The British Council.

Jackendoff, R.S. (1977) *X-Syntax: A Study of Phrase Structure*. Cambridge, MA: MIT Press.

Jackendoff, R.S. (1981) On Katz's autonomous syntax. *Language*, 57, 425–25.

Jackendoff, R.S. (1985) *Semantics and Cognition*. Cambridge, MA: MIT Press.

Jackendoff, R.S. (1990) *Semantic Structures*. Cambridge MA,: MIT Press.

Jesperson, O. (1924) *The Philosophy of Grammar*. London: Allen and Unwin.

Johannson, S. (1993) 'Sweetly obvious': some aspects of adverb–adjective combinations in present-day English. In M. Hoey (ed.), *Data, Description and Discourse: Papers on the English Language in Honour of John McH. Sinclair*. London: HarperCollins, 39–49.

Johnson-Laird, P.N. (1983) *Mental Models*. Cambridge: Cambridge University Press.

Joos, M. (1961) *The Five Clocks*. New York: Harcourt, Brace and World.

Kamp, J.A.W. (1975) Two theories about adjectives. In E. Keenan (ed.), *Formal Semantics of Natural Language*. Cambridge: Cambridge University Press, 123–55.

Kaplan, R.M. and Bresnan, J. (1982) Lexical-functional grammar: a formal system for grammatical representation. In J. Bresnan (ed.) *The Mental Representation of Grammatical Relations*. Cambridge, MA: MIT Press, 173–281.

Katamba, F. (1993) *Morphology*. London: Routledge.

Katamba, F. (1994) *English Words*. London: Routledge.

Katz, J.J. and Postal, P. (1964) *An Integrated Theory of Linguistic Descriptions*. Cambridge, MA: MIT Press.

Kress, G. (ed.) (1976) *Halliday: System and Function in Language*. Oxford: Oxford University Press.

Lakoff, G. (1987) *Women, Fire and Dangerous Things: What Categories Reveal about the Mind*. Chicago: University of Chicago Press.

Leech, G. (1974) *Semantics*. Harmondsworth: Penguin.

Leech, G. (1983) *Principles of Pragmatics*. London: Longman.

Levelt, W. (ed.) (1993) *Lexical Access in Speech Production*. Oxford: Blackwell.

Levin, B. (ed.) (1985) *Lexical Semantics in Review*. Lexical project working papers no. 1. Cambridge, MA: Center for Cognitive Science, MIT.

Levin, B. (1993) *English Verb Classes and Alternations: A Preliminary Investigation*. Chicago: University of Chicago Press.

Levin, B. and Pinker, S. (eds) (1992) *Lexical and Conceptual Semantics*. Cambridge, MA: Blackwell.

Lyons, J. (1968) *Introduction to Theoretical Linguistics.* Cambridge: Cambridge University Press.

Lyons, J. (1977) *Semantics,* vols 1 and 2. Cambridge: Cambridge University Press.

Mann, W.C. and Matthiessen, C.M.I.M. (1983) *Nigel: A Systemic Grammar for Text Generation.* Marina del Rey, CA: ISI/USC.

Mann, W.C. and Matthiessen, C.M.I.M. (1985) A demonstration of the Nigel text generation computer program. In J.D. Benson and W.S. Greaves (eds), *Systemic Perspectives on Discourse,* Vol.1: *Selected Theoretical Papers from the Ninth International Systemic Workshop.* Norwood, NJ: Ablex, 84–95.

Martin, J.R. (1987) The meaning of features in systemic linguistics. In M.A.K. Halliday and R.P. Fawcett (eds), *New Developments in Systemic Linguistics,* vol. 1. London: Pinter, 14–40.

Martin, J.R. (1992) *English Text: System and Structure.* Philadelphia: John Benjamins.

Matthews, P.H. (1981) *Syntax.* Cambridge: Cambridge University Press.

Matthiessen, C.M.I.M. (1985) The systemic framework for text production. In J.D. Benson and W.S. Greaves (eds), *Systemic Perspectives on Discourse,* Vol. 1: *Selected Theoretical Papers from the Ninth International Systemic Workshop.* Norwood, NJ: Ablex, 96–118.

Matthiessen, C.M.I.M. (1988) Representational issues in systemic functional grammar. In J.D. Benson and W.S. Greaves (eds), *Systemic Functional Approaches to Discourse.* Norwood, NJ: Ablex, 136–75.

Matthiessen, C.M.I.M. (1990) Lexico(grammatical) choice in text generation. In C.L. Paris, W.R. Swartout and W.C. Mann (eds), *Natural Language Generation in Artificial Intelligence and Computational Linguistics.* Dordrecht: Kluwer Academic Publishers, 249–92.

Matthiessen, C.M.I.M. (1996) *Lexicogrammatical Cartography.* Tokyo: International Language Sciences Publishers.

Matthiessen, C.M.I.M. and Bateman, J.A. (1991) *Text Generation and Systemic Functional Linguistics: Experiences from English and Japanese.* London: Pinter.

Meara, P. (1980) Vocabulary acquisition: a neglected aspect of language learning. *Language Teaching Abstracts,* 15(4), 221–46.

Meteer, M. (1992) *Expressibility and the Problem of Efficient Text Planning.* London: Pinter.

Muir, J. (1972) *A Modern Approach to English Grammar: An Introduction to Systemic Grammar.* London: Batsford.

Palmer, F.R. (ed.) (1968) *Selected Papers of J.R. Firth.* London: Longmans.

Palmer, F.R. (1986) *Mood and Modality.* Cambridge: Cambridge University Press.

Perkins, M.R. (1983) *Modal Expression in English.* London: Pinter.

Pollard, C. and Sag, I. (1987) *Information-based Syntax and Semantics,* vol.1, Stanford: Center for the Study of Language and Information.

Proctor, P. (ed.) (1987) *Longman Dictionary of Contemporary English.* London: Longman.

Pulman, S.G. (1983) *Word Meaning and Belief.* London: Croom Helm.

Pustejovsky, J. (1991) The generative lexicon. *Computational Linguistics,* 12 (4), 409–41.

Quirk, R., Greenbaum, S., Leech, G. and Svartvik, J. (1985) *A Contemporary Grammar of the English Language*. London: Longman.

Radford, A. (1988) *Transformational Syntax: A First Course*. Cambridge: Cambridge University Press.

Renouf, A. and Sinclair, J. (1991) Collocational frameworks in English. In K. Aijmer and B. Altenberg (eds), *English Corpus Linguistics*. London: Longman, 128–43.

Rosch, E. (1978) Principles of categorization. In E. Rosch and B.B. Lloyd (eds), *Cognition and Categorization*. Hillsdale, NJ: Erlbaum, 27–48.

Scott, F.S., Bowley, C.C., *et al.* (1968) *English Grammar: A Linguistic Study of its Classes and Structures*. London: Heinemann.

Sells, P. (1985) *Lectures on Contemporary Syntactic Theories: An Introduction to Government-binding Theory, Generalized Phrase Structure Grammar, and Lexical-functional Grammar*. Stanford: Center for the Study of Language and Information.

Shank, R.C. (1972) Conceptual dependency: a theory of natural language understanding. *Cognitive Psychology* 3, 552–631.

Siegel, M. (1980) *Capturing the Adjective*. New York: Garland.

Sinclair, J. (1966) Beginning the study of lexis. In C.E. Bazell, J.C. Catford, M.A.K. Hallidy and R.H. Robins (eds), *In Memory of J.R. Firth*. London: Longman, 410–30.

Sinclair, J. (1972) *A Course in Spoken English: Grammar*. Oxford: Oxford University Press.

Sinclair, J. (ed.) (1987a) *Collins COBUILD English Language Dictionary*. London: Collins.

Sinclair, J. (1987b) Collocation: a progress report. In R. Steele and T. Threadgold (eds), *Language Topics: Essays in Honour of Michael Halliday*. Amsterdam: John Benjamins, 319–32.

Sinclair, J. (1987c) *Looking Up: An Account of the COBUILD Project in Lexical Computing*. London: Collins.

Sinclair, J. (1988) Sense and structure in lexis. In J. Benson, M. Cummings and W. Greaves (eds), *Linguistics in a Systemic Perspective*. Amsterdam: John Benjamins.

Sinclair, J. (1991) *Corpus, Concordance, Collocation*. Oxford: Oxford University Press.

Sperber, D. and Wilson, D. (1986) *Relevance: Communication and Cognition*. Oxford: Blackwell.

Spitzbardt, H. (1965) English adverbs of degree and their semantic fields. *Philologica Pragensia*, 8, 349–59.

Starosta, S. (1988) *The Case for Lexicase: An Outline of Lexicase Grammatical Theory*. London: Pinter.

Stubbs, M. (1996) *Text and Corpus Analysis*. Oxford: Blackwell.

Tench, P. (1991) *The Roles of Intonation in English Discourse* (Forum Linguisticum 31). Frankfurt: Peter Lang.

Tucker, G.H. (1988) Initial specification of lexis for prototype generators 0, 1 and 2. COMMUNAL Report No. 5, Computational Linguistics Unit, University of Wales, College of Cardiff.

Tucker, G.H. (1992) An initial approach to comparatives in a systemic functional grammar. In M. Davies and L. Ravelli (eds), *Advances in Systemic Linguistics*. London: Pinter, 150–65.

Tucker, G.H. (1996) So grammarians haven't the faintest idea: reconciling lexis-oriented and grammar-oriented approaches to language. In R. Hasan, D. Butt and C. Cloran (eds), *Functional Descriptions: Language Form and Linguistic Theory*. Amsterdam: Benjamins.

Turner, G. (1970) A linguistic approach to children's speech. In G. Turner and B. Mohan, *A Linguistic Description and Computer Program of Children's Speech*. London: Routledge and Kegan Paul.

Vendler, Z. (1968) *Adjectives and Nominalizations*. The Hague: Mouton.

Vossen, P., Meijs, W. and den Broeder, M. (1989) Meaning and structure in dictionary definitions. In B. Boguraev and E.J. Briscoe (eds), *Computational Lexicography for National Language Processing*. London: Longman, 171–92.

Weeransinghe, A.R. (1994) Probabilistic parsing in systemic functional grammar. Unpublished PhD thesis, University of Wales, College of Cardiff.

West, M. (1953) *General Service List of English Words*. London: Longman.

Whorf, B.L. (1956) *Language, Thought, and Reality*. Cambridge, MA: MIT Press.

Wierzbicka, A. (1980a) *Lingua Mentalis: The Semantics of Natural Language*. Sydney: Academic Press.

Wierzbicka, A. (1980b) *The Case for Case*. Ann Arbor: Karoma.

Wilks, Y. (1975a) Preference semantics. In E. Keenan (ed.), *The Formal Semantics of Natural Language*. London: Cambridge University Press.

Wilks, Y. (1975b) A preferential pattern-seeking semantics for natural language inference. *Artificial Intelligence*, 6, 53–74.

Wilks, Y. (1977). Good and bad arguments about semantic primitives. *Communication and Cognition*, 10, 182–221.

Wilks, Y., Fass, D., Cheng-Ming Guo, McDonald, J., Plate, T. and Slator, B. (1987) A tractable machine dictionary as a resource for computational semantics. In B. Boguraev and E.J. Briscoe (eds), *Computational Lexicography for Natural Language Processing*. London: Longman, 193–228.

Winograd, T. (1972) *Understanding Natural Language*. Edinburgh: Edinburgh University Press.

Wittgenstein, L. (1953) *Philosophical Investigations*. Oxford: Blackwell.

Name Index

Subject Index

Lightning Source UK Ltd.
Milton Keynes UK
UKOW05n0822050614

232894UK00010B/197/A